A Moment's Grace

A Moment's Grace
Stories from Korea in Transition

TRANSLATED WITH COMMENTARY
BY

JOHN HOLSTEIN

East Asia Program
Cornell University
Ithaca, New York 14853

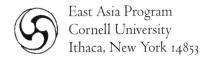

The Cornell East Asia Series is published by the Cornell University East Asia Program (distinct from Cornell University Press). We publish books on a variety of scholarly topics relating to East Asia as a service to the academic community and the general public. Standing orders, which provide for automatic notification and invoicing of each title in the series upon publication, are accepted.

Address submission inquiries to CEAS Editorial Board, East Asia Program, Cornell University, Ithaca, New York 14853-7601.

This publication was supported in part by a grant from the Korean Literature Translation Institute.

Number 148 in the Cornell East Asia Series
Consulting Editor for this volume: Doug Merwin

ISSN: 1050-2955
ISBN: 978-1-933947-18-1 hc
ISBN: 978-1-933947-48-8 pb
Library of Congress Control Number: 2009936456

Contents

Preface

The stories gathered here tell us about the most dynamic period in Korea's transition to modernity. I have defined this period loosely and somewhat arbitrarily as the period bordered by two significant events in this transition, Liberation in 1945 and the Seoul Summer Olympics in 1988. Society had been evolving, of course, over the centuries, and influential developments occurred during the nineteenth and early twentieth centuries,[1] but possibly the most concentrated and formative period of transition—the crucible in which the particular character of modern, second millennium Korea was forged—might be regarded as the years between Liberation and the Seoul Olympics, give or take a few years at either end.

Two sources for understanding of a cultural period are its history and its literature. These two kinds of knowledge have a symbiotic relationship, in that each increases the significance and understanding of what the other tells us, and each makes the reading of the other more rewarding. It is with the intention to provide this enhanced understanding and experience that I have assembled these short stories together with a chapter on the stories' social and historical background. In the background chapter, the four basic aspects of Korean society that influenced and were influenced by the period—people and the state, belief systems, human relationships, and standard of living and quality

1. The definition of Korean modernity varies from scholar to scholar, as do opinions on what periods were most influential in bringing about modernity. For an enlightening discussion, see Karlsson's review of Kyung Moon Hwang's *Beyond Birth: Social status in the emergence of modern Korea.*

of life—are described in their relation to corresponding points in the stories.

In this book, then, you will find an introduction to the literature of the period, written by Bruce Fulton (translator of Korean fiction and professor of Korean literature at the University of British Columbia); the stories; an article on my experience in translating one of the stories; and the chapter on the social and historical background of the stories.

A Few Notes about the Book

The stories featured here were all translated by the author of this book. Eight of the translations have been published before but have since been revised for this volume, and four of the stories appear for the first time here.

"Korea" refers to South Korea, unless specified as "North Korea."

The McCune-Reischauer (M-R) Romanization System[2] is used for Romanizing Korean words. If the spelling of a proper noun is already established (names of characters in the stories, for example, and personal names), that spelling is used, even when it does not follow the M-R system. The M-R system provides transcription; it focuses more on how the language is pronounced than on how it is written. But it does not represent every sound variation. The Korean plosive consonants represented by this system as *p*, *k* and *t*, for instance, are pronounced at different places on a spectrum between voiced (e.g., [b]) and unvoiced (e.g., [p]), depending on their environment. Generally, the closest pronunciation is halfway between voiced and unvoiced. The consonant represented as *ch* is pronounced somewhere between [ch] and [j], and the consonant that is represented by *s* is somewhere between [sh] and [s]. Vowels are pronounced as they are in Latin; vowels with the diacritic (ŏ and ŭ) are unrounded vowels (as in b*ough*t and b*oo*k, respectively).

2. For rules and tables of this system, see "McCune-Reischauer Romanization System" in "Recommended Reading." For a detailed description and history of other Romanization systems used for han'gŭl, see Holstein, 1999, in References.

In an effort to minimize interruptions to the reading eye, endnotes for items (mostly source citations) in the background chapter are not numbered. In "Endnotes," at the end of the book, they are marked with the page number and phrase that correspond to the item to which they refer.

Acknowledgments

Without the assistance of many erudite and generous people, this book would not have been possible. University of British Columbia Professor Bruce Fulton wrote the Introduction, provided expert counsel in semantics and style in the short story translations, and inspired and encouraged from beginning to end. Ahn Yong-seok devoted many hours helping to improve my understanding and rendering of both the stories and the transition period with his greater knowledge and clearer perspectives. Others who gave freely of their time in providing help with essential details and insights were Kenneth Kaliher and Sungkyunkwan University Professors Lee Young Oak, Yue Mahn-gunn, and Yonsei University Professor Dwight Strawn. Semantic accuracy in the stories could not have achieved the level that it has without the assistance given by Professor Lee Young Oak, Kang Yŏn-ju, Lee Byŏng-hyŏn, Dr. Bae hŭi-jin, Kim Yŏng-no, Gary Rector, and Kang Yŏn-hŭi. Sungkyunkwan University Professors Song Chían-gyŏng, Han Chung-hyŏn and Kim Yong-chŏl also provided welcome pointers for my better understanding of the stories and the period. Sungkyunkwan University Professor Robert McPherson made substantial improvements in English style, and Kenneth Kaliher contributed the benefits of his journalist's eye and his deep knowledge of the transition period. One mention here is so very little in return for the invaluable help which these friends contributed. I am also deeply indebted to the Korean Literature Translation Institute for its generous grant and to the Institute's Dr. Park

Hye-ju, Yanna Kim, Kim Ye-jin, Park So-yŏng and Park Mil for their continuous guidance, encouragement and patience in getting this book through its early stages. Doug Merwin deserves my sincere gratitude for his expert editing of the entire manuscript in its earlier stage. One scholar whom Cornell asked to evaluate the manuscript kindly spent many unpaid hours writing important suggestions in the margins of my translations; I hope one day to express my deep gratitude in person. In the end, though, all of our efforts might have gone to naught were it not for Cornell East Asia Studies managing editor Mai Shaikhanuar-Cota, whose wisdom, patience and devotion guided this book into print. Even if publication of this book brings me nothing other than her friendship, I will feel immensely rewarded.

Introduction

Bruce Fulton

The stories in this volume span seven decades of Korean fiction, from the 1930s to the 1990s. If we accept the year 1917—when Yi Kwang-su's novel *Mujŏng* (Heartlessness) was serialized and Kim Myŏng-sun's story "Ŭishim ŭi ch'ŏnyo" (A suspicious girl) was published—as the starting point of modern Korean fiction, then the nine authors and twelve stories collected herein constitute a representative sample of that tradition. They are representative in the sense that they reflect not only the outward, physical changes in a modernizing society but the psychological, emotional, and spiritual changes as well. Modern Korean fiction is notable in terms of the vast amount of information it offers us about Korean history, society, and culture, especially as these have been affected by the upheavals that have marked twentieth-century Korea. It is also notable in describing for us the world-view of those who have been influenced by these upheavals.

There is in modern Korean fiction, and indeed in the Korean literary tradition from earliest times, a propensity for writers to bear witness to the times, to help in the inculcation of the society's mores in young people of high school, college, or post-college age (who, surveys suggest, constitute the majority of the readers of Korean literature). This tendency is in large part responsible for Korean literature being what we might call a more culturally specific literature, a literature that is more often than not about Korea than about the larger world. (It may also be responsible in part for the failure of Korean literature to reach the kind of international audience that, say, Japanese and Chinese literature have access to.) One way of reading the authors and works in this collection, therefore, is to understand them in terms of the period in which the stories were written, whether this be the colonial period (for the stories by Kim Tong-ni), the post-Liberation period (Hwang Sun-wŏn), the postwar period (O Sang-wŏn, Yi Pŏm-sŏn, and Kim Tong-ni), the Hangŭl Generation (Ch'oe In-hun and Sŏ Chŏng-in), the years of military dictatorship (Sŏng Sŏk-je and Kong Chi-yŏng), and the democratic era of the post-1987 years (O Chŏng-hŭi). This is not to say that periodization is the best or only way to understand modern Korean fiction. Rather, a periodic approach will better enable us to understand the recurring tendency, intentional or not, of modern Korean fiction writers to attempt to illuminate their society and its changes in their works.

Kim Tong-ni (1913–1995), firstborn among the writers represented in this volume, offers us a window through which to observe the conflict between tradition and modernity that takes place in every modernizing society, a conflict that has been taking place in Korea at least since the Enlightenment Era of the late 1800s and early 1900s. By virtue of his upbringing and education he seems to have been ideally suited to this task. He was born near Kyŏngju, capital of the ancient Shilla kingdom and a repository of early Korean culture. Initially educated in the local village school, or *sŏdang,* he also spent time at a Buddhist temple as well as in the new Western (by way of Japan) schools. And then as a young man he moved to Seoul, eventually becoming a professor at Chungang University.

Already by 1936, the year in which his classic story "The Shaman Painting" (Munyŏdo) was first published, Christianity had taken firm root in Korean soil, especially in what is now the Democratic People's Republic of Korea, or North Korea. In doing so it came to co-exist with, and sometimes challenge, existing religions and cosmologies, in particular native Korean spiritualism centered in the person of the female shamans known as *mudang*. The confrontation between Western religion and native spirituality plays out tragically in "The Shaman Painting." The emphasis in "Loess Valley" (Hwangt'ogi, 1939) is less on conflict between ideologies and more on the primeval passions that seem to underlie native spirituality in any form. The periodic bouts of drinking and fighting that punctuate the lives of the two men in "Loess Valley," as rare as they may be in modern Korean fiction, resonate both within and without Korea, in urban as well as rural settings, as may be seen in literary works as far afield from Korea as Chuck Pahlaniuk's novel *Fight Club*. "The Visit" (Ŏttŏn mannam, 1951) is less ambitious than the two earlier stories but equally effective, a sketch of a brief and inarticulate wartime encounter between a farmer and soldier son. The story reveals Kim's knack for character development, evident in his very first published story, "A Descendant of the Hwarang" (Hwarang ŭi huye, 1935).

The life of Hwang Sun-wŏn (1915–2000) mirrors many of the vicissitudes of modern Korean history. He was born to a landed Christian family outside of Pyongyang, went to college in Tokyo (Waseda University), moved with his family from Pyongyang to Seoul in what is now the Republic of Korea (South Korea) in 1946, lived with his family as refugees first in Taegu and then in Pusan during the Korean War, and subsequently settled in the Seoul area, where he taught first at the high school and then the university level. It is unfortunate that Hwang will forever be linked in the Korean imagination to a single story, "The Rain Shower" (Sonagi, 1952), by virtue of its inclusion in the middle-school reader studied by generations of Korean schoolchildren. Understood, appreciated, and ultimately delimited by most of these readers as a romantic and lyrical recorder of a pastoral and bygone Korea, Hwang is quite probably the most versatile and accomplished of modern Korean short fiction writers, and the more than one hundred stories he published from the 1930s to the 1980s reflect not only his personal life, as just outlined, but also the major historical events of twentieth-century Korea. Hwang's stories from mid-century are especially interesting, and comparatively little known. Those from the *Haebang konggan,* the post-Liberation "space" dating from the end of the Pacific War in 1945 to the establishment of separate regimes in southern and northern Korea three years later, offer glimpses into one of the most chaotic periods in Korea's modern history, a time when Koreans were confronted with the sudden exodus of their colonial masters and with such social problems as massive refugee influxes, changes in land tenure, economic chaos, and ideological rivalries. These stories, gathered in Hwang's *The Dog of Crossover Village* (Mongnŏmi maŭl ŭi kae, 1948) collection, were followed in the mid-1950s by *Lost Souls* (Irŏbŏrin saram tŭl, 1958), five stories that can be instructively read as theme-and-variations on the motif of the outcast in a highly stratified society—an appropriate subject at a time when Koreans had recently sustained a horrific civil war.

Written in March 1948, "The Game Beaters" (Morikkun) is closer to the *Dog of Crossover Village* collection in its reflection of the vicissitudes of life in the post-Liberation period but looks ahead to the more experimental narratives of his subsequent fiction in its use of a limited third-person narrative that functions like a first-person narrative that constantly shifts from one character's point of view to another's. In an October 16, 1997, interview Hwang explained to me that the onlookers whose remarks constitute much of the narrative are the game beaters, the urban hunters, in this story. In their changing pronouncements and fickle behavior and in the confounding of their expectations we see in microcosm the political and ideological vacuum of the immediate post-Liberation period, as well as a reminder by the author of the fallibility of presumption and, by extension, of narrative omniscience.

O Sang-wŏn (1930–1985) came of age during the horrors of the Korean War. A French literature major at Seoul National University, he like some of his contemporaries, notably Chang Yong-hak, was attracted to French existentialism for the possibility it offered of an understanding to the absurdity of war and fraternal conflict. Essentially a writer of short fiction, he published most of his work between the mid-1950s and mid-1960s. "A Moment's Grace" (Yuye, 1955) was one of his first stories, and is striking for its use of stream-of-consciousness technique that alternates between first-person and "over-the-shoulder" third-person narrative. It is fitting that O, a native of North Korea, should be remembered for this story set near the border between the two Koreas during the civil war. Westerners who visited Korea in the 1950s describe a desperately poor land littered with the wreckage of war. Fiction from that decade portrays the psychic as well as physical damage of the 1950–1953 conflict, and is often set in a landscape devoid of moral signposts. Here was fertile ground for French existentialism with its emphasis on individual existence as one's only certainty in life. One man's existence is at the center of "A Moment's Grace" and when that existence is extinguished, the story comes to an expected but still jarring end.

Yi Pŏm-sŏn (1920–1982), like O Sang-wŏn, was a native northerner who began publishing fiction during the postwar period, which in Korean literary history usually means the 1950s after the cease-fire in July 1953 that was supposed to have ended hostilities in the Korean War. (As of today, a permanent peace treaty has yet to be signed and North and South Korea remain technically at war.) Yi's best-known story, "A Stray Bullet" (Obalt'an, 1959), is as grim a piece of fiction as one will find in modern Korea, a deterministic story about a family undergoing physical, moral, and mental breakdown. The ending of the story, in which the protagonist is likened to a stray bullet discharged by a disengaged deity, was deemed blasphemous by government officials and the author lost his teaching job as a result.

But there is another side to Yi Pŏm-sŏn. Unlike his fellow northerner O Sang-wŏn, whose fiction-writing career was essentially over by the mid-1960s, two decades before his death, Yi continued to write until his death in the early 1980s; he was especially prolific in the 1960s, publishing some three dozen stories during that decade. And like other Korean writers—Yi Hyo-sŏk (1907–1942) and O Yŏng-su (1914–1979) come readily to mind—Yi found creative inspiration in the rural Korea and Korean tradition, and it is this aspect of his literary life that will most likely sustain his reputation. That such writers, and Koreans in general, were able to find stability in a tradition whose written record dates back two millennia, helps us understand how the people on the Korean peninsula could have survived ongoing historical, political, and societal crises and, in the case of South Korea, to be thriving as never before at the outset of the new millennium. What is striking about "The Gulls" (Kalmaegi, 1958) is the mood of permanence and stability underlying the various traumatic experiences recounted in this short piece—a deadly typhoon; the resettlement of the protagonist (a refugee from North Korea) on a coastal island in the South; the separation of a father and his son during wartime, and their chance reunion in the island village where the story takes place.

Ch'oe In-hun and Sŏ Chŏng-in, though born in the same year (1936), nevertheless represent diverse approaches to fiction. Like several of the writers in this volume, Ch'oe produced mature fictional work at an early age. His *The Plaza* (Kwangjang, 1961), a novel about a young Korean War veteran as existential hero, has never quite lived up to its earlier reputation as The

Great Korean Novel, but subsequent fiction has revealed Ch'oe to be perhaps the most gifted practitioner of intertextuality in modern Korean literary history. Starting with "A Nine-Cloud Dream" (1962), echoing Kim Man-jung's eighteenth-century novel *Kuun mong*, Ch'oe has worked his way through a repertoire of Korean fictional favorites from both premodern and modern times, including "The Tale of Nolbu" (Nolbu tyŏn, 1966), "The Tale of Ch'unhyang" (Ch'unhyang tyŏn, 1967), and *A Day in the Life of Kubo the Writer* (Sosŏlga Kubo sshi ŭi iril, 1970–1971). Though he draws on the Korean literary tradition for much of his fiction, Ch'oe is a sophisticated writer keenly attuned to contemporary Korean political realities. An early story, "Imprisoned" (Su, 1961), shows remarkable psychological insight, and in retelling the celebrated Ch'unhyang story Ch'oe makes use of the subversive inner themes of that tale, in which a low-born girl transcends class boundaries to marry a nobleman's son. Ch'oe is among the generation of writers who chafed under the strictures imposed on the people of South Korea by President Park Chung Hee from 1961 to 1979 as he pushed forward his program of export-led industrialization. It should come as no surprise that Ch'oe responded to the repressive intellectual atmosphere of the 1960s and 1970s by drawing on the Korean oral tradition and its legacy of satirizing the hypocrisy of the elite. Ch'oe's interest in the oral tradition is also suggested by the plays he authored from the late 1960s to the early 1980s.

"House of Idols" (Usang ŭi chip, 1960) is another early work, a sophisticated sketch of a sociopath who takes into his confidence "victims" such as the narrator with fictitious stories of love, death, and war. Knowing of Ch'oe's propensity for allegory, one cannot help suspecting that the confident man in this story symbolizes the authoritarian leaders of postwar South Korea who used a national narrative of civil war and territorial division to victimize a gullible populace who themselves had been wounded, uprooted, and separated from loved ones. "End of the Road" (Kukto ŭi kkŭt, 1966) is a very different story. Taking place mostly on a bus, it begins with a wide-angle view of the Korean countryside, then switches to successively narrower shots of an American military base camptown, to a young woman who works in that compound, and finally to her younger brother, who waits at the end of the road for the bus that is supposed to be bringing her home. The urban, internal landscape of "House of Idols" gives way in "End of the Road" to a sketch of the rural, physical landscape and the conflicts of those who inhabit it. Together these two stories offer a three-dimensional view of a society and a culture in flux.

In modern Korea it is the short story that cements a fiction writer's critical reputation and the novel that brings popular recognition (and, especially in the case of multivolume sagas, critical acceptance as well). Sŏ Chŏng-in during a forty-year career as a creative writer has restricted himself to short fiction and not coincidentally is probably the least known of the authors in this volume to a general Korean readership. And yet as a storyteller he ranks among the most accomplished of modern Korean writers. Perhaps because of the trauma that modern history has visited upon the Korean people, the response of fiction writers has tended to originate more in the interior landscape than in the outside world. Correspondingly, authors such as Sŏ, a master of physical description, dialogue, and plot, are rare. In his best stories, such as "The River" ("Kang," 1968), included here, and "On the Road" (Haengnyŏ, 1976), the interior landscape tends to be implied rather than explicit. South Korea in the 1970s was being propelled by President Park's economic strategy of converting from a traditional agrarian society to a modern industrial state. No less profound than the rapidly developing urban landscape in South Korea has been the loss of population in the countryside. Emblematic of this population shift, described at length by authors such as Yun Hŭng-gil (b. 1942), Hwang Sŏg-yŏng (b. 1943), and Yang Kwi-ja (b. 1955), are the brother and sister in "On the Road," who have left their ancestral village for the capital.

Sŏng Sŏk-che (b. 1961) was originally a poet and began publishing fiction in the mid-1990s. The title of his first published story, "The Last Four and a Half Seconds of My Life" (Nae insaeng ŭi majimak 4.5 ch'o, 1995), which takes place inside a car careening through a guard rail and over the side of a bridge, signaled the arrival of a distinctive fictional voice. Utilizing a variety of narrative formats (including one based on the traditional *chŏn,* a tale about an individual's life) and focusing often on drunkards, gamblers, and womanizers, Sŏng has developed a humorous world-view that ties him to the earthiness of the Korean oral tradition while setting him apart from mainstream modern Korean fiction writers. Inheriting the premodern literatus's obligation to enlighten the unlettered masses and at the same time prove himself worthy among his equally accomplished literary peers, modern Korean fiction writers have for the most part adopted serious fictional personae so as to be consistent with the gravity of historical events in twentieth-century Korea, events that, indeed, often form the subject matter of their narratives. Writers, especially those of a younger generation, display humor in their works at the risk of being judged frivolous. For Sŏng and like-minded writers, the hope remains that with increased stability on the Korean peninsula and in the minds of its inhabitants will come the security and self-confidence that allow for increased freedom of artistic expression. At a time when the Korean Wave of popular culture threatens to overshadow the literary arts, voices like that of Sŏng are more important than ever before.

Sŏng's "First Love" (Ch'ŏssarang, 1995) is a remarkable story if for no other reason than it treats male same-sex desire. Korea has long had the reputation as the most neo-Confucian society in East Asia. Ritual veneration of ancestors is a fundamental element of neo-Confucianism, so much so that a man's failure to produce a male heir is potentially catastrophic, for it is the male heir who is ultimately responsible for conducting the all-important ancestral rites. In an ideology concerned above all else with the practical matter of correct relations in a social hierarchy, homosexuality serves no immediate and obvious function. This is not to say that homosexuality is absent in Korean society past or present. Rather it occupies an anomalous position, one that is shared by *paekchŏng* (outcaste persons), mixed-race individuals, military camptown prostitutes, and others who have no clear location within a tightly ordered social system. Only comparatively recently has same-sex desire appeared openly in Korean fiction, in stories by mainstream writers such as O Chŏng-hŭi and Kang Sŏk-kyŏng as well as in works by more experimental writers such as Chang Chŏng-il and Pak Min-gyu (though some readers might argue that there are homoerotic undercurrents in some of Yi Kwang-su's early stories). The halting transition in Korea today to a more tolerant society is perhaps symbolized in "First Love" by the confusion of the narrator, who is both the object of desire by an older youth and the subject of heterosexual desire of young women in his neighborhood.

Kong Chi-yŏng (b. 1963) has been linked in her readers' imagination with the 1980s and the student activism that coalesced following the May 1980 government massacre of citizens in the southern city of Kwangju. A veteran of the student movement that has served as the youthful conscience of South Korea at least since the April 1960 student-led popular uprising that forced heavy-handed president Yi Sŭng-man (Syngman Rhee) to step down, Kong has in her fictional works been equally concerned with professional women such as herself who attempt to forge meaningful and independent lives in a traditional patriarchal society. An enduring image in contemporary Korean cinema is a wife's one-punch knockdown of her two-timing husband in the 1995 film adaptation of Kong's 1993 novel *Go Alone Like the Horn of a Rhinoceros* (Muso ŭi ppul ch'ŏrŏm honja sŏ kara; the title is derived from an early Buddhist sutra). The tension in her stories sometimes originates in the conflicting demands of the student movement with its emphasis on societal responsibility and the women's movement and its concern for gender equity. An example is the title story of her 1993 collection *Human Decency* (Ingan e taehan yeŭi), in which the journalist protagonist finds herself torn, in terms of the subject matter of her next magazine feature, between a self-fulfilled female artist and a male political dissident recently released from a long term of imprisonment. After a hiatus of several years in her writing (a not uncommon phenomenon among Korean writers who have shouldered the burden of producing works considered relevant to the times) Kong reappeared on the literary scene in the new millennium with a new realization of the variety of human experience in the world today—owing partly to a year she spent in Berlin, which resulted in her story collection *Field of Stars* (Pyŏl tŭl ŭi tŭlp'an, 2004). With that awareness has come a much broader range of thematic interests. *My Sister Pong-sun* (Pongsuni ŏnni, 1998) examines continuing class-based prejudice. *Our Happy Times* (Uri tŭl ŭi haengbokhan shigan, 2005) concerns a death-row prisoner and reflects the author's desire to confront what she believes is the psychopath latent within each of us. And at the time of this writing she has just completed a novel in collaboration with a Japanese writer—perhaps a first in modern Korean literature, and a fitting partnership in view of the sudden popularity of Korean popular culture in Japan and elsewhere in Asia.

Kong's "What's To Be Done?" (Muŏs ŭl hal kŏs inga, 1993) looks back to her debut story, "The Coming of Dawn" (Tongt'ŭnŭn saebyŏk, 1998) and ahead to her 1994 novel *Mackerel* (Kodŭngŏ) in its focus on young people involved in the student and/or labor movement. Kong's gift in these works is her pitch-perfect narratives of young women whose sense of obligation to the hierarchical and ultimately patriarchal dissident movement conflicts with their evolving awareness of themselves as potentially independent and professional individuals. As important as the student movement was to the eventual triumph of participatory democracy in South Korea in 1987, the age-based structure of the student dissident organizations, exemplified by the distinction between *sŏnbae* (group members older or earlier in membership than oneself) and *hubae* (group members younger or subsequent in membership), and the difficulty of erasing gender-role expectations within the movement, invest these stories with undertones of frustration and ambivalence.

O Chŏng-hŭi (b. 1947) will go down in Korean literary history, along with Pak Wan-sŏ, as the writer who made possible the 1990s breakthrough by women fiction writers in the predominantly male Korean literary establishment. Her contribution to the development of contemporary Korean fiction has included breaking the stereotype of Korean women's fiction as sentimental, using nameless first-person narrators to simultaneously distance readers and draw them close, sharpening the use of stream-of-consciousness narrative, and portraying the societal costs of rapid industrialization and urbanization in terms of damage to the family structure. O has always been interested in the Korean oral tradition and her stories have made reference to the herdboy/weaving girl folktale ("The Weaving Woman" [Chingnyŏ, 1970]), the Ch'ŏyong story ("A Portrait of Magnolias" [Mongnyŏnch'o, 1975]), and the Ko Chumong myth ("Fireworks" [Pulkkot nori, 1987]). At the same time, her characters are often alienated in ways we associate with a modern urban lifestyle, their nuclear family vulnerable to death, divorce, sterility, abandonment, and insanity. In this way O Chŏng-hŭi, like the first author in this volume, Kim Tong-ni, is both traditional and strikingly modern.

In "The Face" (Ŏlgul, 1999) O revisits territory she charted in one of her most successful, and disturbing, stories, "The Bronze Mirror" (Tonggyŏng, 1982). As birth rates decline and the Korean population ages, we see more elderly couples like those portrayed in these two stories. In traditional Korea old age was a triumphant time, for advanced age in a traditional neo-Confucian society brings veneration for a life lived long and well. It is a time when elders are largely freed of the need to be deferential to those older than oneself, a time to speak one's mind and to enjoy the attention of an extended family. How sobering, then, to see the elderly husband in "The Bronze Mirror" symbolically silenced by the removal of his teeth in favor of dentures, and the husband in "The Face" bedridden and capable of communicating only through dream and memory. For many elderly Koreans, both in the homeland and in the worldwide Korean diaspora, the comforts of an extended family are absent.

Korean literature faces an uncertain future. In South Korea, visual culture dominates the landscape in the new millennium. The image is everywhere, on cell phone, computer monitor, television monitor, movie screen and in print media. The written word as creative medium is losing ground. On the other hand, the "feminization" of Korean literature, deplored by the conservative Korean literature establishment since the mid-1990s, is now a reality, and women's voices are finally gaining parity with those of men in the literary marketplace. Diaspora literature is increasingly drawing attention to ethnic Korean voices overseas, and it may be that in time those voices will be heard in Korea itself and begin to mingle with domestic literary voices, which to an untrained ear may sound like a monotone. In any event, for better or for worse fiction in Korea promises to remain anchored in the realities of contemporary Korean life. In that respect, it will continue to offer a bridge to Korea for those beyond the peninsula.

THE SHAMAN PAINTING

Kim Tong-ni

(1936)

1

Low hills slumbering on night's distant horizon. Broad river winding black across the plain. Sky spangled with stars about to rain down on hills and river and plain as this night approaches its climax. On the broad sandy riverbank under a large canopy a crowd of village women held in thrall by a shaman's magic dance for a lost soul, sadness and hope in their faces and a weariness that tells of coming dawn. In their midst the shaman caught up in the ecstatic throes of her dance, spinning weightless in her swirling mantle, pure spirit freed of flesh and bone. . . . This painting was made before I arrived in this world, around the time my father married. Before this, people looked on our family, with its wealth and lineage, as one with a "good pedigree." The manor was always alive with literati gentry, and we had what was said to be one of the best collections of precious calligraphy and antiques in the country. This love of art was handed down along with the family's wealth from generation to generation, father to son to grandson.

Grandfather was not the kind to concern himself with the material condition of the estate, and he kept up this family tradition even after our family's fortune had begun to wane, around the time he turned over authority as head of the family to Father. He continued welcoming others who shared his love of the arts, as if the good times had never ended. And so there was always one or another itinerant highborn poet or wandering lowborn artist enjoying a few days or months of his hospitality in the gentlemen's quarters.

It was around that time that a peculiar-looking stranger appeared at our door. He came at dusk, I remember, on the day the apricot tree by the vegetable patch in the yard had just blossomed—one of those days in early spring when the gritty loess wind blew from dawn to dusk. About fifty, or so he seemed, small of build. With no long coat he was improperly attired for the road; on his head sat a straw commoner's hat held down by an old silk kerchief tied from the top down round his chin. One got the impression that he had been traveling a long time with no special place to go. In his hand he held the reins of his donkey, and on that donkey sat a girl with a very pallid complexion, about sixteen. The two looked like a rustic servant escorting his master's daughter.

It was not till the next day that the man got around to introducing the girl. "I thought we might visit your lordship because people say this young one here—my daughter—they say she is quite good with a brush . . . "

"What's your name, dear?" Grandfather asked. She simply looked at him for a moment with her big almond eyes, and Grandfather later recalled the young girl's intriguing face, whiter even than the white clothes she wore, and at the same time tinged with a shadow of sorrow.

"Well then, how old are you?" But that one glance was all she was prepared to give, and she remained silent.

Her father answered for her. "My daughter's name is Nangi, sir, and she is sixteen." Then he lowered his voice. "She can't hear too well, you know."

Grandfather nodded. He asked the girl's father to stay a few days and let him get a better look at what the girl could do. So father and daughter stayed on for over a month, daughter painting and her father recounting to Grandfather the sad details of the girl's hard life.

On the day they left, even when Grandfather gave the unfortunate pair some very expensive silk and a generous sum of money for the road, the face of that silent young girl seated on the pony was filled with the very same grief that appears with tears . . .

But now, let me tell you the story that they left behind with the painting, the one Grandfather called "the shaman painting."

2

About a half hour's walk outside the walls of Kyŏngju, ancient Shilla's capital, there is a tiny village. Some knew it as Yŏmin, and to others it was Chapsŏng. At any rate, in one isolated corner of this village lived a sorceress whom people called Mohwa. They called her this because it was the name of the place she had come from.

Mohwa's house was quite unlike the others in this hamlet. It hid deep in the weeds that crowded a large yard encircled by a long rock wall crumbling in places like the ancient fortress wall that snaked along the mountain ridge nearby. The roof of this old house was blackened from one end to the other with shingle mushrooms that gave off a pungent stench of humus. One corner of the decrepit dwelling was in a state of impending collapse. The flourishing jungle that surrounded the house was overrun with all sorts of vines and herbs, and nameless grasses and weeds grew so high a person could get lost in them. This jungle was fed throughout the year by pools of old rain water covered with black-green algae. In the nocturnal world beneath all this vegetation worms as big as snakes slithered and frogs as hoary as toads prowled, and except for these creatures, no living thing—no human anyway—seemed to have lived there for decades, even centuries.

The shaman Mohwa lived with her daughter Nangi in this weary, rundown haunted house. The solitary pair had little to do with anyone from the outside. Practically their only visitor was Nangi's father, who had a seafood shop on the coastal road a few hours' walk from Kyongju. They said Nangi was the only thing of any meaning in his life, and she was so dear to him he could not bear to be away from her for very long so in the spring and fall he would come visiting with precious foods from the sea, like tasty bundles of dried kelp and seaweed. Until Mohwa's son Woogi returned after several years away, mother and daughter had no other visitors to their goblins' den except for the occasional woman, from town or from afar, who wanted Mohwa to exorcise a demon or summon the spirits for protection.

On these rare occasions that someone came to ask Mohwa to perform a rite, the visitor would peek in the outside gate and call, "Mohwa, you in there? Mohwa . . . ?" and when there was still no answer come into the yard and call a couple more times. Then she might approach the house, maybe lean with one hand on the low, narrow porch and reach over with the other to open the door . . . but just then the door would open and peeping out would be the young girl Nangi, staring at the visitor without a word. The girl might have been painting all by herself and then, when she heard someone calling, dropped her brush in surprise and blanched with fear, and finally crept to the door, trembling from head to toe.

It was always like this, Nangi sitting alone all day at home and Mohwa spending all day outside. Mother was up and out the very moment the sun breached the ancient fortress wall, and it was not till that sun sank behind the west ridge that she could be seen coming back home, tipsy, with some peaches in a knotted wrapper, slowing now and then into her dance, intoning in her doleful chant,

> Daughter, my daughter, Mr. Kim's daughter,
> Sea Kingdom Flower Spirit, my daughter Nangi . . .
> Let me into the Dragon King's Palace
> Twelve gates all locked
> Open up, open up you twelve gates.
> Please open up . . .

"Had one today too, Mohwa?" the villagers greeted her, and she smiled and clasped her hands in front and twisted her shoulders demurely, "Yes, on my way home from the market," and then bowed politely. When she was not doing an exorcism or summoning the spirits she was usually at the wine shop.

She liked drinking so much and Nangi liked peaches so much that she came back drunk every day, in mid-summer always with a few peaches. "Daughter, daughter, my little daughter . . . " calling Nangi with this chant all the way into the house. And Nangi would attack one of these luscious peaches and gobble it up, just as she used to go so hungrily for her mother's breast when she was much younger.

To hear Mohwa tell it, Nangi was an incarnation of the Sea Kingdom's Flower Spirit. In a dream Mohwa had a visitation from the Dragon Spirit, who ruled the Sea Kingdom, and he gave her a peach to eat. Nangi was born seven days after this. Now the Sea Kingdom's Dragon Spirit had twelve daughters. The first was Moon, the second Water, the third Cloud . . . and so on till the twelfth, Flower, and these daughters were betrothed to the Mountain Spirit's twelve sons—Moon to Sun, Water to Tree, Cloud to Wind—each pair betrothed and to be married in their turn, but Flower, the last daughter, who had a romantic sort of nature, could not wait her turn and grabbed Bird, the eleventh brother and darling of Flower's elder sister Fruit, so the bereft Fruit and the twelfth brother Butterfly complained so pitifully to the Dragon Spirit and the Mountain Spirit that the Dragon Spirit got angry and punished Flower by making her deaf and then even banishing her from the Sea Kingdom, which of course turned her from Flower Spirit into an ordinary peach blossom, and though she bloomed in rich hues every spring by the river and in the forest, and Bird Spirit came every spring to perch on her branches and sang plaintively over and over of his love for her, all that is left now of Flower Spirit is her deaf and dumb reincarnation, Nangi.

At times Mohwa would be in the wine shop drinking, or dancing with the male shamans, when all of a sudden she would stop, then run off as if she were losing her mind. When they shouted "Now what's got into you!" she would yell back at them over her shoulder as she hurried off: Nangi was calling from home. The Dragon Spirit, who was after all the Great Mother and Nangi's first and real parent, had entrusted Mohwa with Nangi for only a while, and Mohwa knew that if she did not take care of this girl she would feel the fury of the Spirit's wrath.

Nangi was not the only incarnation around. Mohwa might pounce on anyone she came upon, admonishing, "Don't forget now, you're an incarnation of Tree Spirit," or "I hope you know you're a son of Rock Spirit." And then she reminded them to pray often to the Seven Stars Spirit or the Dragon Spirit, who had given them all they had.

There were times that she saw everyone and everything as if they were the spirits themselves. It was not only to the grown-ups that she demurely twisted her shoulders and bowed in respect; even children awed her, and upon occasion even a dog or a pig would be the object of her embarrassing demonstrations. Cats too, and frogs, and worms, or a lump of meat, a butterfly, a potato, an apricot tree, a fire poker, a clay pot, a stone step, a straw shoe, the branch of a jujube tree, a swallow, a cloud, wind, fire, rice, a kite, a gourd ladle, an old straw cattle-feed pouch, kettles, spoons, oil lamps . . . and so on and so forth. When she was in this mood everything she chanced to meet became her neighbor, no less worthy of being a spirit than her neighbors who happened to be human and whom she exchanged glances and greetings with, and talked and fought with, even envied and cursed.

3

From the day Woogi came back home Mohwa's goblin den began to seem more like a place where people lived. Nangi, who used to hate to set foot in the kitchen, now came up with an occasional meal for Woogi. And at night now, a paper lantern hung from the corner of the sagging tile roof and provided a faint glimmer of light where there used to be only the black gloom of the yard and the stars far above.

Woogi was born of a relationship that Mohwa had with some man when she still lived in Mohwa Hamlet, before her spirit took possession of her. Even when Woogi was still very young everybody around remarked what a precocious one he was, but Mohwa was so poor she could not send him to the classics primer school that most of the children in the village went to. When he turned nine, though, an acquaintance of Mohwa's got a temple to take him in as a novice. After that there was no news from him at all until that day ten years later he appeared again out of the blue.

Nangi was his half sister. When she was around five, before Woogi left and she got sick, she was always calling his name and tagging along after him everywhere he went. It was soon after Woogi went off to the temple that Nangi took to her bed with her sickness. She came out of it three years later unable to hear much at all, though no one was ever able to tell exactly how bad her hearing was.

For a while after Woogi left she would stammer to her mother, "Wh-where is Woogi?"

"Temple," Mohwa would shout. "Studying in the temple."

"Wh-what temple? Wh-where?"

"Jirim. Very big . . . "

That was not true, though. Mohwa herself had no idea what temple Woogi was at, but she did not want to admit it. So she just said the first thing that came to her.

One day, arriving home from the market, Mohwa found a beautiful eighteen-year-old boy in the yard. When she was finally able to make out who the lad was, she panicked, and her booze-darkened face blushed an even deeper shade of scarlet. She turned to bolt, but then stopped, then shuffled a moment in hesitation—and abruptly turned back toward him. Those long arms on her long willowy frame spread open, then she ran to Woogi and embraced him like a big hen drawing her chick to her breast.

"Who can this handsome young man be? Whoever . . . ? Oh my son, my dear son!" She let the tears flow, oblivious to everything around her. "Look who's here! My son!"

"Mother!" Woogi buried his cheek in his mother's shoulder. "Mother . . . " And he cried too, long and hard.

Before Mohwa came back home Nangi had been sitting by herself in the family room when this strange young man opened the door and looked in, and he scared her so bad her heart stopped and she sat there pinned in the corner unable to utter a sound, unable even to show her fear except in her violent trembling. Nangi saw the boy had Mohwa's slender waist, her long neck, and she guessed who he might be. But that beautiful face that gave him such a noble countenance did not belong to a person who had undergone the lonely rigors of working in a temple for several years. She had seen a clear resemblance to Mohwa, yet it was only now that she was fully able to comprehend this young man was truly her lost Woogi. When she saw her mother smothering this boy in her embrace and sobbing "My son, my son!" through her streaming tears, she felt the tears coming to her own eyes. This young man that was able to bring out such tender feelings from this crusty sorceress had to be her brother Woogi, and an indescribable thrill ran through her.

Within a few days, though, Woogi had become an unsolvable riddle to his mother and Nangi. When he was about to eat, or go to bed, and then again when he got up in the morning, he never neglected to mumble some strange long incantation. And at times he would pull a small book from his breast pocket and bury himself in it.

On one of these occasions Woogi saw Nangi's puzzled expression and a smile lit up his beautiful face. "Here," he offered, opening it up and showing it to her, "you can read it too." Though it was not all that easy for her, Nangi could read—she had already been through the classic "Tale of Shimch'ong" a few times—but this was the first time she had ever seen that word "Bible," there on the cover. Woogi saw her puzzled look and that whole exquisite face of his lit up in one big beatific smile.

"Do you know who made you?"

Though Nangi could not hear what he said, she was able to get the general idea through his gestures and the expressions on his face. But what he really meant—well, this was difficult, something she had never thought of before.

"All right then, do you know what happens to you when you die?"

She just stared in reply.

"It's all here, right in this book." And then he pointed at the sky. The only word she could just barely make out was "God."

"God is the one who made us. And it's not only us He made, He made everything on the earth and in the sky. And we return to Him when we die."

It was not long before this god of Woogi's roused Mohwa's suspicion, even repulsion. Four days after he arrived, when he was just about to say his prayers over the food she had put in front of him, she ventured, "I never knew they had that stuff in Buddhism." Apparently she was thinking that he had been in the temple all those years and that this was some sort of arcane Buddhist practice.

"No, Mother. I am not a Buddhist."

"Well then, what else is there besides Buddhism?"

"Mother, I ran away from that temple because I could not abide seeing another Buddhist."

"Couldn't abide . . . ? Buddhism is the Way. So what are you, a Taoist, some Taoist immortal maybe?"

"No, Mother, I am a Christian."

"Christian?"

"They call it Christianity up north. It's a new religion."

"So you're one of that Donghak cult?"

"No, not Donghak. Christian."

"Sure, sure. In this Christianity or whatever you call it do they do this incantation every time they sit down to eat?"

"That is no incantation, Mother. I was offering a prayer to God."

Her eyes bulged. "God?"

"Yes. It's God who made us."

His mother blanched. "Oh my, the boy's gone and got possessed by some drifter demon!" And that put an end to her questions.

The next day Mohwa went to the house of someone possessed by one of those drifter demons who latch on to one victim and torment him for a while till they get chased off to another victim. She had taken care of this demon with her rice-water cure and had just returned home. Woogi saw how worn out and disheveled she was, and asked, "Mother, where have you been?"

"Pak Kŭp-ch'ang's. I did them an exorcism."

Woogi silently thought to himself for a while, then asked, "And does the demon leave when you tell it to?"

"Well, the man has returned to his senses so it must be gone," she replied in a tone that wondered what sort of silly question he was going to come up with next.

Until now in this area she had conducted countless exorcisms and cured hundreds, even thousands possessed by every sort of demon, and not even once had she ever doubted the power of her spirits or her power to use them. Chasing away those drifter demons came as naturally to her as offering a cup of water to a thirsty person would to you or me. And Mohwa was not the only one who believed this. The one who asked for her services, and all those related to the one possessed, thought the same way. It was simple: When you got sick, you went to Mohwa before you went to any doctor. Everyone knew that Mohwa's exorcisms and conjurations worked a lot faster and were far more effective and far cheaper than any medicine or needle they had in any clinic.

Woogi, bowed in thought, now raised his head and looked straight into his mother's eyes. "Mother, it is a sin for you to do that—it is Jesus who does that sort of thing, not people. Look, right here in Matthew, Chapter 9 Verses 32 and 33: If we bring the deaf mute to Jesus he will cast out the evil spirit and the dumb shall speak again and . . .

But before he was able to finish, Mohwa got up and went

over to the altar she always kept in the corner of the family room.

> Great spirits,
> rulers of heaven and earth,
> north, south, east and west,
> above and below,
> what you've made to fly flies,
> what you've made to crawl crawls.
> No more than beasts in human clothes are we,
> tenuous lives hanging by a thread.
> In your bosom we find protection;
> you guide us along the righteous way,
> grasping good and spurning evil.

Mohwa's eyes gleamed like jewels, her whole body began to tremble violently, as she rubbed her hands in prayer.

> House Spirit gives us land, Hearth Spirit gives us fire,
> Family Spirit gives us good fortune, Seven Stars Spirit
> gives us life,
> and Maitreya protects this tenuous life.
> Lead us along the righteous way,
> the broad and level way.

As soon as she finished her wild prayer the spirit who now possessed her grabbed the dish of rice water from over the altar, took a mouthful, and sprayed the demon in Woogi with it head to toe. Then "Shoo-o-o-o-o!" she shrieked at him,

> Shoo, demon!
> You're in Yongju here, place of the gods,
> at Biru Peak, highest of all—

Too high for the likes of you!
Sheerest cliffs, fifty fathoms of blue sea—
Too deep for the likes of you!
A sword in my right hand, torch in my left,
Out, evil spirit, on your way.
Shoo and away with you!

Woogi, stunned at Mohwa's frenzied raving, bowed his head in a short prayer. And then, without another word, he got up and left the house.

Long after Woogi had gone, Mohwa went on ranting, as she sprayed the demons from every corner.

4

Woogi decided it was about time to find out if there were any Christians in the area. Mohwa thought he would be back soon, but the sun set and the night deepened without his return. Mohwa and Nangi slumped gloomily in a corner of the family room waiting for him to come back.

"Is that Jesus demon book here somewhere?" she asked Nangi. The child shook her head, she did not know, but wished at the same time that he had left it with her, that thing he called the Bible and Mohwa called the Jesus demon book because she was sure Woogi was possessed.

Woogi was thinking the same way about them. He believed this demon of Mohwa's had probably gone and possessed Nangi too, had even struck her dumb. But he remembered: "In his time, Jesus cured people possessed by the devil and rendered deaf and dumb," and determined with all his heart that he would pray to the Lord as much as it took to get Him, through Woogi, to cure his mother and little sister.

> When Jesus saw that the people came running together, he rebuked the foul spirit, saying unto him, "Thou dumb and deaf spirit, I charge thee, come out of him and enter no more into him." And the spirit cried, and rent him sore, and came out of him: and he was as one dead; insomuch that many said, "He is dead." But Jesus took him by the hand, and lifted him up; and he arose. And when he was come into the house, his disciples asked him privately, "Why could not we cast him out?" And he said unto them, "This kind can come forth by nothing, but by praying and fasting." [Gospel of Mark, Chapter 9, Verses 25–29]

And so Woogi believed that if he only prayed persistently, God would chase the demons out of his mother and little sister. Straightaway he wrote a letter to Reverend Hyun and Elder Lee in Pyongyang, who had taught him about Jesus.

> Dear Reverend Hyun,
>
> Through the bountiful grace of God I have found my mother. However, since the word of our Lord has not yet spread to this area, so many here are possessed by the devil and they worship idols. Without a church—as soon as possible—these people will never hear the Good News.
>
> I am embarrassed to tell you this, but both my mother and sister are possessed by demons. One demon has turned my mother into a sorceress and another has stricken my sister deaf and dumb. As Jesus instructs us in Mark's gospel, Chapter 9, Verse 29, I am praying to Him very hard to chase away these demons, but it is very hard to pray here without a church. I sincerely hope that a church will be built here as soon as possible.

It was this Reverend Hyun, from America, who clothed, fed and educated Woogi. In the summer of the year Woogi turned fourteen the boy had announced at the temple that he was going to Seoul and quit his life as a novice, but instead of going to Seoul he wandered here and there through the country, and in the autumn of the year he turned fifteen found himself in Pyongyang. That winter he met Elder Lee, and Elder Chang introduced him to Reverend Hyun.

A couple years later, when Woogi told Reverend Hyun he was going to have to try to find his mother, the minister sat him down and told him, "Within three years I will be returning to America. If at that time you wish to go with me, you're very welcome to."

"Thank you, Reverend. I would like very much to go with you."

"All right, then. Go find your mother, and return as soon as you can."

But the house he found his mother living in was of a totally different world from the one he had known with Reverend Hyun. In place of those bright, cheery sounds of hymns and the organ and voices reading the Bible and the happy, smiling faces of people sitting together at a table of wholesome food and giving thanks to the Lord, here was this forlorn crumbling wall surrounding a yard of twisting vines and tangled weeds crawling with frogs and worms around a stale old house suffocating under a roof creeping with dark-green shingle mushrooms, and every time he saw these two women in the midst of all that—mother possessed by the sorceress demon and daughter possessed by the deaf-mute demon—Woogi immediately wondered whether he himself had not been bewitched into that goblins' den.

A while after Woogi finally came back home one day from meeting the Christians in the area, Nangi started to change. All day long Woogi could sense this girl with her lithe body, smooth skin as fair as paper, languishing in the corner without a word, without a smile, following Woogi's every movement with her big gleaming eyes. Then when night came and the paper lantern glowed dimly from the roof corner and Woogi went out for some air, Nangi would stroll into a dark corner of the yard and watch him. Before long the blood-starved mosquitoes started swarming round her with their mad singing, and she flew from them to Woogi for protection. Her lips sought his neck, and her ice-cold hands startled him as they found his breast; he pulled her hands away, and she backed off some but then, whole body trembling, moved in again. After a while Woogi took her hand and led her into the light of the lantern, both of them confused and embarrassed at what was happening to them.

From the time Nangi started behaving this way Woogi grew paler by the day, and in his face showed the confusion that was working inside him. After a couple weeks of this he abruptly left home, without a word of where he was going or when he would return.

Two days after he left, in the middle of the night, Mohwa woke, sat up, and let out a long sigh. She looked at Nangi, lying next to her, and shook her awake. In a voice heavy with gloom she asked, "When did Woogi say he was coming back?" When she saw Nangi had nothing to say, she grumbled, "How can we expect him to come back if you don't have his supper ready like I asked you to?"

Every day that he did not come back she got more anxious. In the middle of the night she would suddenly get up and go to the kitchen, set aside the dinner tray they had prepared for Woogi, pour some more mint oil into the ritual lamp saucer and light the wick. She raised her hands above her head and then bowed.

Our own Household Spirit, our own Seven-Stars Spirit,
our own Hearth Spirit . . .

She rubbed her palms together in supplication and bowed again, then straightened and began to work slowly into her dance to beckon the spirits.

I pray to you, and to the Guardian Spirit of this family
I pray.
Heaven has its stars, the sea has its pearls,
and this house has its prince,
Precious as gold and silver, beautiful as jade, child of
auspicious star.
We pray for him to the Birth Spirit for long life,
to the Seven Stars Spirit for glory,
to the Family Spirit for good fortune,
to the Dragon Spirit for virtue,
to the Hearth Spirit for enlightenment,
to the Homesite Spirit for talent.
Stars in the heavens, pearls in the sea . . .
Birth Spirit, Hearth Spirit won't refuse
to come and cast out the Jesus demon,
craving fire demon 10,000 li from the west.

Now she was ranting, wheeling and whirling madly about.

He burns, look at him burn—whoosh! whoosh! he burns,
the fire demon up in flames!
And when he's finished burning, my child of auspicious
star is sitting over his ashes,
unscathed, shining like gold and silver.
Yes, Birth Spirit is on his way,
here comes Hearth Spirit!

The commotion in the kitchen would waken Nangi, and she would get out of bed and go to the door that connected the family room and the kitchen. She peeped through the hole in the window paper, holding her breath, enthralled, and before she knew what was happening her whole body began to twitch and tremble. Soon she jumped up, possessed by her mother's spirit. She took off her upper clothes. Then her lower clothes. One step in tandem with her mother, then another, and one more, and soon she was with her mother step for step, gesture for gesture, chanting the same lyrics to the same notes to the same rhythm, daughter in the family room, mother in the kitchen. And then at dawn after one such night, when Nangi returned to her senses she found herself off her sleeping mat and spread out on the bare floor, completely naked, now a sorceress.

One day around this time Mohwa was on the porch trying on a new pair of shoes that she had been given to wear for her next ritual. She looked up, and there was Woogi, a smile on his face. The mother put down her shoes and got up, and, just as when he had returned the first time, beckoned him with outspread arms, then wrapped them around Woogi's slender form, enfolding him like a big mother bird protecting her chick. And she wept. She uttered not a word of resentment, not a sound other than the quiet sobs of her relief and happiness. That usually ghostly ashen face now glowed with warmth, and in place of the crudity of the possessed sorceress showed the wholesome bearing of a mother.

"Well, uh . . . ," said the uncomfortable boy as he extracted himself from her embrace, "I think I'll get some rest now."

After Woogi went to his room Mohwa went back to the porch. For a long time she sat there, legs spread out in front of her, head hanging, lost deep in thought. And suddenly it came to her. She raised her head with an "Ah . . . !", got up and went into the house and started rummaging for that thing among Nangi's paintings.

Later, in the middle of the night, Woogi's hands sought the Bible that he always slept with at his breast, and when they found nothing there he began to stir from his sleep. At the same time a muffled chanting teased his slumbering consciousness. He woke, sat up, and looked for his Bible, but no, it was not there. Then he noticed that his mother was not there either, where she usually slept between Nangi and himself. An ominous premonition chilled him. And there, that sound again, clearer now, a ghost's wailing babble from the very bowels of the earth—a witch's incantation. Without another thought he was up and peering through the hole in the paper window of the door to the kitchen.

Jesus demon, craving fire demon 10,000 *li* from the west!
Torch in my right hand, sword in my left.
Vagabond, you drifter, no way to escape,
Dash here, blocked by the Mountain Spirit.
Dart there, Dragon Spirit waits.
Up to the Seven Stars—
they block your every probe.
Break through the clouds? Ride the wind?
Cloud Spirit, Wind Spirit, they're already there.
Down to the Dragon Palace—all Twelve Gates locked.
Rattle the first, four devas jump out,
fierce eyes flashing, iron maces high.
Pound on the second, firedog mates pounce:
Male spits flame, female spits hot coals.
Bang at the third door and water dogs spring out,
Male's bark douses the flame,
Female's bark douses the coals.

Mohwa was in her sorceress outfit, a mantle over white garments. She rubbed her palms together as she bowed and danced in languid, beckoning moves. On the hearth the ritual flame in its offering dish was burning clean on its wick in mint oil, and above this was a tray with one offering dish of water and another of salt. To the side of this Woogi detected a blue curl of smoke rising from a flame's dying flicker on the thick cover of his Bible. One corner of the cover had already turned to ash, along with the pages inside.

That eerie scornful grin on Mohwa's face showed a crazed determination to meet the Jesus demon's challenge. She swung by the tray and picked up some salt out of the dish and sprinkled it on the black ashes, which had now stopped smoking. Her voice was hard with hatred.

> There you go Jesus demon, craving fire demon 10,000 *li*
> from the west,
> to our village shrine to get some money for the road,
> to Kwanu's shrine to take your leave.
> Bells on your ears, keep in step,
> ding-a-ling one-two, ding-a-ling one-two!
> Cross the mountains, cross the seas,
> move onward, forward.
> And once you go, you'll never return,
> your feet will be too sore.
> The flowers may be back next spring, not you;
> in that leanest month your hunger will keep you there,
> 10,000 *li* away in the west.

Deranged babble from a witch's brew, her song sent a shiver of revulsion through Woogi. His heart was wrenched by that coy coaxing in those eyes hard and cold as gems and those lurid gestures in rhythm with the swinging folds of her mantle. He could bear it no longer and, like one struggling out of the throes of a nightmare, he burst out with a cry and in the next instant bounded blindly outside and around to the kitchen door, kicked it open, and made for the dish of water on the offering tray next to Mohwa to save his Bible. But Mohwa whirled round at him and before he could reach the dish the big kitchen knife in her hand flashed him a warning to back off. She waved it tauntingly in his face, between him and his Bible, as she stepped slowly back into her dance.

> Shoo, demon . . . Get out!
> You can't fool me,
> craving fire demon 10,000 *li* from the west.
> You're in Yongju here, place of the gods,
> at Biru Peak, highest of all—
> Too high for the likes of you!
> Sheerest cliffs, fifty fathoms of blue sea—
> And a patch of thorny ash for your feet.
> This is no place for you.
> A sword in my right hand, torch in my left,
> Away, you drifter demon from the west.
> Shoo-o-o-o! And away with you!

And she slashed at Woogi's face. He felt the blade cut the edge of his left ear and he grabbed the water dish from the tray, threw the whole thing into Mohwa's face to bring her to her senses. Then he saw that he had knocked over the ritual flame and the paper door was burning so he jumped up on the hearth to stop it. Mohwa, her face dripping water but burning with rage, followed Woogi up onto the fireplace swinging her knife, and Woogi, trying to smother the spreading flames, felt the blade slash his back. He straightened, turned, and fell straight into his mother's arms and the last thing he saw was the ghost-white face of a fiendishly grinning witch.

5

The wounds from Mohwa's frenzy still showed on Woogi's head, neck and back, and with each day he grew thinner until he was just skin and bones with two sunken eyes. But it was not his wounds that made him so sick.

Mohwa nursed him with all her energy, running here and there day and night to see to his every need. Sometimes in desperation she pulled him up and squeezed him to her breast. But he did not respond. Of course she fed him all kinds of medicines, performed every rite she knew and recited her most eloquent incantations over him. But Woogi did not get better.

The more Mohwa devoted herself to Woogi the weaker became the spirit that possessed her. When someone asked her to do an exorcism or summon the spirits she usually declined—she had to nurse her son. The couple times she consented to perform a rite they said later that the spirit was not with her like it used to be.

Around this time a preacher came to the county seat and a small church was built. Evangelizing teams were dispatched to every village and Christianity spread like wildfire. And one day the word reached even to Mohwa's village in the person of an American missionary.

"Brothers and sisters, thanks be to the Lord for letting us meet. God created each and every one of us, he loved us so. Yet we are all sinners; in our hearts lurks only wickedness. And to save us from our wicked selves Jesus offered himself up to be nailed to that cross. Thus only belief in Jesus Christ will save us. We must glorify him with joyful hearts. And now, let us pray to the Lord our God."

They said it was more fun to watch this American with his weird blue eyes and his parrot's beak than it was to watch a circus monkey.

"And he doesn't charge a thing. Come on!"

They gathered in droves.

Elder Yang, who had brought the missionary here, paid a call at every household. As a sign of the changing times, he was accompanied by his wife, granddaughter of a respected patriarch of the town. He exhorted the villagers, "Believing in shamans and fortunetellers is a sin before our Father, the one and the only Master of heaven and earth. What power has the shaman? She prays and grovels to a rotted old tree, to a deaf and dumb stone image of the Maitreya Buddha. What power has the fortuneteller? This one who cannot see what is right in front of him and gropes his way with a cane claims to guide a person with eyes that see. The almighty who put us on this earth is the absolute one and only Heavenly Father. And what then did our Father tell us? 'Thou shalt not have strange gods before me.'" And he poured forth endlessly on how God's only son Jesus cast out every demon, healed the leper, the cripple, the deaf, and about how Jesus rose from the dead and ascended into heaven only three days after he died on the cross.

When Mohwa overheard any talk about these preachers she sneered, "Worthless drifter demons." Disdain their derision and slander as she might, though, it hurt deeply, and she banged her large gong and she banged her small gong and ranted . . .

Shoo, demon! Away!
You leech off my people,
the poorer the better for you.
But you know Mohwa, so you'd better listen.
If you don't vanish right now I'll wrap you and all your
descendants in the hide of the White Steed Spirit
and throw you into an ash briar patch,
into a boiling cauldron,
into the fifty-fathoms deep blue sea.

Your grandchildren and their grandchildren,
they'll never again see the light of day,
and never beg again.
Away, demon, get away while you can!
Burn the road up with your feet;
Shoo you, 10,000 *li* back west,
A ball of fire on your tail,
A bell on each ear, ding-a-ling ding-a-ling . . .

But the Jesus demon was not driven away; in fact, his followers multiplied. Worse, he began taking possession of those who had come to Mohwa for her magic, until no one came anymore.

In the meanwhile a revivalist had arrived in town. They said he had the skill to cure an illness with a prayer and so everybody in the county started to flock here. He laid his hands on the head of the sick and intoned, "It is your sins that are causing you to suffer so," and prayed over them. They told far and wide of women who had their female maladies washed away with their sins, of the blind who saw again, the crippled who walked again, the deaf who heard, the dumb who spoke, and the paralytic and the epileptic and all those others who, depending on the strength of their faith, had their sins washed away and their afflictions along with those sins.

Day after day the women placed their silver rings and gold rings in the offering box on the dais at the preacher's feet. Contributions poured in. They said the show Mohwa put on could not begin to compare with this one.

"So our phonies from the West have brought their magic show," Mohwa sneered. Her own patron spirit had given her, and not these scoundrels, the power to summon the spirits and exorcise demons. But where she saw the spirits—in the old tree, the rock, the mountain, the river—they saw only craven idols.

And in her they saw an enemy: "Believe in the sorceress and the fortuneteller and you sin in the face of our one and almighty God the Father!" When those Jesus demons put on one of their drum-beating, pipe-squealing anti-superstition parades and slandered Mohwa and her gods, Mohwa went off by herself and danced and chanted to the rhythm of her gongs:

> Shoo you, 10,000 *li* back west,
> You drifter demon.
> A ball of fire on your tail,
> A bell on each ear, ding-a-ling . . .

6

As fall turned to winter that year Woogi got even worse.

Mohwa watched her son waste away a little more every day. At times, faced with her utter powerlessness, she broke down and mourned in a trembling voice, as if her heart were going to break, "Poor thing, you poor thing, what's happening to you? Come from so far away to find your mother, and look what you get for it!"

When Woogi saw this helpless grief he held her hand and, through his tears, said quietly, "Mother, don't fret yourself so. When I die I will go to our heavenly Father."

Mohwa might ask him if there was anything he wanted, but he would only shake his head quietly. Now and then, though, when his mother went out and he was alone with Nangi, he clutched her hand and uttered, "If I only had my Bible . . . "

The following year, four days before Woogi finally departed this world, the one he had longed so to see again arrived from Pyongyang. As soon as the American missionary was led into the yard by the village's Elder Yang he winced at the desolate scene and the fetid stench. "How on earth can Woogi live in such a place?" he wondered to himself.

Woogi's eyes lit up as soon as he saw the man. "Reverend Hyun! You're here!"

The missionary's face flushed crimson and his brow knitted against the tears that wanted to come. He took Woogi's emaciated hands in his own, closed his eyes and said nothing for a while, trying desperately to control the emotions that were overwhelming him.

Elder Yang attempted to ease the strain. "Ah yes . . . yes now, Reverend Hyun, isn't it all thanks to this brave young man's distinguished service that the church in Kyongju was established so quickly!" He went on to review how Woogi had pleaded for a church in his letter to Reverend Hyun, how this letter got Reverend Hyun to approach the Daegu Presbyters Council and propose construction of a church, and how Woogi at the same time rallied the faithful in Kyongju to present a united appeal to the Council, with the result that construction had progressed faster than anyone could have hoped.

After a few whispered words with Woogi, Reverend Hyun got up, promising to come back with a doctor. Woogi asked him, "Reverend, please, get me a Bible."

"Of course, of course. But in the meanwhile you can use this one," and he pulled his own Bible out of his bag. Woogi took it and clasped it to his breast. His eyes closed and two tears formed, like drops of dew.

7

Just as in the past, ancient frogs and other creeping things prowled the entangled weeds in Mohwa's yard. Now that Woogi was gone the house was back to normal.

But Mohwa was not performing any rites in public now and spent all day every day banging away on her gongs and dancing with her spirits in her decaying, dilapidated house in the weeds, and people were saying she had gone mad. Her kitchen was now a perpetual ritual site, hung with five-colored streamers and Nangi's ritual paintings of the Mountain Spirit, Seven Stars Spirit and many others. She had stopped eating, as if she had forgotten how, and her face turned sallower day by day even as the flame in her eyes burned hotter. And every day the spirits that possessed her ranted and raged to the furious beat of her gongs.

Going, Jesus demon, 10,000 *li* back to the west.
A ball of fire on your tail,
A bell on each ear ding-a-ling-a-ling.
Shoo demon, off with you.
And if you don't go I'll wrap you and all your
  descendants in the hide of the White Horse Spirit,
throw you into an ash briar patch,
into a boiling cauldron,
into the blue sea fifty fathoms deep.
Shoo, demon! Shoo-o-o-o!

Once in a while a neighbor, remembering how much Mohwa used to enjoy drinking, dropped by with a jug of wine. "How you can bear such a loss, that dear boy . . . " To which Mohwa would only mumble, "Taken off by that Jesus demon . . . ," and put an end to the conversation with a long sigh.

Her neighbors mourned that she had completely lost her mind. "She was so good. Will we ever see her do another rite?"

Before long, though, word spread throughout the area: Mohwa was going to conduct one more rite, her last. The daughter-in-law of some rich gentry family in the county seat had thrown herself into the river, where the current had carved a deep pocket in its bed. Legend had it that the black fathomless depths of these slowly turning waters that locals called Yegi Pool took for themselves one person every year without fail, and deep in the bowels of this pool quietly stewed the sufferings and secrets of generations. The family wanted to send the tormented soul on to her rest, so they had pressed Mohwa with two silk outfits to use in conjuring up the soul, and she had consented to do just this one last service. At the same time, the rumor went, Mohwa was going to restore her own daughter's hearing.

"Hmph. Now we'll see who's for real—that Jesus demon or the spirits," she asserted.

The rite was to be held on the sandy beach near the pool where the young woman had drowned herself. The big night finally came, and the people turned up in droves, out of both curiosity and expectation. They came from over the mountains and across the river with a mixed sense of excitement and nostalgia.

The beach swarmed with taffy vendors, rice cake vendors, drinking stalls and food stalls equipped with their awnings and their mats, and in the center of this was the big canopy where Mohwa would summon her spirits to help rescue the young woman's lost soul. Silk lanterns like green, red, yellow, blue and white flowers had been strung all over the tent, and lined up under these lanterns was an array of offering tables, one for each spirit that would be called upon. There was the table for the Host Spirit, with its rice cake steamer, jar of wine, and carcass of a pig. There was a table for Chesŏk, guardian spirit of the drowned woman's family, with its bowl of uncooked rice, spool of thread, plate of tofu, and skewer of dried persimmons. There was a table for the Maitreya Buddha with apples, pears and mandarin oranges, snowy white rice cake, cooked vegetables, vegetable soup, salted fish, and hard honey cakes. There was a table for the Mountain Spirit with twelve kinds of wild herbs, a table for the Dragon Spirit with twelve different seafoods, and a table for the Lanes Spirits with one dish for each of a variety of foods. There were a few more large and small offering tables, and a table for Mohwa, with just one bowl of plain water.

Tonight Mohwa's face was suffused with a dignified and serene countenance that had not been there before. People gabbed how, for a woman who was mourning her son as if he had died only the day before and was at the same time bearing every abuse and insult imaginable from these Christian interlopers, she had assumed quite an air of dignity. This was the face they knew from long ago, of that shaman ennobled by a few nights' vigil under the light of the moon. She did not gad about and fawn over everyone as she used to, nor did she make a big fuss about every detail; she only stood there quietly, waiting. At one time, surveying the sumptuous offering tables with contempt, she sniffed at her assistants, "Lowlifes, thinking a few offering tables is all you need."

When the women who gathered there saw this new Mohwa they started whispering that a new spirit possessed her.

"It's the spirit of that young lady," they grudged.

"Will you just look at that stoic composure, so demure—kind of prissy if you ask me—and when was Mohwa ever that pretty. That young woman's spirit has got into her all the way."

Others gossiped among themselves of how tonight Nangi would speak again, and still others debated the rumor that Nangi was with child, whoever the father was. And all of these women were eager to get answers tonight to all these questions buzzing about.

Mohwa's spirit began by recounting, in a more plaintive voice than anyone ever heard from her, all that had happened to Lady Kim from the day she was born till the day she drowned in Yegi Pool. Then the sorceress moved into a frenzied dance accompanied by the fiddle, flute and bamboo oboe, and it was not too long before she lost herself to an ecstatic trance steeped in the anguish of the dead woman's soul. Her human body metamorphosed into pure rhythm, uninhibited by skin or bone, only a phantom of fluid motion. The blood of the mesmerized spectators pulsated in harmony with the folds of the shaman's mantle undulating in tempo with her racing blood. The stars turning in the heavens and the water flowing in the river paused in witness.

Yet, as the night wore on, the young woman's soul was not responding to Mohwa's invocation. Her male assistants and her apprentices had tied a rice bowl to the spirit line made from pieces of the young woman's clothes, thrown it into the pool, retrieved it a few times, but in the bowl they could not find the strands of hair that would announce the soul's recovery.

With an anxious look one of Mohwa's assistants whispered in Mohwa's ear, "We can't fetch her spirit. Now what?"

Mohwa showed no concern at all. As if she had expected this she calmly took up her spirit pole and walked to the edge of the pool. The male shaman with the spirit line maneuvered the rice bowl here and there in the water in the directions indicated by Mohwa's spirit pole. Mohwa called to the dead soul.

> Rise, rise up,
> thirty-year-old wife of Master Kim from
> Wolsong.

She stirred the water with the spirit pole and continued in a voice now husky with emotion.

> When you were born under that auspicious star,
> offerings were made to the Seven Stars Spirit.
> You came into existence like a flower blossom,

and you were cared for like a precious gem.
But then you jumped into these dark waters,
deserting your parents, your infant child,
so even the Dragon Spirit turned from you.
When your skirt ballooned 'round you as you hit the
 water,
what on earth were you thinking?
That you were mounting a lotus blossom?
That you would float on to eternal life?
Oh no, you're just a water demon,
hair let down like a scraggle of hemp.

Mohwa followed the spirit pole a little deeper and then a little deeper into the river. The turning water took one fold of her mantle and twisted it round her, left the other bobbing on the surface. The dark waters covered her waist, covered her breasts, rose higher, and higher . . .

Going, I'm going now,
a farewell cup of white dewdrop wine and I'm gone.
Young lady, gone before me, call me to you.

Her voice began to fade and her thoughts seemed to stray.

Nangi my daughter, dressed in your mourning white,
when it's spring on the river's bank and the peach
 blossoms bloom
come and ask after me.
Ask the first branch how I am,
ask the second . . .

And that was the last anyone could make out, because the pool took Mohwa, along with her song, to itself.

Her mantle floated on the surface for a while, but soon that was gone too. Only the spirit pole floated there, turned a while, then flowed on with the river.

Ten days after Yegi Pool took Mohwa, a small man said to be running a seafood shop in a back lane in a town on the east coast came up to the old goblin house, riding a donkey. Inside he found Nangi lying in bed, eyes sunken in her ghost-pallid face, still suffering the agonies of the shaman initiate.

The little man made her some rice gruel. It was not until she had eaten a spoonful that she fully recognized him, and uttered, "Fa . . . Father . . . ?" Whether Mohwa had actually given the girl her speech back, as the rumor had prophesied, this was the first time in years that anyone heard the girl speak anything that could be understood.

Ten more days passed. Out in the yard the little man pointed to his donkey. "Up you go now." Nangi silently did as her father bade her.

After the man and his daughter left the house, no one came there again. And now, at night, in that jungle of weeds, those swarming mosquitoes are the only sign of life.

LOESS VALLEY

Kim Tong-ni

(1939)

Two barren ridges descend from Solgae Pass, one running 15 *li* to the northeast and the other 10 *li* to the northwest. At their northern extreme stands Mount Kŭmo. And in the midst of this lies Loess Valley. Here the vital forces of the surrounding highlands culminate in the legends they inspire, legends passed down by old men sitting at the bank of the stream that winds through their valley.

They tell the tale of the Wounded Dragons. Two yellow dragons, having waited a thousand years to be anointed to the highest order, were beginning their ascent to heaven when a rock fell from Mount Kŭmo and smashed into them. Blood gushed forth from their sides to flood and color the whole valley.

And these old men pass on to us the Legend of the Mating Dragons. In this tale, too, a brace of yellow dragons was about to begin that ascension to heaven that they had waited for so long. But the Emperor of Heaven learned that they had defiled this occasion by mating the night before, and in his rage he seized their magic stones and stowed them away deep in his realm. The dragons went wild with grief and tore into each other with such fury that the blood they shed inundated the entire valley and left that reddish hue for eternity.

And then there is the Legend of the Severed Vein. They say that many centuries ago a great general of Tang China observed Mount Kŭmo and saw that a Korean mighty enough to trouble even China would one day issue from the area dominated by this mountain. So the general drew his sword and cut through the mountain to its heart. Torrents of blood coursed throughout the entire region for a hundred days, and gave its earth the color it has today.

* * *

Across Dragon Creek, in Loess Valley's foremost paddy, was a white line of about twenty people stooped over pulling weeds. On the paddy's banks stood one man with the village flag and a group of four others banging away at their gongs and cymbals. Already the sun was shimmering high in the center of the sky and the green of the hills stretched as far as the eye could see.

Bang, bang! Kabam, jjang!

A farmers' band to be sure, but they had only a gong, a drum, and a cymbal. The racket they made, though, winding tirelessly from bank to bank and stimulating the workers in the paddies to song was more than enough to break the natural silence of the fields.

And over this way at the foot of the ridge, far apart from the group working together, was a lone man bent over his work in the middle of his paddy. A closer look would reveal the great size and extraordinary might of his torso and limbs, his shoulders—his entire body. His hair was already sprinkled with gray.

The man's name was Ŏkswae. In keeping with his size, which set him apart so from others, he worked apart from others.

Ŏkswae knocked off his work and came up the bank, looking a couple times in the direction of the ridge. He still could not see Buni. He stuck a cigarette in his mouth and lit up, listened to the raucous buzz of the cicada from an elm tree on the bank.

After a couple cigarettes he gave up waiting and was just getting up to head for the wine house when he saw Buni coming through the pine trees. She was carrying a small jug of makkolli on her head.

As she approached he asked her testily, "Where you been so long?"

"What do you mean where I been?" Buni threw back at him, lowering the jug of brew from her head. She reeked of the stuff, and her earlobes and the area around her eyes were flushed.

"Guzzling again," Ŏkswae mumbled to himself.

"Here, have some." That weird smile came to Buni's lips as she handed a bowl of makkolli to Ŏkswae. The brew sloshed up and out of the jug as Ŏkswae snatched both it and the bowl from Buni's hands.

She fumed, then snarled, "Hmph! We'll see about that bitch . . . " Ŏkswae knew this was about Sŏlhŭi. What gibberish!

He poured another bowl for himself and drank as if this were no business of his. Meanwhile, glaring at Ŏkswae with her spite-filled eyes, Buni ground out again, "Just let me get my hands on a knife, and those two . . . "

Ŏkswae scolded, "What the hell kind of talk is that?" and Buni flew back, "Was I talking about you? I meant Tŭkbo."

Now he was even more confused. "Go on, tell me another one. You mean you're going to talk that way about your own uncle . . . or whoever he's supposed to be?"

"My uncle!" she retorted, nostrils flaring. "So what if he is?" and she went over and sprawled on the grass. She was snoring away as soon as her dazzling white legs appeared from below her raised skirt.

In the elm tree the cicada let loose with another round of buzzing. Ŏkswae stared vacantly at the tree with the third bowl of makkolli in his hand, Buni's "get my hands on a knife" turning in his head. He was baffled—how could she be so jealous?

Ŏkswae slammed down the makkolli jug and lit up a cigarette. Just then Tŭkbo appeared descending the ridge, the carcass of a wild boar dangling by its rear legs in his hand.

"Been up on the ridge?" Ŏkswae asked in greeting.

Tŭkbo flung the boar down at Ŏkswae's side. "With my bare hands . . . " and he went over to where Buni was sleeping and plunked down in front of her.

Tŭkbo completely dwarfed the ordinary man. Although shorter than Ŏkswae, his shoulders spread even wider. And his face was a heavy copper color which showed a fearsome brawny strength. Tŭkbo's hair was jet black and he looked six or seven years younger than Ŏkswae.

"Have a drink." Ŏkswae indicated the jug with his chin.

Tŭkbo came over and picked up the jug. He poured himself a bowl and drank it off. "Ahhh . . . !" he exclaimed. After downing a second bowl he glared at Ŏkswae. "How much you got left of this batch?"

"Still a lot left."

Tŭkbo glared at Ŏkswae. "Okay, we'll finish it off tomorrow." A flame kindled in both their eyes, an awesome flame that would melt brimstone.

The following day was hot even for summer. Red clouds of every form billowed in the sky like smoky blooms of fire.

Annae Meadow is in a cozy valley over the ridge from Loess Valley. There is a stretch of white sand along the creek which boarders the meadow, and green grass, and shady old pines, which make it a superb place, perfectly suited to Ŏkswae and Tŭkbo's feasting, carousing and fighting.

The two, clad only in shorts, were drinking in the shade of one of the pines. They started out congenially, one ripping off a foot of the boar for the other, both pouring each other makkolli with the best of camaraderie. Once or twice every season they drank this way, but there had never before been such a day as this, with their hearts so fit to burst with pleasure and contentment. They wouldn't have traded this joy, this utter contentment, for anything. Compared with this, Buni's or Sŏlhŭi's beauty would seem no more than a little extra thrown in to liven up the activities a bit.

This was their bloodletting feast.

The language coarsened gradually as the two got higher. "Hey! There's booze here too, you butcher!" . . . "Well, why don't you have some then, instead of stealing all the meat."

Thus would begin the taunting. Even so, they kept on exchanging cups and throwing bits of meat to each other.

Tŭkbo was usually the one who got the fight going. Tossing a boar's foot at Ŏkswae, he said, "Here, glutton, choke on it . . . Old guy like you strutting around with a female on each arm—disgusting!" He knew that he could provoke Ŏkswae best by getting on him about Buni or Sŏlhŭi.

"You son of a . . . You don't watch your mouth you're not going to be needing it much longer," Ŏkswae menaced as he poured Tŭkbo another cup.

"Look at you sucking away at that old pig there like it was some woman. Dirty old lecher." And with that Tŭkbo was on his feet, scattering everything in one kick. Ŏkswae followed right on, throwing his half-eaten pig's foot in Tŭkbo's face. "Finished with that. Now for you."

An indescribable tension appeared on their faces. Now the fight was on.

His fists bobbing, leveled at Ŏkswae's face, Tŭkbo whinnied, "Yippee! Poor old guy's done for! One flash o' this fist . . . " He bounced around in front of Ŏkswae, advancing, retreating.

"Come on, I'll give you a free punch with that putty fist of yours," Ŏkswae said disparagingly. He was planted there firmly, supremely unperturbed.

"One flash o' this fist . . . this guy's skull's going to shatter like a dried-up gourd." That instant Tŭkbo's fist caught Ŏkswae's left eye and his nose in a roundhouse. A welt formed immediately and blood began to collect in his eye.

"There you go, boy. Take a few more of those putty punches . . . stuff yourself . . . come on!" And Tŭkbo's fist smashed a second time, into Ŏkswae's right cheekbone. His third punch was another roundhouse into the eye he got the first time.

Then Ŏkswae, watching Tŭkbo in his withdrawn position, suddenly bared his teeth and guffawed like a lunatic. But Tŭkbo kept up his whinnying, hopping and bobbing out of reach. Even when Tŭkbo's fourth punch caught him above the right eye, and the fifth one got his nose again, Ŏkswae went on roaring with laughter. "Hey! Let's see you move this mountain with that putty fist!"

Six times, seven times, no matter how often, it was always the same: "One flash o' this fist . . . ," again and again, jumping in and smashing Ŏkswae's face and throat and chest and stomach with all his might. Ŏkswae took every punch with only a slight reflexive motion, never even showing a sign of punching back. He just stood there beaming with boundless glee, bursting into howls of laughter, until the whole upper part of his body was drenched in blood.

Tŭkbo, coming on even stronger than ever, was getting at Ŏkswae's thighs and lower stomach with the feet he was now using in unison with his fists. Ŏkswae guessed what he going for and knew he had better keep an eye on those feet.

Tŭkbo hopped around, frothing at the mouth, and whinnied in a kind of chant:

Was a bird, the Phoenix bird,
'round the world in a flash.
Now he's here, now he's there . . .

Ŏkswae just planted himself there like a totem pole painted with blood, taking the punches and kicks of the onrushing Tŭkbo. Then the fourth kick found Ŏkswae's groin and his knees buckled for an instant.

"You *bastard!*" The whole valley rang with Ŏkswae's shout.

He managed to get his arm around Tŭkbo's neck and catch him up in a headlock. Then the singing and laughing of these two entangled in one hunk left off abruptly, and all that could be heard was the heaving and gasping of their breath and the crunch of muscle on muscle. Blood began to gush like a fountain from both their noses at almost the same time, and it formed in their eyes and welled up from their throats. Their faces, shoulders and chests, which had been glistening with sweat, were now streaming with blood.

Tŭkbo bashed Ŏkswae in the jaw and tried to wrench himself out of the headlock. But Ŏkswae threw all his power into a lightning blow just below Tŭkbo's lower left rib. With this sledgehammer punch Tŭkbo's face went ashen; he staggered backward a few steps and doubled over right there on the sand.

Ŏkswae just stood there absently, cupping his hands under his chin to catch the blood running from his nose and mouth. Then he sat down vacantly. But shortly he leapt back up in a fury and was on the fallen Tŭkbo in the same stride. He dug his teeth into Tŭkbo's right shoulder and tore some flesh away. Vivid red blood coursed down Tŭkbo's arm toward the elbow and he stirred a bit, but finally crumpled back, spread-eagle, unable at all to get up.

Ŏkswae chewed a little more on the flesh he had torn from Tŭkbo's shoulder and then spat out the bloody chunk. He got up and drank a couple more bowls of makkolli from the jug. Then he collapsed.

No one had called surrender, nor had either side suggested a break. The two forms were sprawled out there just as well, though—not sleeping, not dead, just in a helpless stupor.

It was only when the evening breeze rose from the drifting creek and the cry of the cicadas in the tall pine trees sharpened that the two finally came to, shuddering, as if trying to shake off a bout with some witch's brew. Then they were back again at what was left in the jug from that morning.

Usually Ŏkswae got the evening round going, and tonight, too, he got the first punches in. It was not long before the blood was flowing again.

Tŭkbo danced around in his jig, just out of Ŏkswae's reach.

> This bird, this bird, old Phoenix bird,
> back and forth 'cross the River Styx . . .

"Tŭkbo! Come here and fight!" Ŏkswae bellowed, setting the whole valley ringing again.

But Tŭkbo kept on edging in toward Ŏkswae, now shouting his chant.

> Roaring, soaring up and away,
> could round the world in a flash.
> And I'm gonna take this fist o' mine
> and make your noggin tater mash . . .

Then, for whatever reason, Tŭkbo let his guard down and approached Ŏkswae in his happy dance until he was right up to the man's chin. Ŏkswae jumped him, catching him in another headlock. Then Tŭkbo got Ŏkswae in a headlock too, and the two crashed to the ground with the thud of a felled oak.

Ŏkswae, now rolling this way and that with Tŭkbo in tow, suddenly erupted in a loud guffaw. Where his ear should be was only torn skin and blood. Half of his ear was in the mouth of

Tŭkbo who, though busy with Ŏkswae, seemed to be savoring it too much to let it go.

They fought on and on, and even when the sun sank and the mountain shadows deepened the two bloody hunks were rolling back and forth in the streaming blood without a thought of stopping.

* * *

Ŏkswae and Tŭkbo had first met one day in the spring of the year before, and from that very day began their lives together. Before this each of them had merely been existing; now they were living.

Take Ŏkswae. Fifty-one years old, his beard and hair had gone half gray. He had been living in Loess Valley since the day he was born, suppressing that inferno in his breast all those years till the day he met Tŭkbo. It had been raging inside, straining to burst free, to spread like a rainbow to the ends of the sky.

The year he turned twelve he set the whole village in an uproar when he easily hefted a field rock which the grownups could hardly manage.

"Gods, what strength!"

"We've got a Hercules right here in Loess Valley!" The word passed quickly from one busy mouth to another, and by the very next day the elder had dressed themselves up and gathered together at a village meeting.

"It's always been said that if a man like this were born in Loess Valley he would be a good-for-nothing son, or maybe a rebellious subject."

"That's right, but what about when that old general cut through the heart of our mountain? He took care of the problem then."

"Nonsense. Why, somebody in my family around our great-grandfather's time got himself tagged a Hercules. Be darned if they didn't drag him off to the county office and finally send him away with a broken arm."

The nastiest of them all was Ŏkswae's great uncle. He attacked Ŏkswae's father, "You know what's going to happen when word gets around what we've got here? If only you'd never had the kid . . . Ahhh, the whole family ruined, and for what!" Ŏkswae's father just sat it out without a word in reply. Ŏkswae was his only son, but what could he say to an elder?

In the end, after everyone had his say, it was concluded that Ŏkswae would have to have a little acupuncture in the muscle of his right shoulder.

That night Ŏkswae's mother took him by the arm and chided him tearfully, "You poor little dolt you, what did you go and do a fool thing like that for? If you only knew what this is doing to your father."

And the next morning his father called him. "You're twelve years old now. If you want to stay in one piece don't go showing yourself around like that everywhere. Son, your whole life and our whole family will be ruined if you don't curb yourself . . . Well, whatever happens now is all up to you."

These words engraved themselves in Ŏkswae's heart, and after this he never showed up at the village wrestling matches, tug-of-war games or weight lifting contests, and was never around when there were rocks to be removed from the paddies. But sooner or later it had to happen. When he was a little over nineteen the power which was welling up inside became too much for him. So he would go out alone at night and carry some huge rock to the top of the hill and back, sometimes working away at this till dawn. He was beginning to look deranged, eyes bloodshot and topknot down in a tangled mess. But even after a whole night of this, with the coming of day he would still want to lay someone flat or annihilate whatever caught his eye. These demonic fits that raged inside him were unbearable. It was not at all a desire to show off his strength, though, just a craving to try it out.

As soon as the rumors about his behavior began spreading again throughout the valley, Ŏkswae's great uncle told his father, "One of these days the kid's going to go too far. If you'd handled him like I told you, nothing like this would have happened. So now who's going to take care of this . . . ? Okay, since he's your son, you take it on yourself. I'm not staying in this valley any longer." And with that he moved away, across the heights.

Hearing of this, Ŏkswae went deep into the hills and sobbed his heart out. When he returned home he sharpened a scythe. Then, keeping out of his father's sight, he slashed his right shoulder and watched the blood flow. When his mother found out what he had done she scolded in frustration, "Whatever good is that going to do now? And is being strong all that bad? It all depends on how you handle it . . . Good gracious, just another useless fuss when your father finds out."

His grandfather's last words to him were very simple. "Use your strength prudently." And his father, on his deathbed, admonished him in the same way, but more explicitly: "When you were a child I asked someone your fortune. He said your life would be a stormy one, and that you'd be asking for trouble if you didn't harness that power of yours. But to a man, strength is a real treasure, and if you realize that and handle it that way, there'll be a day when you can use it in a big way. So wait, quietly, for that time." These very last words struck Ŏkswae like some divine revelation.

"There'll be a day when you can use it in a big way . . . wait for that time." He never forgot those words. Forever suppressing the energy which welled up in him so maddeningly, he waited for the day he could use it once in that big way. Today? Tomorrow? But before that day ever came, his hair and beard had turned more than half gray with waiting.

It was around this time that Ŏkswae started frequenting wine houses and drinking with the girls who worked in them. One day he was drinking at the crossroads wine house with the comely Buni.

Buni excused herself for just a minute because a customer was asking for her. Finally, when she still had not come back after a while, the clamor of fighting erupted outside. Ŏkswae opened the door to find that some stranger had the wine house owner by the neck. The customers gambling in the backyard had swarmed out and gathered around, jabbering away, eventually taking up the argument themselves.

The owner bawled, "Some guy you never seen before in your life comes up and claims that one of your girls is his daughter, and so he's going to take her off with him. Ever heard such nonsense?" Then an onlooker shouted, "And you know for sure the guy's just fallen for a pretty face. But everyone else likes her too, so where does he get off snatching her all for himself without even paying? Something's got to be done about this freeloading . . ."

So one of them smacked the stranger in the jaw; the stranger grabbed him by the throat and laid him out right there. That gave everyone second thoughts about tangling with him, but finally, since they heavily outnumbered him and boasted a couple pretty fierce characters among themselves, they realized there was no reason to give in to the man. So first one and then another would approach just close enough to egg him on, trying to lure him into the group, but he just polished them off one at a time before he could get sucked in. The yard was soon littered with the casualties—a cracked skull here, a kicked in belly there, a bruised rib, a swollen jaw . . .

Ŏkswae, pretty high now, could not just sit there and do

nothing. He came up roaring, "Who's causing all this racket out here?" and the house shuddered with his voice. The stranger saw him out of the corner of his eye. "Huh! Another one . . . " and even before the words were all out he jumped at Ŏkswae, staggering him with a crashing butt to his brow. Ŏkswae was stunned, but in the next instant had the man's throat clutched in his right hand. This fellow was damn big, and he obviously knew how to fight . . . and he was every bit and more than Ŏkswae could have hoped for. With the realization that he had found a match for his own awesome power an exhilarating joy welled up in his breast, and his hand slipped from the man's throat.

* * *

It was from that day that this stranger Tŭkbo settled in Loess Valley to be near Ŏkswae. Ŏkswae provided Tŭkbo with a shack facing the creek road, and they laid some stepping stones across the creek which flowed between it and Ŏkswae's own place.

After several days passed Tŭkbo came over and said, "It's really a shame that a guy who's already turned half gray hasn't got even one kid. You know, I've got nothing else to give you for all your help, so I brought along Buni here. Take her on as your own kid—or whatever."

Ŏkswae smiled awkwardly. "But you . . . ?"

"You going to worry about me, old man? Hell, just a word of thanks'll do . . . and you can treat me to a nice binge now and then." Then, grimacing, he clicked his tongue. "Sure, I've got no one, but I'd never go and live with my own niece."

Ŏkswae felt a little easier when Tŭkbo referred to Buni as his niece—a man does not usually take one of his kin, no matter how distant, as his mate. But he was still embarrassed by the offer and had to grope around for something to say. "Yeah, well . . . anyway . . . You think you've got to look after an old man like me, huh? You're not getting any younger yourself . . . I mean, well, I've been noticing you ought to nicen up your language some. And listen here, you think I'm too old to take care of something like you if I'd half a mind to?"

"This old boy's really got a way with words!"

As the two sparred like this, Buni busied herself preparing makkolli from Ŏkswae's vat. With this she marked the beginning of her wedded life with Ŏkswae.

When Ŏkswae got a little high on the makkolli, he said again to Tŭkbo, "You just going to live by yourself?"

"You think there's no other girls around?" he said in a voice full of confidence.

"You think they're going to rush up and form a line for a guy with a fierce puss like yours?"

"The only problem is what to do with them all. That's why you got Buni . . . and I can't get on with a jealous one like her, anyway—she's more your type, you farmer."

Ŏkswae did not know how he was supposed to take Tŭkbo's reply. First Buni was being offered in return for the house Ŏkswae had given him, next it was because he could not live with his own niece, and now it was because he could not get along with anyone so jealous. That first time, at the wine house, Tŭkbo had said Buni was his daughter, next she was his niece, and now she was a jealous partner. At any rate Ŏkswae's circumstances now called for a second wife and, seeing as he had had his eye on Buni ever since she started in the wine house, he could not see any special reason to up and refuse her now.

Just as Tŭkbo had alternately referred to Buni as his daughter and his niece, Buni's way about Tŭkbo was also pretty weird. Sometimes she would call him "uncle," sometimes "that man," and in extreme cases she would even call him just plain "Tŭkbo."

One night, after it had been going on like this for a while, she said, "Oh, it's nothing. He's some distant relative on my mother's side, nothing close. They say he's my uncle's stepbrother." Then one day, drunk as usual, she said, "Who says I can't have a child? Go and ask Tŭkbo there—what about that beautiful little boy that Buni bore him when she was fifteen? You think the problem's with me? Huh! It's that he-man who can't perform."

Seeing Buni always bringing Tŭkbo into everything this way really riled Ŏkswae. But since he knew when he married her that she was not exactly a virgin, there was nothing to do but pass this talk off as though he had not heard anything.

Piecing together what the two let drop here and there, Ŏkswae was able to get a general idea of their pasts. Tŭkbo originally worked with his brother in a smithy in a town on the east coast, about 80 *li* from Loess Valley. Once they got into a fight, and Tŭkbo hit his brother on the head and killed him. With that he was on the run to Seoul. In Seoul he worked as a servant for some important family, and it seems that he got something going with the wife. After a while the affair was discovered and he was off again, back to some place around his hometown. He had almost gotten back into another smithy job when the rumor spread that he had killed his brother some time before, so he could not hang around there any longer. The only course left was to take to the road again.

Buni claimed that Tŭkbo took off because he had gotten her pregnant. But who could tell, with Buni's strange ways, even if she had such a relationship with her distant uncle Tŭkbo, and even if she did become pregnant by him when she was no older than fifteen. Ŏkswae could not believe that a guy with a character like Tŭkbo's would let a mere embarrassment like this cost him a job he had gone through so much to get. So who knows but that it was not a combination of the two—the rumor about his brother and Buni's thing—that put him back on the road.

Tŭkbo's name never left Buni's lips. Her heart was with Tŭkbo, and where the heart goes the body usually follows. Soon Ŏkswae found himself a widower again twenty nights out of the month. And during the day Buni would leave her housework to go over and help wait on the customers or maybe cook up a leg of pork at the wine house. Considering her past, this was not so difficult for him to take. What really got him, though, was the way she was spending every night at Tŭkbo's, not a stone's throw across the creek from her own husband's house . . . no matter what kind of some "distant uncle" he was supposed to be.

Ŏkswae got on Tŭkbo about this. "What the hell's Buni doing at your place all the time?"

"Aren't you a lecher for your age," Tŭkbo said, spitting at his feet.

"Hey, why don't we have a look and see if there isn't something wrong with that beak of yours."

"Okay, maybe you'd like to take care of it tomorrow. And if you can't, you're handing Buni over to me for good."

Ŏkswae snickered, as if there would be no problem with a guy like this. With such a good excuse, all one of them had to do was to prepare the brew and something to eat, and the fight was on for sure the next day. Their relationship thrived on an occasional fight, and the way Buni carried on was great for stirring them up. Tŭkbo may have had this in mind even in the beginning, when he turned over his "niece" to Ŏkswae. Buni, though, paid no attention to the two going at it like this all the time, and just kept on crossing back and forth over the creek as if nothing was happening.

But it was Tŭkbo she wanted, and she hung on tight. Ŏkswae was bewildered at the way she was constantly harping at Tŭkbo about his other women, and Tŭkbo was just as constantly bragging that women were the most plentiful thing under the sun. Sure enough, Buni or no Buni, Tŭkbo never went without.

It was not unusual for Tŭkbo to bring some totally strange girl back with him after a few nights out, but before the girl was there more than a couple days she would be run off by Buni's obsessive pestering. "Where'd my hair switch go to . . . ?" "Who stole the chopsticks . . . ?" "What'd you do with my ramie skirt . . . !" "Okay, hand over my silver ring . . . !" And before the girl knew it she would be relieved, one by one, of her bits of jewelry and clothing. If this did not work in getting the girl out of the house soon Buni would resort to batting her around, pulling her hair and tearing her clothes.

"Tŭkbo'll never get a wife if you go carrying on this way," Ŏkswae scolded her. Buni would flare up at him, "Now I've heard everything! You want me to just go and make those thieves feel right at home!"

There was one girl who seemed to be quite taken with Tŭkbo, and she had been holding out against Buni for a month already. If Buni started in on her, she would just open up and show Buni the bundle she had moved in with. And she was on the big side, strong for a woman. Buni was pretty good at hair pulling and tearing a person's clothes to shreds, but somehow she could not handle this girl; several times Buni tried to force her way in close enough to get at her hair, but in the end she always had to give up. After every one of these tussles Buni just planted herself in the corner of Tŭkbo's room and sulked a few days, not moving a muscle.

Then some nights, whatever they were up to inside there, Ŏkswae could hear banging and thumping and crunching sounds. Sometimes they would keep this up the whole night and appear the next day with disheveled hair and swollen, bloodshot eyes. "Perverts!" Ŏkswae would mumble to himself, spitting in contempt as if he were trying to get rid of something bitter in his mouth. At dawn once there was a sharp cry of pain. "Murder!" It was Buni's voice. And then the thumping, bashing sounds of another free-for-all started up again.

Despite her obsession with Tŭkbo, you could not really say that Buni neglected her husband Ŏkswae. Whether it was some idea of giving to her lover what was her lover's and to her husband what was his, she could often be seen lugging the dishes from Tŭkbo's to prepare meals for Ŏkswae and her mother-in-law and taking her laundry paddle and bundles of dirty clothes down to the creek. And to think that she ever refused Ŏkswae her body? Never.

But she did complain what a bore Ŏkswae was in bed.

* * *

As Buni went back and forth across the creek like this, Ŏkswae in his heart gave her up for lost. In her stead, though, he finally won over Sŏlhŭi, whom he had been longing for deep down quite a while.

In Ŏkswae ran the blood of a farmer, and it showed in everything he did. So it was not only in bed that he and Buni could not hit it off—there was nothing they could find in common. He felt shame at not being able to give a grandson to his aged mother, and there was his own desire, too, to leave behind something of himself. But what could he expect from Buni, with her ways? She killed even the desire in him to open up to her about these things. And so without a word to Buni he had taken to seeing Sŏlhŭi.

Buni, of course, was furious when she found out. She fumed, "Humph! Think it's me? It's him that's all dried up down there. Show me what's so special about that woman's you-know-what!"

Sŏlhŭi was a beautiful woman. That and her modest demeanor made her the talk of everyone in town. She was twenty-two when her husband died and left her with only his father. But she refused the men's overtures and the propositions that came from every matchmaker for miles around, and devoted herself uncomplainingly to her father-in-law. Not too long before, however, the old man passed away and Sŏlhŭi, having no one and nowhere to turn to, at last surrendered to Ŏkswae's persistent attentions.

It was not only Ŏkswae that yearned for her. Among the many was Tŭkbo, supremely confident that he could take her for his own . . . until he heard with dismay that Sŏlhŭi had taken up with Ŏkswae.

"Old buzzard, swaggering around with a girl on each arm. Your heart isn't going to stand for this kind of greed much longer. You're giving one over to me . . . fast!" he growled at Ŏkswae on the way back from Annae Meadow.

"Watch your mouth . . . " was all Ŏkswae replied, but in his heart he worried, "This guy's never going to give up."

Late at night in a drizzling rain Ŏkswae approached Sŏlhŭi's house. The reddish light shown in the doorway as usual, but from inside came the sawing of a man's snoring. "Now what?" he exclaimed to himself. And then he was stunned to make out in the dim light those familiar huge straw sandals sitting next to the door. His fists clenched tightly by themselves and all the blood in his body pounded up into his breast.

Ŏkswae had his trembling hand on the door, about to yank it open, when he thought he heard someone over in the corner of the yard. He turned quickly and was able to make out easily the white form of someone standing beside the dark heap of manure. Taking a couple steps in that direction he soon found it to be none other than Sŏlhŭi.

She came up close, till she was right under his chin. "It's Tŭkbo. He's been here since early this evening," she whispered.

"He asked for you and I told him you weren't here, but he just came right on inside anyway. Then he started in with that nonsense of his and just wouldn't let up, so all I could do was tell him I was going to the outhouse, and come hide out here in back."

"Hmmm," Ŏkswae grumbled, but inside thought, "I'll kill the bastard." Ŏkswae wondered whether he shouldn't just bust open Tŭkbo's head right there in his sleep. He entered the room, but Tŭkbo kept on sleeping. His huge snoring bulk was spread out over the whole room. The weak rays of a white light played over his beet-red, bloated face, and on that potato nose sat a huge fly. Ŏkswae's eyes followed the fly as it started to crawl up the bridge of Tŭkbo's nose and then buzzed heavily over to alight on the acorn-sized welt near the left eyebrow, which was left from one of Ŏkswae's punches in their fight the March before. From nowhere a wave of melancholy arose and swept over him.

He kicked Tŭkbo in the rump. "Tŭkbo!"

Tŭkbo stirred a bit, but went right on snoring. Ŏkswae bellowed, "Tŭkbo!"

With this Tŭkbo's bloodshot eyes opened and scanned the room once, and then he stretched and worked himself up into a sitting position.

"Where the hell do you think you are?" Ŏkswae shouted this time.

Only then, glaring at Ŏkswae out of the corner of his red eyes, Tŭkbo asked sarcastically, "Where?"

"Why you . . . " Ŏkswae's eyes riveted in Tŭkbo's face. A cold smile came to his lips but was gone as quickly as it appeared. "Your day's coming." And then, "But in the meanwhile, we'll have a drink," and he called Sŏlhŭi to bring the jug.

From that day Tŭkbo was a bit more proper to Sŏlhŭi. At the same time, though, his visits became more frequent. "Anyone home?" Tŭkbo would call from outside, and Sŏlhŭi, knowing he had come for her, would always answer, "He's not here." Tŭkbo would just come in regardless of whether Ŏkswae was there, so that eventually Sŏlhŭi would just open the door and let him in without a word. Having weaseled his way into the house, Tŭkbo would start off with some pretty risqué stuff, but when he went too far Sŏlhŭi would silence him with a withering glare. Then Tŭkbo would let off and all of a sudden be spread out on the floor, snoring away.

"I'm warning you . . . " Ŏkswae might growl menacingly, at which Tŭkbo, disgusted, would raise some phlegm and spit it out. "Practically in your grave and you get so excited because your friend wants to rub a little ass with your woman."

But Ŏkswae remembered that Tŭkbo had shown this casual attitude about Buni too, before he stole her back. Glaring ferociously, he would threaten, "Keep it up, boy, you just keep it up," and then Tŭkbo would challenge, "Okay, we'll settle who gets her tomorrow," again in the same manner he had handled the matter with Buni. It was not at all the same with Ŏkswae, though. These days Ŏkswae's warning carried a far different meaning.

And so it was that ever since Sŏlhŭi entered their relationship the fights were over her. Though Sŏlhŭi, like Buni before her, might in this regard have been no more than a pretense for rousing a good fight, the fact was that the two went at it a lot more seriously over her.

When with Sŏlhŭi, if Ŏkswae got a little high he would fret, "I don't know, something's got me worrying over you," furtively trying to determine her real feelings. Every time Sŏlhŭi just bowed her head without saying a word.

But there was one time they were talking about Buni, when Sŏlhŭi said, "Why can't you just make an end of it with her?"

Ŏkswae, by now high as usual, said half in jest, "Sure, and then what do I do when you run off to Tŭkbo?"

She blushed deeply and then, after a long silence, sighed, "A woman with a fate like mine . . . what's the use of trying for anything better than what I'm stuck with here? It would be futile to tamper with things anymore." She wiped away her tears with her handkerchief. Even drunk, Ŏkswae knew what she meant by her "fate." Stroking his gray beard he mumbled, "Sorry . . . I'm sorry," at a loss for anything else to say.

* * *

During the days that Tŭkbo was haunting Sŏlhŭi's house so persistently, the figure of a woman might be found at night glaring at the dimly lit door. On moonlit nights she hid in the shade of the backyard locust tree, and on moonless nights she stood out in the darkness. A venomous luster, icy as the winter's moon, glowed on her face, and a weird gleam shone in her eyes. At her bosom, wrapped in a small piece of cloth, was a finely honed dagger.

* * *

There was a change in Buni's manner and countenance since Ŏkswae and Tŭkbo began contesting so heatedly for Sŏlhŭi. Gone were her incessant nagging, her affected pouting. Whatever for, she would stay out all night, only to return the next morning and spend all day buried under her blankets sleeping. Never seen fixing anything to eat for herself, she simply seemed to have given up all thought of food. Her face had the life and color of paper and there was no longer any trace of that familiar beaming smile. Ŏkswae, of course, could not help but notice the change in her. His mother had become very sick, though, and he was too distraught over her deteriorating condition to concern himself with Buni.

He was nursing his mother late one night when the stillness

was pierced by the sounds of fighting from Tŭkbo's house. Then came Buni's cry of pain, and the racket stopped abruptly. At Buni's cry Ŏkswae's old mother struggled to her elbows and grabbed Ŏkswae's sleeve: "That noise, Ŏkswae, what's that noise . . . ? Ŏkswae . . . !"

From that moment her condition worsened drastically, and on the third day after she heard Buni's cry, at the same hour, she breathed her last.

* * *

Ŏkswae's mother joined her husband in the family plot on the ridge above Loess Valley. The night of the burial Ŏkswae and a few relatives were gathered in the clearing, watching the glowing brazier. It was then that poor Sŏlhŭi, finally with child, lost her troubled life, the glinting blue blade of a dagger buried deep in her throat.

While Sŏlhŭi's body was still warm, Buni, her hand and sleeve and whole blouse all stained with blood, hurried through the pitch black shade of the locust tree after Tŭkbo. The kitchen knife from Sŏlhŭi's house gleamed in her right hand. As she came out from under the locust tree she hid the knife in her skirt.

At that moment Tŭkbo was deep in a drunken slumber in his darkened room. He had been out all that day helping to carry Ŏkswae's mother's coffin and dig her grave, and was rather well rewarded with wine for his services.

Buni came up to Tŭkbo's door. She heard his snoring and her breast began to beat madly, just as when she grabbed the handle on Sŏlhŭi's door a short time before. She reeled as a smell like the earth she had eaten furtively sometimes in her childhood welled up in her. Then in the next instant, half out of her senses, she dashed in and plunged the knife into the darkness at the throat of the snoring Tŭkbo. But the knife missed its target and sank a few inches below into the left side of his breast.

Tŭkbo gasped at the hot sting. Then something fell on his chest and tried to embrace him. Buni flashed through his mind and, as if fighting his way out of a nightmare, he flung off the thing with all his might. Buni landed at the doorstep. Only then did Tŭkbo waken fully; instinctively his hand went to his breast, where he felt a hot, sticky wetness. A shiver of realization shot through him, and he plunged back into unconsciousness.

The sight and pungent smell of the blood-spattered room assailed Ŏkswae when he barged in, out of breath, the next day.

"Tŭkbo!" he yelled.

Tŭkbo's bloodshot eyes opened and stared at Ŏkswae.

"Tŭkbo!"

Tŭkbo just kept on staring, blankly.

"You're alive, anyway."

Instead of answering Tŭkbo rubbed his breast, where a dark red crusty clot of blood had formed. Then, from near his hip, he produced the knife sheathed in hardened blood. Ŏkswae picked up the knife. As he examined it, the blood on the floor seeped through his sandals and into his socks.

Buni, sprawled out on the pile of tindering straw in the kitchen, was startled awake by Ŏkswae's voice. Stealthily she rose, then disappeared, never to be seen again.

* * *

After about a month the wound in Tŭkbo's breast was nearly healed on the surface, but for some reason it actually seemed to be getting worse inside. His cheekbones protruded sharply out over sunken hollows, his complexion was like some jaundiced old leather, and his forehead was cruelly furrowed with wrinkles, so that there was no hint of the former Tŭkbo there. In one month he had become an old man.

"What about Buni?" Tŭkbo asked Ŏkswae every time he saw him. At first Ŏkswae thought that Tŭkbo was looking for her to get his revenge, but the expression on Tŭkbo's face the third and fourth times he asked made Ŏkswae wonder whether Tŭkbo did not also miss her.

Ŏkswae would always answer, "I'll find her." It was not at all that easy, though. At various times he heard that she was in her hometown on the east coast, or working in some wine house to the south, and one rumor had it that she had fallen to her death in a well near Yongchon.

So Tŭkbo often flared up at Ŏkswae, "Well, what are you stalling for? You could've been looking for her all this time." But Ŏkswae never did get around to it.

Spring came. Before lunar New Year's Tŭkbo was seen occasionally in the market, but as soon as the grass greened in the fields and the mountain azaleas blossomed he took off abruptly down the road. Ŏkswae waited anxiously for Tŭkbo from the day he left, and went to the wine house every day just for word of him.

Spring then turned to early summer. One day around May Festival, when every branch on every tree was unfolding to turn the world into a lush green, Tŭkbo returned to Loess Valley. To Ŏkswae's surprise, Tŭkbo brought along with him a young girl about eighteen. This girl, dressed up in a full pink skirt and dark green top, was the "beautiful boy" Buni had when she was only fifteen.

"And what about Buni?" Ŏkswae asked.

"Looks like she's done for," Tŭkbo answered simply, dispirited. But even after this Tŭkbo would go off, not returning for six or seven days.

"Where've you been?" Ŏkswae would ask. And Tŭkbo would

always reply, dejectedly, "Oh, around," but Ŏkswae could sense clearly that he had been off looking for Buni.

When Tŭkbo was at home and not out looking for Buni, he was forever sending the girl to keep an eye on Ŏkswae.

"What's he up to?"

"Just lies there."

This was the extent of the conversation between father and daughter. When she reported that Ŏkswae was not home, Tŭkbo just sent her right on back, and he could not rest until she came back and told him that Ŏkswae had returned.

Tŭkbo dropped in on Ŏkswae once on his drunken way home from the wine house. He shoved his big fist up under Ŏkswae's chin: "You, you're nothing. Nothing!" But Ŏkswae in his excitement could only break out into his usual loud guffaw. Exasperated, Tŭkbo buffed him solidly on the cheek with his fist and yelled in a voice charged with rage, "Old man, dirty . . . !"

"Okay," Ŏkswae bellowed, cutting off his flippant laughter. "You go and sober up. Then I'm going to take care of you for good!"

Tŭkbo's eyes lit up. "You're not kidding me now?" he pressed, as if he could not believe what his ears were telling him.

But Ŏkswae did not show up the next day, or the day after. In fact, it was already half a month later when Tŭkbo came after Ŏkswae and told him that he had won enough money at gambling for them to do some drinking. Ŏkswae was up for a drink anyway, so he was glad to join him. Tŭkbo seemed really uptight for some reason, though, and Ŏkswae guessed it was because he still could not get Buni off his mind.

"Buni's dead," he told him. "Forget her and get a hold of yourself."

Tŭkbo jumped on him, "What Buni? Can't you get the women off your mind, just once?"

"Okay, okay. But how long's it been already since she drowned in that well at Yongchon? You miserable dope," Ŏkswae retorted.

"First it's Buni, now it's Yongchon," Tŭkbo said. "You never heard of Onyang?"

So it was Onyang, not Yongchon, and that's why he's been boozing it for the last month like that. When Ŏkswae ventured, "Well, you'll have to go into mourning," Tŭkbo sat there without a word, as if he were mulling something over. He finally just let out with a snicker.

They had been at the booze for a long time when all of a sudden Tŭkbo slammed a dagger down on the table. Its blade glinted a steely blue. "You really don't see it . . . you really don't think this is your fault?"

In spite of himself Ŏkswae showed not the least confusion or fear, almost as if he had been expecting this. He even suppressed his urge to burst into laughter, which at other times would be set off by the most trivial thing. "All right, Tŭkbo," Ŏkswae pronounced steadily, solemnly. "I been saving you for a time like this." There was fire in Ŏkswae's eyes.

Tŭkbo took in the burning eyes and solemn voice with indescribable satisfaction. Hiding his glee, though, he scorned, "If you don't want to get squashed like a worm in here get outside and fight like a man." He shoved the dagger back into his belt.

Ŏkswae sent Tŭkbo on ahead to Annae Meadow and stayed behind to get the booze and some meat. The owner's wife poured him a glass of hard stuff to try out. "Ah, great! This stuff sure does pack a wallop!"

"This is about all we've got today," the wife said, bringing out a few dried cuttlefish legs.

"Cuttlefish'll do just fine." Ŏkswae bunched up the legs and stuffed them into his pocket, then slung the big bottle of soju over his shoulder and took off after Tŭkbo. Probably because of that shot of soju on top of the makkolli he had with Tŭkbo, his heart was dancing and his step was as light as that day—seemed like so long ago—he married.

"One of these days we're both going all the way and finish this farce for good," Tŭkbo had recently sworn, spitting out his bitterness with his phlegm. This and the thought of the gleaming dagger which Tŭkbo had slammed on the table plunged Ŏkswae into a deep reverie and stopped him in his tracks. He imagined Tŭkbo plunging the eight-inch dagger into the middle of his chest and he could feel it gouging around in there, scraping out down to their roots the burning and itching liver and lungs of his tempest. His body thrilled at the thought.

When he lifted his head again, a gossamer sun was already hanging low over Loess heights. There, maybe a *li* ahead, Tŭkbo plodded on alone toward Dragon Creek.

THE GAME BEATERS

Hwang Sun-wŏn
(1948)

Down in the deep bed of Chŏnggye Channel three kids are stooped over poking around in its shallow waters. They're wearing rags as filthy and gray as the water of this city drainage ditch. Anybody can see they're street urchins.

But what on earth are they up to? It looks like they're hunting those useless minnows, the way they're going about it.

After the monsoon you can occasionally see these street kids grabbing those dim-witted minnows with their bare hands. When a boy cups one in his hands and holds it close up to see, his face lights up with the energy of that wriggling bit of life. The black body of this fish from that black water flops around in the boy's cupped hands and splashes sparks of sun into his eyes. The kid's eyes flash too. Under protruding ribs and sun-darkened skin, this skinny kid's heart leaps with the fish. Scale-skinned fish gleaming in the sun with the boy's glistening skin turned smooth and sheeny from peeling and peeling again. Suddenly the pulsating heart of this boy holding the flapping fish bursts: "Hey guys, this is great! Look at 'em—look at 'em jump!"

But there's a season to go wading around in that water, and this is only the middle of March. These kids could have picked some warmer weather for hunting fish.

So what could they possibly be looking for now? From time to time you'll find these street kids rummaging in this stream's dark waters for old cans or wire or other scrap like old nails. In the dingy gray bed of this stream a boy might come across a piece of white porcelain. He digs it out and holds it up for inspection and finds it's chipped, and ends up throwing it back with a disappointed "Ehyee!" with an instant of flashing white teeth like chips of porcelain in that sun-blackened face. It looks like there's no particular season for street kids to be scavenging in the black bed and black waters of that stream, and that's probably what these kids are doing.

One boy crouched over his work now lifts his head and his eyes dart left and right with the alertness of a little animal. Something catches his attention and he whispers to his companions. All three rush off toward the yawning jaws of a sewage pipe emptying into this stream. The first one there scoots into that gaping mouth.

* * *

Across the stream, a middle-aged gentleman walks out of a lane that opens onto the main road running along the channel. He happens to glance across the stream and catches a glimpse of the backs of two lads, one about to disappear into the gaping mouth of the drainage pipe and another that looks ready to follow.

What are those little rascals up to now? he wonders. Maybe hide and seek . . . ? Nobody wants to stop them from playing around, but really, what's to be done with kids like that, playing in such filth. He takes a right onto the main road. Soon his eyes are drawn back to the stream and fall upon a building across it, and he stops dead in his tracks.

"Hey, you little bums!"

At the man's shout the one now almost hidden in the pipe comes back out and he and his partner split off right and left, then start up the embankment. They scamper up those neatly laid stones that offer nothing to grab or get a foothold like they're running up a ladder, then slip off neatly into nearby lanes.

But the third one isn't coming out of that pipe.

The gentleman puts a little more gravitas into his voice. "You in there—out right now, or else!"

A man riding by on a bike stops to see what all the commotion is.

The kid's showing no sign of coming out.

"You in there—last chance!"

Mr. Bike wonders what this gentleman could be raising such a commotion about.

The gaping jaws of the sewage pipe just yawn in silence.

The middle-aged gentleman speaks, half to himself and half to Mr. Bike. "Just a minute ago some kids got into that thing over there . . . "

Mr. Bike doesn't look like he's catching on. "Well you see," pointing at the building across the stream, on the other side of the dike, "that foreigner's house has already been targeted by hoodlums like that."

"Ah," he says, nodding. Yes, now Mr. Bike understands. These sly street kids with all their tricks these days, burgling Westerners' houses and all that. Now he gets to see it for himself.

"I shouted at the three of them as they were going in, and two of them flew off like bats out of Hades. But one is still in there."

Nobody can pass by without stopping. One more coming down the street sees the crowd gathered there and hurries his step in hopes there's something worth seeing, and asks one after another, "What's up? What's going on?" Somebody drop something in the stream? Somebody find something big? Maybe an infant's corpse like we're coming across all the time these days?

Mr. Bike addresses the crowd in an accent straight from the

provinces. "A street boy went inside that drain pipe there," pointing at its gaping mouth. "And you know what for . . . ?" He covers the crowd with a quizzing look of You don't, do you? Then he takes new aim with his pointing finger and jabs it at the building across the stream: "Fixing on that foreigners' house is what for."

Isn't that something, the crowd nods just like Mr. Bike did before, and that certainly does make sense.

The middle-aged gentleman shouts again, "Hey kid, still not coming out?" to let everyone know he's the one that saw those urchins first. And with that everyone's eyes are back on the mouth of the drainpipe.

That drainpipe just sits there like before, its black mouth wide open but telling nothing.

"Those cursed street kids are sly as can be."

"You're telling me. Tough little bastards, those . . . "

"Heck, ought to sweep litter like that off the streets. All of them, one swoop. It's them that do all the pickpocketing and everything."

"That's what I say."

"Heard the one about the tofu granny? She's there on the street trying to sell her tub of tofu when all of a sudden these two scamps run up and start fighting right in front of her. The bigger one knocks the other down and is beating away on him, and he's going to kill the guy if no one stops him, so granny can't stand it anymore you know and she gets in there and separates them. Well, later when she's got a buyer for her tofu and goes to her purse—you know how they strap that thing around their waist, and under the skirt, mind you, not outside—she goes there to get some change . . . and its gone. Vanished. And she's sure it was there before those two hooligans came along. Nipped it off her as smooth and easy as a leper's you-know-what. So if all that hitting and getting hit wasn't a scheme I don't know what it was. Not a thing those sly little bastards can't get away with when they set their minds to it."

"They say they're getting really smart these days at lifting things from those Yankees. At one army barracks there's this steel drum rolling along, but nobody rolling it, the weirdest thing, just rolling along all by itself. They were watching it wondering what was up and it got so far and all of a sudden out pops this little urchin bugger. He'd gotten inside and drove it here and there like it had that round steering thing inside if you know what I mean."

"And they say lately those devils have discovered a way to get into a house and burglar it by crawling right up the sewage pipe . . . " Everyone's eyes follow the talk back to the drainpipe. But it's keeping mum.

"Can't someone teach them how to behave?"

"Let's *us* teach 'em a lesson," says a very well-groomed young man with a fashionable fedora.

Everybody looks at him to tell them exactly how they're going to teach that kid a lesson, but he goes off without another word and crosses over a nearby bridge, leading to the big house.

Mr. Bike, who was about to leave, decides to see what will happen next.

A young man in a brown fighter pilot's jacket he must have finagled off some American is crouching at the mouth of the sewage pipe, looking inside. "Out here quick, you wily little rat . . . !" and back to those still up on the bank, "Wish we could fire a blank in there. That'd give him such a scare he'd come crawling out begging for his life." This one probably has one of those new GI carbines in mind. The younger fellows in the crowd imagine what a thrill it would be if they could set that sewer pipe ringing with a blank or two.

Now a young one in a black shirt shouts in his rough southern accent, "If you don't come out we're going to shoot!"

"We're shooting if you don't come out!" the crouching young man in the fighter jacket passes the warning on in.

They are answered with the sound of something moving deep down in the bowels of that black hole, and suddenly a loud hiss announces a rushing stream of water. It's not one or two buckets of rice-wash either, it gushes out like somebody has hitched a hose up to a fire hydrant and let her go. And it keeps on gushing. That young man in the fedora must have gone over and alerted the Westerners.

The eyes of everybody in the crowd are fixed on the sewage pipe. Now there is no way that little urchin will be able to stay in there.

"That'll teach him," says the young man in the fedora. How did he get back so fast?

The water keeps on surging out. Now that filthy water in the pipe has all been washed out and in its place is a steady flow of clear water. But they still don't see that sly rascal crawling out.

How can the little bastard hold on like that, don't care how wily he is. The season being what it is, that water must be awfully cold. Maybe there's nothing in there after all and we're making such a fuss over nothing? Sure seems like it, anyway.

But that doubt is dispelled right away. Here comes something floating down out of the pipe. Must be the kid! . . . No, just a couple rags. In pretty sad condition even for rags, but you can tell they're definitely somebody's clothes.

The clothes that kid was wearing. So what about the kid?

"Okay now, if his clothes are coming out he'll be following them soon enough." That's Mr. Bike. Mr. Bike's face shows that since the middle-aged gentleman seems to have left he owns the distinction of being the only here now that's witnessed this whole thing from the beginning. As long as that's the case, he makes up his mind to stay to the end. He can make up for his lost time by pedaling a little faster.

That scamp refuses to come out of there and they need to teach him a lesson.

A young man with a smart pair of Lloyd's horn-rims says, "Boy oh boy, that little guy sure is one tough customer. But everyone, do you know why this urchin of ours isn't coming out and just sending his clothes out? There's a logical reason for it. If you're in the water, clothes or anything you're wearing adds a lot of weight. So he stripped them off." And he flashes a smile that shows the gaps in his white teeth.

"Look—over there!"

Now who could that be? And where did he come from all of a sudden? He snatches those rags from where they got snagged on something and goes splashing off back up the stream. Another street kid. Maybe one of those that ran off into the lane across the stream before.

The young fellow in the black shirt dashes off right away along the top of the dike, and now he's caught up even with the kid down in the bed of the stream. The two engage in a *pas de deux*—he's going to cut him off, the kid doubles back, the young guy doubles back, catching up and cutting the kid off again. The kid doubles back again, the young guy does the same, cutting him off again. The kid feints, and the young man parries. Kid bolts right, man follows; kid bolts left, man follows. As they go on like this an animal's keen glare charges the boy's eyes and the vigor of a creature of light energizes his every move. A pulsing rhythm possesses his whole being.

"Not coming up, huh?" Then I'm coming down there to get you, he signals. The kid knows he'll never come down there but still makes to break away. And his stalker moves with him. And the kid just nimbly doubles back. Finally the young man stops and gives up trying to block the kid, and in the bat of an eye the kid vanishes beneath the bridge.

Meanwhile the rush of water has slowed. But there's still

nothing showing up at the drainpipe. That clever scamp is one clever scamp.

"Looks like he hasn't had enough yet." The young man in the fedora walks quickly off across the bridge again, toward the foreigners' house. Seems like he might be able to speak a word or two in English, and they hope he'll tell those foreigners to turn the water on stronger this time.

Suddenly a shout from the one in the fighter jacket, "Gotcha, you little rat!" along with, "Ow-w-w-w!" He's got one of the kids by his collar. Same ragged clothes, dirty face, height—the same one that ran off under the bridge before. But then again, maybe it's the other one. You really can't tell these rascals apart. What could make it worth the risk for them to come back here? Buddy's rags? And this second one now, to see if you can help out? As loyal as they are identical.

"Come on you little rat!"

"Ow-wow-wow! I ain't done nothin', sir. Ask anyone. Ow-w-w-w! Ain't done nothin' wrong. Just passin' by. Ow-w-w!"

The young man in the jacket starts dragging him off to the police box. He twists the kid's collar to get a tighter grip, but the skinny squirming life under those rags won't give up.

"Ow-w-w-ch. Please, I'm innocent! Ask anyone. Ow-w-w. Really. Sir! Just passing by. Hey, you're gonna rip my clothes. Ow-w-w!"

Gradually the abject wailing and the babbling and the resistance of this skinny creature slacken—and then in a wink the cowering boy straightens, twists out of the young man's grasp, shoots off like a kite that has snapped its string. The young man is left standing there with that rag of a coat in his hand.

* * *

Meanwhile the flow from the drainpipe has slowed a lot. But—wait a minute—what's that red there? Isn't it . . . ?

"It's blood!" someone shouted. Does that mean the kid in there . . . ?

"Now, now, everyone, there's nothing to worry about. It's just that he's putting up such a fight to stay in there his fingers and toes are bleeding from scraping on that cement bottom," Four Eyes says, as if it were perfectly obvious.

"That kid sure is a tough little devil."

Another surge of water gushes from the pipe. The blood disappears into it right away. Just a rushing stream of clear water now.

By now everyone has had a change of heart.

Up to this point that scamp in there has been amusing and teasing them with the question of whether he'd end up crawling out. Now they're rooting for this wily kid to show how really wily he is and stick it out.

But their hopes are soon dashed. From inside the pipe floats the limp, lifeless body of that little street urchin. A useless piece of flotsam.

THE VISIT

Kim Tong-ni

(1951)

Black rubber slip-ons, baggy white cotton trousers and vest under a threadbare black overcoat, grimy dingy fedora faded past any discernible color over a face of 43 or 44 years, with a sparse stubble of beard—you could tell at a glance that this smallish man with the build of a country yokel stepping onto the wharf from the coastal ferry was a farmer.

In his right hand he held a bundle wrapped in a kerchief, so small it could be carrying an infant's pillow. But it was rice inside. He was now down to about a third of what he'd left home with. Except for when he had to pay for a room at a roadside inn, the traveler had been leaving some rice wherever someone was good enough to put him up for the night.

"Can you tell me where this is?" As soon as he was off the wharf he asked this of a fellow passenger.

The passenger beheld this farmer—Sŏkgyu was his name—with a sidelong glance. "This is Yŏsu," the passenger grudged.

Sŏkgyu had been asking everybody this same thing ever since their boat began its approach to the harbor, and then asked a few more times as they were getting off the boat.

"Yŏ–Yŏsu, you say?" Sŏkgyu asked again. This time there was no answer. Other passengers standing nearby just rolled their eyes at each other.

It was evening now. Spring had just arrived, but the apricot trees were not in bloom yet, and a chilling wind was blowing down from Mount Chiri.

"How far is it to Kwangju?"

Again, no answer.

"Will I still be able to get a bus today?"

"Probably not."

Then a young man in a uniform offered, "Try the bus station tomorrow morning," and a middle-aged woman in homespun and headscarf chimed in, "Sure, go there tomorrow morning and find out."

"Then maybe you can tell me how far it is to Kwangju?"

"Three days to walk it, even for a man."

"Three days!" the farmer exclaimed.

Sŏkgyu was on his way to meet his son Pongho. He'd heard that Pongho was in some unit in X Division, which was headquartered in Kwangju. Mister Yang, the blacksmith in the county seat near Sŏkgyu's farm, had a son in the army, too, who enlisted together with Pongho. So one day in early February Sŏkgyu dropped by Mister Yang's to ask about the kids, as he usually did on his occasional trip into town. When Mr. Yang saw Sŏkgyu at the door he ran up to him, flushed with the news that Pongho was stationed in Kwangju. He could not remember exactly which unit, but at least . . .

Sŏkgyu was stunned. "P . . . Pongho? In Kwangju!"

Mister Yang's son Yŏngbok had been wounded by shell fragments, and was in the army hospital in Pusan. When Mr. Yang got the news he rushed there and found that the boy's arm was hurt, and one eardrum was damaged, but he was expected to be released in a couple weeks, and it was from his son's lips that he heard about Pongho, that he was in Kwangju in such and such a unit of such and such a regiment of such and such a division.

Pongho's parents hadn't heard a thing from him ever since he left for the war over six months before. Mother's tears and father's sighs had been sapping them of the strength to work their farm, and it had even got to the point where they could not expect much of a crop this year. But now, with this news of their boy, a bright new world dawned.

"Go see him, now," Pongho's mother told Sŏkgyu. "Forget the farm, go see our son. Who cares what happens . . . " And Sŏkgyu agreed with his wife.

So Pongho's mother threw herself with a fury into getting Sŏkgyu ready for his trip. She mended Sŏkgyu's clothes for the trip and put them in to soak and found so many other things to fret over that Sŏkgyu grumbled, "What's all this fuss with rice cakes and this and that when we're not even sure where the boy is, or whether he's even still wherever it is he's supposed to be? I mean, it's already been two months since Yŏngbok saw him, and Mister Yang can't remember anything about where he is except 'some unit in some battalion in whatever corps it is.' So even if he's still there, how do we know if I can find him?"

"Well then, go to Pusan first and ask Yŏngbok again." Sŏkgyu had thought of that already, of course, but all the extra time and expense of going by way of Pusan . . . it would just be too much. He could not help worrying that this weary body of his, which had been wasting away with the cough that began just after Pongho left for the army, might go and break down under the strain of long boat rides and bus rides, and hiking it when he could not get a ride. And even if he were healthy, he was still an ignorant farmer who had done nothing except hack away at the soil for the last thirty years since leaving school after fourth grade, and the thought of going from Haman in Kyŏngnam Province all the way to Kwangju in Cholla Province was as unsettling, as frightening, as going to a foreign country. He did not need a detour to Pusan to add to all this.

He went into town for some help. "How far is it from here to Kwangju?" He asked the clerk at the township office, the county chief, and any of the older people around who were said to know anything about that world outside. But he got a different answer from each one he asked. The clerk guessed about 500 *li*, the county chief told him 600 *li*, Mister Yun said 700 or 800. Of course, no one knew for sure how far it was from Masan to Yŏsu—he got estimates from 200 to 300 to 400. So they would know even less about how far it would be from Yŏsu to Kwangju, and the guessing ran anywhere from 150 all the way to that devastating pronouncement of 600 *li*.

This was not helping any, so Sŏkgyu decided he would just go and discuss his problem with Mister Yang, and borrow some money for the trip while he was at it. The blacksmith was also not all that sure how far it was—maybe 300 by boat from Masan to Yŏsu, and on land from Yŏsu to Kwangju another 300, and he would also have to reckon from here to Masan—but he thought it would be best to figure on at least 600 *li* to get anywhere close to where Pongho was.

"Six hundred *li*!" To Sŏkgyu 600 *li* might just as well be 6,000 *li*. "W . . . Well then, how long do you think it would take to get there?"

"Who knows? You'll have to take the boat to Yŏsu, and then you'll be taking a train or bus from Yŏsu to Kwangju. So that would be a day from Masan to Yŏsu, and then if it takes you a day by bus from Yŏsu to Kwangju . . . but then you can't expect those boats and buses to be sitting there waiting just for you. Who can tell, you might find yourself waiting three or four days and never get a ride. And nobody can promise nothing will happen to you along the way. So you'd better plan on at least five or six days one way . . . "

"Then how much would I have to bring with me?"

"When it comes to something like a trip, the more money you bring, the better. Once you get there you're not just going to turn around and come back right away, are you . . . ? I'd say you'd better figure on around twenty or thirty thousand won."

Sŏkgyu did not have even ten thousand won, so twenty or

thirty thousand was an awful lot of money. For basic farm expenses like fertilizer and such he could always find some place to borrow enough money, but that was the limit of what he could borrow and have any hope of repaying. Put the farm money into a trip, though, and there would be no way he could borrow what he would need for the farm. If he was not very careful about this borrowing business, that awesome interest would turn around on him and gobble up his farm.

Then again, money is money, and a man's son is his son. Whether or not they lost their farm—they would just have to worry about that when the time came. Right now the important thing was to see Pongho.

"All right. Loan me thirty thousand, will you?"

* * *

It took Sŏkgyu four days to get from Yŏsu to Kwangju. The first day he covered 20 *li* on foot, then found an inn at sunset. The second day, after he'd covered 30 *li*, he hitched a ride on a truck going to Sunchŏn. When he reached Sunchŏn, around noon, he found that the bus to Kwangju had already left that morning. So he set off again on foot. The next day around noon, when he got to Busŏngni, he managed to get a ride on another truck to Bosŏng. And early the next morning in Bosŏng he got a ride in a car to Kwangju.

He went into a small inn for lunch. After he ate, he asked if anyone knew Kim Pongho in the Third Regiment of Fifth Division. One of the customers told him he would have to ask at division headquarters. "Then the Fifth Division really is in Kwangju?" Yes, it was. He felt a bit of relief, then asked how to get to division headquarters.

It was already dusk by the time he found his way from division headquarters to regiment headquarters, where he was told there was a Kim Pongho in the reconnaissance unit of a battalion 20 *li* further out, "at the foot of those mountains there." With this, Sŏkgyu started walking again, down another unfamiliar road in the gathering darkness, and it was not until the middle of the night that he arrived in the village near Pongho's unit. He stayed the night there in the village office.

Sŏkgyu was at Pongho's unit early the next morning. The boy was not expected back till that evening. But they knew him there, he had found his son! Sŏkgyu said he would return later, and then went off to the foothills nearby and found a patch of grass to lie down and get some rest.

That evening, when he returned to the unit, there was Pongho, in that uniform and that overturned stew pot which all but hid his gaunt face, standing at the barracks gate.

Then Pongho saw his father.

"Father!" He walked up to Sŏkgyu.

"Pongho . . . ?" Sŏkgyu greeted his son.

Pongho removed his helmet and bowed solemnly to his father.

"Been rough, has it?" Sŏkgyu asked.

A fiery blush reddened Pongho's face.

" . . . Well then, you must be hungry."

"I'm fine."

" . . . "

" . . . "

"Well . . . why don't we go someplace," Sŏkgyu finally managed.

"I can't leave the compound now, Father. I'll get a pass for tomorrow afternoon and meet you then . . . "

* * *

The next morning Sŏkgyu was waiting again outside Pongho's unit. Pongho finally came out at two o'clock, and when Sŏkgyu saw him he felt the same pang he had the day before.

Pongho walked over to where Sŏkgyu was waiting. He had a two-hour pass, and had to be back by four o'clock. He had orders to go off somewhere the next day at seven in the morning, and wouldn't be returning for another two or three weeks.

Sŏkgyu took Pongho off down the road where there were some shops. Sŏkgyu bought some rice cakes, taffy, an apple, a pear . . . but with every purchase, Pongho objected he was fine, had just had lunch. And he asked the same questions about his mother and his kid brothers and sisters that he had asked the day before.

They went to a roadside inn and ordered a rice soup.

Sŏkgyu had some rice wine.

He placed the rice cakes and taffy and fruit in front of Pongho.

Each had his soup.

Nudging a rice cake toward Pongho, he urged, "Go on, have one . . . Here, how about a pear . . . ? You ought to have something."

"I'm fine, Father," Pongho said, pushing the treats back. "Bring them back for the kids."

They sat in silence.

Sŏkgyu finally managed, "So, when do you think you'll be coming home again?"

Pongho blushed. "I don't know, Father . . . "

And they sat in silence.

After a while Sŏkgyu asked, "You think you'll have to stay in till the fighting's over?"

"I don't know, Father."

Silence.

Pongho had about thirty minutes left on his pass.

"Well, I guess it's about time you got started back now."

"Yessir," Pongho said, as soon as the words were out of his Father's mouth.

The two got up and left the inn. They walked back toward Pongho's barracks.

"Better get on back home, Father."

"Guess I better."

They stopped. Pongho beheld his father. Sŏkgyu beheld his son. But it hurt and they dropped their eyes.

"Guess you better go."

"Yessir . . . Good-bye, Father."

Pongho removed his helmet and bowed, as he had when they met the day before, then turned and walked off. Sŏkgyu took a few steps after him. Pongho looked back, and Sŏkgyu stopped. Pongho looked back a couple more times.

Sŏkgyu stood there in the middle of the road, watching, till his son was out of sight. Suddenly he felt himself gawking and dropped his eyes, hurting but not knowing really why, or who for.

He shuffled a few absent steps off toward the side of the road. At the corner of the warehouse just off the road he unzipped and relieved himself on the wall.

A MOMENT'S GRACE

O Sang-wŏn

(1955)

One more hour and it's all over.

Lying there curled up beneath the old straw rice sack. Hands and feet cold as ice. From the bottom of the deep pit, every wall frosted white, he glimpses the cold sky through the cracks in the log trapdoor far above.

That sour stench—must have kept somebody down here, not more than a couple days ago. After they lowered the ladder and dumped me here, on their way back up the ladder one of them said Just like the other guy. Same one they were going to execute when I fired at them? Who else would it be?

The cold grabs hold and shakes him violently. His bones are frozen to the marrow.

The interrogation flickers on and off in the haze clouding his mind. Your unit, Lieutenant? How much school? Hometown? Why did you volunteer? What do you think of communism? What do you think about Americans? . . . No, comrade, that makes no sense at all. You've still got that bourgeois mindset—now don't think I'm blaming you for being born into that class—problem is it's bred too deep in you. I'm going to give you some time to reflect. What you tell me an hour from now is going to settle everything.

One more hour and it's all over . . . Led along that crumbling wall in back of the thatch-roof house, snow crunching under every step, muzzle of that gun in my back, now this prison in a pit. An hour from now they'll be pulling me out of here and leading me along that paddy dike. That's how they do things. They exchange a few words, commander says Okay, turn around, walk straight ahead, don't look back. I walk, I hear the snow crunching under each step. They'll probably want my clothes—torn a bit, but U.S. issue, original color still there—tell me to take them off, so I walk along the snow-covered dike, stripped, skin blushing red with the cold. A few shots ring out, I drop right there. Bright red blood silently stains the white snow. Clutching the white snow, maybe a groan or two. Then I get tossed into some shallow grave and forgotten forever. And that's it. They'll turn away, glad it's done with, shoulder their rifles, go back to camp, kick the snow off their boots, step into their quarters rubbing their hands. And a couple minutes later they'll be warming those hands at the charcoal stove, lighting a butt, stretching, as if nothing happened, won't matter that somebody's just died, it's all the same to them.

What is this shivering—shaking all over—every muscle? The cold, or just me? And this rotten stench, like it's in my blood.

I'm not the first, won't be the last. Fighting, and then in the end, dying, that's all there is. What else? For something, to achieve something? That's not it. It's just our nature to fight, to die.

North and farther north, like an arrow from the bow. One battle after another. The search and destroy party he was leading penetrated deep behind enemy lines. But then they started losing contact with headquarters, and it kept getting worse, and every member of the platoon had his mind's eye fixed on the radio operator. The order finally came: Get out! But all the roads were already cut off, so the lieutenant settled on the likeliest place to break through, and they headed south for it. Skirmish after skirmish. One man down, another, then another. To avoid more contact they headed up into the mountains. The platoon shrank as hunger and exhaustion finished off one after another. Snow dumped upon snow. Aimless wandering. They were hit with everything nature could throw at them, desperately battling blizzard after blizzard through waist-high drifts.

They came to a valley, and made their way into a snow-locked village there. Completely deserted. Scattered houses hushed and lonely in their tombs of snow. No sign of the enemy, no sign of any having passed through. Good. Spread out, search every house for food. Just one sack of frozen potatoes. Like biting into a frozen lump of slush. Fatigue and hunger fell on the whole platoon, heavy and sudden as a plate of lead, and they all dropped, unable to go any further. The cold ate into their toes. Night came on—gets dark fast in the mountains—with another blizzard, fiercer than ever. Only the sergeant managed to fight off his fatigue, sat there leaning against that door post keeping watch while the others slept. Quiet, except for that growling blizzard outside. The sergeant closed his eyes for a moment. Good night for an attack.

Nothing that night, though, and the new day dawned. Back to that struggle with the snow and the cold and the hunger. One man fell, then another, nature's prey.

Lieutenant! cried one more as he fell face down in the snow. Hong knelt down at his side and turned him over and looked into his eyes to hold that cold last gaze. Lieutenant . . . Those eyes gazing up into Hong's, that last groping look of desperation, eyes getting dimmer and dimmer as death closed in, eyes icing over. Sir . . . I'm from the north. No wife. No one . . . no . . . in the . . . south. My address . . . in the north—could you . . . ? Crumpled scrap of paper ratty around the edges. Hong clasped his hand, took the address. Nothing more you can do. When it was all over he went through his pockets, feeling like a scavenger.

Only six left now. They left their fallen compatriot lying

there in the snow, and waded on again through the drifts. That feeling of doom was overpowering, but just when it seemed they could stand it no longer, the slope and terrain eased. And before they knew it, they were traversing flat land. Then they saw the road.

As soon as they reached it Sergeant Kim, who had gone ahead to reconnoiter lay of the land and enemy disposition, came hurrying back. Lots of cart tracks and hoof prints and boot prints on the road. He had a horse turd in his hand; it crumbled when he squeezed it, sure sign that whatever unit it was hadn't been by long before. Nothing for it but to wait for dark. Use the cover of darkness to get across the road and make it to the mountain ridge ahead.

Night fell, and they started off, down along the edge of the stream approaching the road to make best use of whatever low land they could find.

No problem crossing the road. Off the road down onto a paddy dike, press fast ahead, fast, from one piece of cover to the next. Now less than 200 meters to that ridge. Push, push, fast, and as they moved along they started to feel a little easier. But then a shot, and the soldier left behind him a cry of pain as he went down. They all dropped to their stomachs in the snow.

A moment passed. Where the hell did that shot come from? The lieutenant couldn't make out the direction. He poked his head up for a better look and another shot whizzed by. From their flank, the road. They shifted around toward it for a better position to return fire. With them situated like this the enemy had the advantage. The enemy had the platoon in their sights, but the platoon was blind.

They had to get out of there fast. Dark it was, but they were silhouetted against the white snow. They low-crawled toward the ridge. On the way they were hit by a hailstorm of bullets.

Lieutenant!

Hong clenched his teeth at the cry of pain behind him. He squeezed his eyes shut against that distraction of death, kept on crawling, sweat streaming down his face like rain. Losing it. But there was the ridge ahead, a soupy white fog of snow-covered shrubs.

When they reached the foot of the ridge the shooting let up a bit. But Sergeant Kim went down. Hong helped, dragging him, stumbling, further up into the trees. Hong finally lost consciousness and dropped right there in his tracks. It was nearing daybreak when Hong finally came to. How far up the ridge had they come . . . ?

Terribly cold in this pit. He tries to shift himself. The cold has frozen every muscle so he can't feel a thing. Sour stench in his nose. Faint crunch of boots on snow. All over now . . . Coming closer. Must be time. He moves to raise himself but is knocked back by a wave of dizziness. The footsteps begin to move away. Nothing. It's nothing. How unbearably cold. But why come then just go away like that . . . ?

His mind fogs, slips back. "What did you major in? Why law, comrade? There's that bourgeois thinking again—have to be a lawyer, a doctor . . . Grow up among people like that and it gets in your bones. Well, get rid of it. Look, we don't want to hurt a good man like you. Our arms are open, ready to accept you as one of us. Just say the word." The wind sneaks in at the threshold and attacks the charcoal stove so it glows red. "Comrade, you seem to be a fine young man. Here, have a cigarette . . . "

"No?" He teases the burning coals with the fire tongs and they flare up in anger. "Well then, Lieutenant, I can't imagine a more pitiful young man. That sorry attitude of yours is quite a disappointment." It's all over now. "And look at that icy glare—

what's that for? Nothing to say, not a word, huh? Lips are sealed, is that it? Fine. But I understand every word you're not telling me, Lieutenant. Just a waste of a good man."

That interrogation, the tiny room, the chipped clay brazier, image after image slips away as they come to him. He strains to shift his stiff, aching body . . .

Both of them out cold, sprawled in the coming dawn. Dawn in the mountains is beautiful, even better with everything covered in snow, every branch capped with snow sparkling in the sun. When the sun climbed a bit Lieutenant Hong woke, shoulder and back spotted black with blood, got to his knees, and crawled over to the sergeant to help him up so they could get going again.

The sergeant's eyes opened. He recognized the lieutenant and a weary smile formed on his lips. Hong hugged the sergeant, pressed his cheek to him. Just us two now. We're all that's left.

"Looks like it's my turn now, Lieutenant."

Hong studied the sergeant's face. Not the slightest hint of unhappiness there. All he could make out was the determined will of one who'd gone through a lot in a long life in the military. This man had drifted from one uniform to another with the flow of time and circumstance. Conscripted into the Japanese army in the Second World War, when Korea was still a colony, saw action in the South Pacific, then he was assigned to the Northern Command in Manchuria. Two months as a POW when Japan surrendered. After liberation he joined up with the Communist Chinese 8th Route Army, switched to Chiang Kai-shek's Nationalists, and finally returned to serve in the army of his fatherland. To the sergeant, who found military life the most fulfilling way to live, battle was the most energizing part of life.

What the sergeant said once comes back now. "You know,

Lieutenant, people are meant to kill each other. That's what history is, a record of people butchering people. Don't you think so? But for me battle is life's most exhilarating moment. When the fighting starts I get so keyed up I can't breathe, and every time I see the heart of the enemy glimmering there in my sights, it's such pure . . . pure—elation. A moment like this, it's like I've become a part of history. People are nothing special. Life is fighting, just fighting and dying." The attitude that ruled his whole life. That was it. Now he'd been shot, and it was all quite simple: it was his turn.

He makes an effort to raise himself, then falls back. A muscle cramps in his upper right arm, he bites his tongue to hold the pain inside. All over now.

"Lieutenant, I guess this is my last stop. Go on now—no sense in worrying about me anymore." Then he dragged himself into a patch of gentle sunlight and leaned against the old oak tree there. His loosely closed eyes were at peace. In his face was nothing of grief or loneliness, just the tranquility of the snow-covered world around them. The sergeant shifted a bit and then slipped from the tree onto the ground. Hong tried to right him. Just then the sergeant's eyes opened weakly. His lips hinted a smile. The sunlight held it there. "Just let me be . . . " His eyes closed. He struggled a minute for air, then he lay still.

Hong pushed on, south, alone now, south, struggling on through the knee-high snow. He couldn't feel his frozen feet anymore. Now and then he blacked out, dropped right there in his tracks. He strayed directionless through day-long blizzards. Anxiety and depression caught him in devastating attacks. Headed the right way? Where am I, anyway? No one at all to talk it over with. Just myself. Well, stop thinking about it and get moving. He labored on through the snow, step by painful step. How much farther like this? How much longer? At night he slept buried in the snow. The sun rose and he forced himself to go on again. Down valley slopes with snow-covered undergrowth that snared and tripped him, up jutting ridges so sharp they must have been hacked out just the day before. He slipped and fell back again and again. Battered knees, torn skin. Hunger, exhaustion. At night the cold and loneliness teamed up in ambush.

A recurring nightmare possessed him in fitful sleep, and he finally came out of it a couple hours later with a groan, opened his eyes to total darkness and desolation. Buried here in this snow, lost forever. This persistent sense of despair was consuming him. But somehow he was making it through another night, somehow another day was on its way. He got up. Forced himself to struggle on through the snow. The mountain terrain got even rougher, the slopes even steeper.

A wrong step sent him tumbling over a twenty-foot drop. He was out for a while, and when he came to he'd bitten clean through his lip. Every bone, every muscle ached and refused to go on. But he pushed himself half up, staggered on all fours a way to finally get up on his feet. Clenched fists trembling, he looked back up to where he'd come over the cliff. Twenty feet, maybe twenty-five . . . much too high to get back up there. Have to, though. He set his jaw in grim determination and started pulling himself back up. Whole body raining sweat; those dizzy spells assailing him again, sky whirling. He grabbed hold of a root, shut his eyes tight to stop the spinning and steady himself, pulled himself up. Clumps of snow and dirt blinded him as his unseeing hands fumbled for roots and bushes. Struggling inch by impossible inch, he finally made it to the top, blacked out, and collapsed.

Night fell. Dawn broke. Now a mindless, worn-out machine, wading through the snow, one step . . . one step . . . each step taking everything he had, each step surely his last. Stop—rifle's too heavy. Tie one end of the strap to the belt. He pulled himself together. One step . . . another step . . . the rifle dragging along behind.

One evening in the dim glow of the setting sun Hong grappled his way to the top of a steep ridge. The next day when he opened his eyes the sun was already high in the sky. He looked down before him, where the mountain's ridge almost completely ringed a valley. His heart leapt at what he saw, a scattering of snow-capped thatched houses dotting the plain. Spent all night up here with this village down there. His breast tightened, tears welled in his eyes. He hurried, letting the tears flow, down to the village.

At the first house he realized that all of them were deserted. Here and there a door hung open. A hinge creaked. Wind in the pines. The village's thick white blanket of snow was smooth, clean of footprints.

But there was a pig pen, a shed for oxen, things people had built. He entered a house. Cabinet doors ajar, things scattered on the floor covered now with dust—the things of people. Torn, worn-out clothing. He picked up a piece and hugged it tight to his breast. The scent of people, that musty odor of people. He looked around the room. So desolate! Can a place for people be so desolate? On the way here he'd seen places just this bad, but he still couldn't get used to how a place where people had been could turn so utterly barren . . .

Wait—footsteps. Outside. Hong flattened himself against the wall, looked out through a hole in the stucco wall crumbling in decay. Nothing there, probably just hearing things. But in the next instant there it was again. Voices. Hope and fear fought in his breast. He looked out again, careful not to miss a thing.

There! A few pushing up the path on the paddy-stepped hill in back of the house across the way. Before they got far they stopped.

Even from this distance he could see they were soldiers. One of them was wearing an American-issue uniform. Friendly territory already? But he kept watching, holding his breath. Something funny here, those quilted uniforms the others were wearing. Need to get a closer look, find out what's really going on here. The house in front offered a better view. He crouched along the wall in the yard, and then nimbly slipped over to the open shed, then to the stack of straw, from cover to cover, and made it to the clay wall surrounding the house. A damaged part of the wall afforded him a peep hole. The image through the tiny hole flickered in and out of focus, but the wind carried their voices. The words comrade and firing squad stunned him and set the scene in front of him spinning. He shook his head to steady things, and looked again, straining to focus. A young man appeared, dressed only in his underwear, gaunt face, long, unkempt hair, bare feet–hands bound behind his back.

" . . . the people's decision. Do you have anything to say?" His authoritative bearing made it clear he was this unit's commander.

The captive's voice rang clear and steady. "One thing: I'm glad. When you took me prisoner you freed me from killing. I didn't have to kill anymore. Nobody's killing machine anymore. I'm going as a human being, not somebody's tool—like you."

A scornful sneer appeared on the commander's face. "Commendable," the commander sneered. "Then walk that way, along this dike. It heads south, you know. Since that's where you were going in the first place you should have no problem with that."

The victim turned. One step, in his bare feet, another step. In back of him two aimed their rifles. He felt those rifles all set to discharge their fiery load into his back but kept walking resolutely forward, shoulders back, down the snowy path. And soon the crack of shots would render this proud young man a limp, wretched clump on that path in the middle of the frozen paddies. Eyes straight ahead, his step never faltering—that composure . . .

Hong's head swam at the horror of it, as if he himself were the one walking that path. He grabbed his rifle. Avoiding a fight now to live one more day is the coward's way. The one walking along that snowy path is me, not him. I'm the one walking that road to death. Have to shoot, no choice. He aimed, drew a steadying breath, and a long volley poured from the muzzle of his rifle. A couple of them fell, definitely two down. He kept shooting. They returned his fire. His forehead ran with sweat, everything spun in front of him, every muscle in his body hopped with each jolt from that rifle butt. He dropped his head to ward off another wave of dizziness and felt himself blacking out. Not *now*. Rifle back up. The rifle's butt punching him in the shoulder told him he was firing again. Head swimming, vision darkening . . . Then their guns fell silent. Must have spread out, closing in now, front, back, left, right. He jumped up, blasting away in all directions like a madman.

Something tore into his body, then another, knocking him back down. The violent explosion of his volley kept ringing in his ear. He felt something wet, clammy oozing down his skin. He heard something approach. A blow to his head. Out again.

A violent pain stabbing his upper right arm brought him to his senses. His left hand moved there and felt the spot. Sticky. He pulled his hand away, held it up to his face. Dark red blood all over his fingers. Voices, murmuring. In a room, dumped here in this room. Air thick with cigarette smoke stealing out through the dusty gossamer spider web covering the hole in the paper ceiling. Now and then through the fog in his mind he could hear footsteps on white snow, then his senses wandered off with them.

After a few interrogations everything was decided . . .

Now, it's all over. So cold, this pit floor, like a bed of ice.

Mind all muddled. Muscles all numb, an occasional cramp. Footsteps. And voices. Must be time. The hatch door will squeak open, sunlight flushing out the darkness, and then, at last, that ladder will slide down. He waits, holding his breath. A moment passes. Silence, not a hint of anything going on out there. What's up? I imagining things? But he's sure he heard footsteps. There—closer, closer . . . sure . . . He struggles to sit up. He looks up at the trapdoor. Blinding sunlight pours in. The ladder.

"What's taking you so long? Out of there, quick!"

So it's not a hallucination. They've already been shouting at him for quite a while to come up out of there. Little by little he manages to clear his mind, rub some feeling back into his frozen knees, and climbs up the ladder out of the pit. As soon as he gets to the opening a strong hand grips him by the collar and yanks him forward, and he sprawls on the snow face first. The cold snow brings him back to his senses. He's resolved that every step from here on out is going to be steady and sure. All over now, have to tough it out, to the very end, finish clean. He gets to his knees, clutches the snowy ground to brace himself, struggles up to all fours, then straightens all the way. He walks, every step steady, a cold, determined glint in his eyes.

A short exchange with headquarters confirms his sentence.

The snow is pure and brilliant and deep on the paddy dike. This path, how many others have already walked it? Wide open plain, and then that hill—all in white—fill him with an exhilarating sense of release. Walk straight on there, Lieutenant. No regrets taking this path—it leads south, right where you want to go. One step, another. Steady now. Each step leaves a footprint behind in the white snow. Prepare to fire! The crackle of guns cocking is as cold as the icy wind. In front all he sees is the white snowy expanse ahead. It's all over now. Have to finish clean, hold strong till the last moment. Can't let go, got to keep it together till the very last second.

His steps follow his determined will. Each step on this path brings him one step closer to death, but this path is not one of futility, anxiety, despair. White snow, walking in a field of white. The hill across the wide open plain. Pure white snow. A volley of shots, but from elsewhere, not here. He keeps walking, step by steady step, into the whiteness. Faint crunch of footsteps on snow. A murmur, a mumble. Someone yanks him up by his collar, wrenching his lower back. But it's not his pain, it's somewhere else, nothing to do with him.

Eyes dimming now. It's all over. They'll turn away, glad it's done with, shoulder their guns, and go back. Shake off the snow, rub the cold out of their hands, go inside. In another moment they'll be warming their hands over the charcoal brazier and, as if nothing at all has happened, roll a cigarette, take a stretch. Whoever it was, once it's over it never happened. Just another life.

Senses fade, fade . . . to nothing.

On the white snow. Sunlight sparkling on the white snow.

THE GULLS

Yi Pŏm-sŏn

(1958)

The huge breakers pounding away in his pillow wake him, and now he'll never get back to sleep.

That light out there should have been extinguished hours ago. What could it be tonight? Something glad, maybe something sad, in this little harbor town.

This small island is actually like one big household, and so, when one family celebrates something, or when another is in mourning, electricity's provided through the night. It stayed on when the fishmonger, a crippled war veteran, finally took a wife, and that day the town leader's mother celebrated the special sixtieth birthday. It stayed on when the kid in the orphanage died, and again that stormy night when one of the fishing boats didn't come back.

Seven years have passed since the refugee Hun came here from the north, through Pusan. Now he's the town's middle school teacher.

At first it had been awfully lonely; and that monotonous sound of wave after wave lapping the shore was nothing but an annoyance. He liked one thing about this island, though—no one had to worry about an identification card or military service card. In those days of war a man on the peninsula valued these cards as he did his life. But here, where even a stranger staying a night at the inn could feel friendship with the island and its shores and townspeople, it was all the same whether one had those cards or not.

Now he and his family are no longer refugees; it's been quite a while since they became islanders. A neighborhood woman, babe in her arms, will greet the teacher warmly when she meets him on the road. Or Ok-hŭi's father and Pretty Girl's big brother, returning with their catch, will pull a red snapper, maybe a conch snail, out of the basket for Hun . . .

"First snapper I've caught me in quite a while. Nice and fresh—still alive."

"And a good size conch here, isn't it? First one of the season."

Then they will set these down for him on the spine of the ox rock at his front gate and go off down the road. That rock does look like an ox just lying there like it does.

Seven years. On this island a year runs its course like one long day. Yesterday just like today, what happens today happens tomorrow. Nothing disturbs that slow flow . . .

"There we go, sir, wouldn't you say they're clean enough? Nothing like salt water for it," the oyster lady said that day as she put aside her work, rinsed her hands in the ocean, then came home with Hun to midwife his child. And now Chong is already five.

* * *

Such an extremely simple life.

Hun wakes in the morning, sits up, and looks out the window at the harbor. The window frames this misty harbor of black and white hues and turns it into a Chinese ink painting. Toothbrush in his mouth, he goes out to the well in the yard to wash. Spot slips out from under the porch, lays down with one of Hun's rubber shoes, gnaws contentedly at its heel. The leaves of the camellia tree on the back hill glisten in the early morning sun, and from off somewhere drifts the call of the magpie.

Friendly cosmos laughs genially from its corner at the turn

in the stone wall. The persimmon tree's luscious vermilion fruit hang three, four, five to every branch, ready now for the Harvest Festival. A leaf as red as the fruit pops off from the end of its twig, spirals slowly downward tracing circles in space, settles delicately to earth. The white cock has just come around past the kitchen door, and he scrambles over and pecks at the fallen leaf. He straightens, and his blood-red comb quivers in the intensity of his watch for his next prey.

After breakfast, book bag in one hand and daughter's hand in the other, Hun sets off through the front gate. The path they take is just wide enough for two to walk abreast; it skirts the cliff rising above them on the left and looks down upon the sea on the right. The two amble along, passing beneath a wild chrysanthemum sprouting from a crack in a rock. Spot is at their heels, whiffing big snorts of the lunch bag daughter is carrying.

Hun's wife and Chong, their five-year-old son, stand watching the threesome from the ox rock. Father and daughter can be seen winding their way along the twisting path till they reach the middle of the horseshoe harbor, so that a really good send-off means standing there until the two have traversed half the length of the harbor's shore. Mother and son have an unspoken agreement between themselves: not until Spot comes bounding back along the path and into the yard do they turn back in through the gate.

* * *

Spot has a rendezvous every morning on his way back from seeing off Hun and the little girl. There is just one house, a dilapidated hovel, halfway along the path leading to the main road. In this hovel live three old beggars. Last year when Hun's brother in high school visited the island during his summer vacation he was struck by the three old men's resemblance to the legendary Taoist Immortals, those Chinese mountain hermits with supernatural powers. So he named them the Three Taos, and the name has stuck.

These three old gentlemen have nothing to do. They just sit all day long gazing out over the sea, as immortals are supposed to do. They're all in their sixties, but that's all they have in common. The one they call the Big Tao is Grandpa Sŏ. His hair, eyebrows and long beard have all turned silver white. He's a tall man, the most distinguished of the three. Middle Tao, Grandpa Pak, has a round face and a scalp scraped clean like a monk's. He always wears an old military outfit. And Little Tao, Grandpa Kim, is the dumpy one, humblest of the three. His face is pockmarked, and he has the beard of a goat. He wears a salvaged gray vest.

At any rate, in each of them is that something deserving of the name Tao. Beggars they are, insistent or bothersome they are not. They even seem to have an agreement that more than one of them will not patronize the same family.

Grandpa Sŏ, Big Tao, has Hun's house. On some days he'll come in the morning, other days in the evening. Hun's wife doesn't know when he'll show up, so she can't really make sure there will be enough for the old gentleman that day. She certainly is sorry if there is not.

Grandpa Sŏ has earned acceptance from Spot, who is actually ferocious enough to have chased away the armed policeman on his sanitation inspection round. Spot doesn't even bother to bark now at Grandpa Sŏ. And returning in the morning from seeing Hun off, as he passes by the immortals' house, Spot gives a look back over his shoulder at Grandpa Sŏ before he continues on back home.

But Spot isn't Grandpa Sŏ's only friend. There was about four days once when Grandpa Sŏ didn't come by Hun's house.

The family thought it strange, so Hun, on his way back from school, took a look in on the hovel . . .

All three of the gentlemen are there. Grandpa Kim is seated at the upper end of the room, facing the wall and weaving a net—whatever he would use a net for—which hangs by one of its loops from a nail in the wall post. Grandpa Pak is seated in the doorway, mending the heel of his rubber shoe. And Grandpa Sŏ is on his back with his feet to the wall at the lower end of the room, seeming even taller than when he's standing. He's stretched out straight as a corpse, and on his leg sits a squirrel cleaning its face with its front paw.

"Grandpa Sŏ doesn't look very well."

Grandpa Pak finally raises his old pumpkin head. "No, he's been like that for a few days now. Stomach's bad," he says, looking over at Grandpa Sŏ.

That evening Hun's son and daughter, with Spot, return to the hovel with a bowl of rice porridge for the old man.

"Such a pity!" Hun's daughter says with a solicitous frown, just like the grown-up second grader she is.

"Such a pity!" Chong agrees.

The next day, as soon as Hun comes back home from school, Chong dashes out onto the porch. "Papa, Papa, look at my squirrel!" And he's pulling Hun by the hand even before Hun can get his shoes off.

Grandpa Sŏ has been by earlier. Knotty wooden cane in one hand and a fine little squirrel in the other, he told Chong's mother, "I thought the child might like this." He has been raising it at home for a year and has treated it so well that, even when he lets it free in his hand, the creature has no thought of running away. Instead, it climbs up to the man's neck and then squirms down inside the shirt to his breast.

And every day now Chong goes into his father's room, diligently empties the tobacco from the cigarette butts there into an old caramel tin till it's filled to the top, and brings it to Grandpa Sŏ. The old gentleman returns the tin filled with acorns.

"Don't you eat them—give them to the squirrel."

* * *

Even this tiny harbor town has a tearoom. Its name is The Gulls. It is in a two-story frame house owned by a Japanese when they occupied the country. A young refugee couple from the North have taken the place. They hammered a nail here, a nail there, and now it's a tearoom.

Hun drops by here once in a while. Coming out the school gate when school is over for the day, he's at the exact center of the horseshoe which the harbor forms. He stands there a while, looking out to sea. Drifting lazily in the center of the harbor is the white hull of a police patrol boat. At the pier just in front of the marketplace four wooden fishing boats, sporting frayed red flags from the top of their masts, rub shoulders. Out farther are two white lighthouses, connected at their girths by the flat horizon. The brimming, dancing waves at Hun's feet spread and flatten as his eyes lift to the horizon. There begins the other sea, the exultant, blossoming autumn sky, so clean and blue and so very deep he gets a giddy feeling of falling into it.

Hun looks just to the right of the light houses and there, almost straight across the harbor from him, without his having to search for it along the rocky cliff path, is his home. A neat, handsome house on the shore, which his fellow teachers call Persimmon Place. A camellia tree stands against the shimmering hill, and the white laundry on the line stands out sharply. And there is his wife on her haunches weeding at the center of the vegetable patch outside the wall, with Chong, in his red sweater, standing in front of her.

On days when Hun can observe them like this he finally turns off in the other direction with the lighthearted feeling of just having come out of the house after seeing to his family.

Hun passes by the post office. He feels like sending off a letter, to anyone, when he sees its red sign. Next is the Chinese restaurant, then the inn, and just a bit further is The Gulls.

A wood checkerboard-sized sign with clumsy white lettering hangs over the downstairs entrance where Hun starts up the creaky stairs to the second floor. Most tearooms these days have hinged doors; The Gulls still has the original Japanese sliding door, veneered. It gives a startled groan as Hun opens it.

The tearoom is usually empty. Often, not even the owner is there. Hun has his favorite table by the window. There is a small cactus plant on the table, and the window is hung with a blue curtain. Pretty fancy for a shop like this.

His eyes follow the road from below this window all the way to where it ends at the sea. He lifts his gaze and finds himself looking directly at the window of his room at home. There is no one in the vegetable patch now. A woman carrying something on her head is passing the front gate.

Just then a gull darts past and sets the tearoom window rattling with its wing. Hun could have reached out and caught it with his hand . . . probably why they call this place The Gulls. Hun absently follows the gull's mad, dizzying line of flight.

A door opens from inside, where the couple lives. The owner's wife comes into the tearoom. There's no way of telling exactly, but the young woman couldn't be past her early thirties. Slender oval face, sparkling eyes. She's tall and slim, attractive in her pink skirt.

"Oh, have you been here long?" She has a sweet, slightly nasal voice.

"Yes, I have—three or four hours maybe."

"There you go again!" She smiles and turns to open the inner door. "Dear, it's the gentleman from across the harbor."

In back of this door is an opening like a bay window, which leads to a small room where the Japanese owner had probably hung the laundry to dry. The young wife goes back and climbs nimbly through the opening into the room, which they now use as the kitchen.

As he waits for her husband Hun regards a picture on the wall. Next to the door leading to the water closet is a print of two naked children. One is standing, the other is squatting and warming his outstretched hands over a fire.

Beneath this picture is the entrance to the "Private Room." Even this tearoom has one. This cubicle used to be a cavity in the wall where the former owner had installed a large cabinet. Now it has a table and chairs and is curtained off with a yellow cloth. On the back wall of this room hangs a faded print of the Mona Lisa. A subtle smile comes to Hun's face when he sees it.

He can hear the wife fanning the embers to bring the stove to life. She's getting his coffee ready. All this work just for one coffee, and he feels a little guilty. The door to the inside room opens, quietly, and now the owner of the tearoom comes shuffling over, step by careful step, across the wood floor. He is blind.

"Is it you, sir?" He gets to the table, feels in front of him with both extended hands. Hun hurries to grasp his hand. Light, smooth, like a woman's hand, and finely shaped even to the nails of its long, thin fingers. "I'm glad you've come—it's been a while now."

"Please, sit down."

Hun scrutinizes the man's face, almost as if he were seeing him for the first time. A few strands of hair sweep low over his even forehead. Gently closed eyes, long eyelashes and black eyebrows—sad eyes. Straight nose. Fine, smoothly sculpted lips, stoic, seeming never to have really laughed.

"How are you getting along these days?" Hun asks.

"Same as ever . . . "

That things are the same as ever is no surprise. In their bleak, solitary life the man and his wife survive only on memories. Last night Hun heard the man's saxophone, "Gypsy Moon" again, just about when the red and blue lamps of the lighthouses began to play their long colored ribbons of light out over the harbor's water. The strains of the saxophone, husky with pathos, rippled through the quiet night sky and tugged Hun's soul relentlessly back, far back into his past . . .

Night after night, even before he knew who was playing it, Hun would sit back against the porch post outside his room when he heard the song of that saxophone, and lose himself in the star-swept sky. Then one day in the tearoom he saw the blind man, who turned out to be the owner of the place, sitting in a corner and fondling that silver sax. It surprised Hun, but just as quickly he felt that somehow a blind person and a saxophone were right together. And from that day on the two men were like old friends reunited after a long separation.

Hun doesn't come to this deserted tearoom for the sugar-water coffee, which the wife has to labor over so each time with that fan at the stove. If it were just the coffee he'd go elsewhere, and save her the trouble. Seven years on this island have almost completely erased his former life, but there are still those times when the shadow of a memory will steal into his heart. What is it in his friend's long eyelashes and tranquil lowered eyes that bring him back to . . . ?

A horn booms far off, softly, like cotton. The tearoom's owner, hands in the pockets of his light gray cardigan, quietly lifts his face. "Evening already."

Hun's eyes follow the man's face. "So it is." He can't see the ferry yet, but about now it must be rounding the base of the cliff.

Then the pumping throb of the boat's engine roils the clear harbor air. Hun looks over toward the front gate of his house and, sure enough, there on the ox rock sits a small boy in a red sweater.

* * *

Chong really likes boats. When the island ferry leaves in the morning and when it returns in the evening his post is out in the yard on the spine of the ox rock. He can watch the ferry easily enough through the window of his room, but all he needs is to hear the booming steam whistle and he's out the front door. Even in the middle of a meal he'll drop his spoon and rush outside. Sitting on that rock, he assumes a countenance of maturity striking in a five-year-old. Chong gathers his knees to his chest, rests his chin on his knees, and in this touching posture fixes steady, unblinking eyes on the boat.

Departing for the mainland in the morning, the ferry gives a blast of its whistle and pushes off from the pier. Out in the middle of the harbor it turns and cuts a broad circle, lining itself up just right with the lighthouses, then proceeds carefully between them. As it reaches the open sea the boat turns its head to the left and passes beneath the cliff, washing its rocky toes in the white breakers. The glimmering yin-yang of the national flag on the boat's tail grows more and more faint as the boat fades from sight, and finally only the horn is heard, far off, like something from a dream.

And then at 4:30 in the afternoon the ferry pokes its nose around the base of the cliff it vanished behind that morning. It gives a blast of its horn and Chong, no matter what he's doing or where he's doing it, stands toward the horizon. He inclines an ear and catches the rasping throb of the engine. His eyes light up and he takes off at a run, as if carried off by some magic spell. Then Chong sits himself on the spine of the ox rock, in the very same posture as ever.

The ferry slips between the two lighthouses into the harbor and turns a broad circle out in front of Chong. It alerts those waiting on the pier with a whistle blast loud enough to stir the leaves on the persimmon tree next to the watching boy. The ferry throws out its tie lines as it eases up to the pier. When it comes to a stop it lowers the gangplank and the passengers in their colorful, fashionable clothes of the mainland step onto the island. Their packages and bundles are rolled over the edge of the boat onto the pier. Before long the passengers have all dispersed and, hustle and bustle of the arrival over, the pier is left deserted. A few gulls let out an occasional squawk as they circle the smokestack of the softly panting boat which seems not to have caught its breath yet. All the while Chong is vigilant, immovable, the storybook child caught up in his dream.

* * *

Hun, eyes on the ferry at the pier, is mesmerized by the delightful scene. The tearoom's owner, head tilted slightly back, is looking at something far off from under his closed eyes. Not a word is spoken.

The wife brings coffee on a tray and looks out the window. "Will you look at that boy—isn't that just like him!"

Hun looks over across the harbor again. Beside the speck of red there is another, a black one. Chong has his arm around Spot. It looks like Spot might be licking Chong's little hand with that revolting white tongue of his . . . "Papa, look—he doesn't bite even if I stick my hand in his mouth!" For all the wonder of it, though, it was a long time before the doubt in the tips of those little fingers dissolved and that exclusive comradeship formed between the two.

"I see him, too," the blind man startles his wife and Hun. "When I hear that ferry's horn I can see a little boy on that rock, sitting there hugging his knees," and he points distantly out the window, just where a person with sight would. His wife's eyes meet Hun's for an instant.

"The little rascal certainly likes boats," Hun says.

"Boats. Yes, I guess so—perhaps the way I like the saxophone. The way they both make you yearn for something out there . . . "

"It could be just that he was born and raised here."

"Columbus was born and raised somewhere too."

"Columbus . . . Yes . . . "

The woman stirs her husband's coffee as she listens, and then her soft hands guide his slender hands around the cup.

* * *

With Harvest Festival only four days off, the big storm hit.

The wind went into a rage, the sea became a tempest. Howling waves the size of a barn piled on top of each other in their race to shore. They smashed themselves on the breakwater and their white spray danced 'round the tops of the lighthouses. The fishing boats had all scurried back to harbor, but even there they tossed against each other. Then the sea gathered itself up, up and lunged across the main road at a man's height. It engulfed even the path in front of Hun's.

The sea took another two days to spend its fury. But today the horizon seems closer, and all is quiet, almost as if the world has stopped turning. The storm has strewn the road by the fire station with large rocks and the main road seems to have been ravaged by a flood. The stone path at Hun's is gone.

Hun is at school. He's heard the news from the boy who does odd jobs there: the couple from the tearoom are dead.

They'd gone out that night the waves were so fierce, and the man was somehow swept into the sea. His wife followed, trying to save him.

In class, Hun can't keep his eyes off that sea outside the window, and every time he looks, there is that other image, of the young couple jumping into the sea, clasped in each other's arms. But no, no one can say how they really died, just as no one knows their past.

* * *

And now it is afternoon of the Harvest Festival. Hun is on his porch smoking a cigarette. Grandpa Sŏ appears, earlier than usual, dressed up in a new calico summer jacket.

"My son is here!" This is all he can say, and Hun hasn't the slightest idea what he can be talking about.

"My son has come back to me!" The old gentleman begins to realize what he has said, and tears appear at the corners of his eyes.

"Your son?"

"Yes, I had—I have a son."

Hun follows the old gentleman out through the front gate. Waiting there is a young soldier, eyes big and round as almonds. He's holding his cap in his hands, and he draws himself to attention and bows smartly to Hun. His captain's bars shine on the collar of his field uniform.

"I'm so very grateful for all you've done for my father, sir."

Hun can only stand there and look from one to the other.

"I had no idea that . . . I mean, I thought my father had passed away." The soldier bows his head again. The excitement of his discovery has drained him.

The two had lived alone together until the outbreak of war, when the boy was called into the auxiliary forces. When the soldier finally returned his home was a pile of ashes and no one could tell him his father's whereabouts. He kept on searching, everywhere, never giving up. But in his heart he knew he was searching for nothing less than a miracle.

He had come upon his miracle just an hour before. Now the young soldier was a captain, assigned security of the island. Just arrived, he was crossing the market bridge in his jeep when he came upon a large crowd and stopped to see what the commotion was. The crowd was gathered around a body they had just pulled out of the harbor.

The soldier got out of his jeep. Ever since he lost his father he never passed the scene of a sudden death without looking into it. But this was the young wife from the tearoom. With a huge sense of relief, tinged with a queer sense of failure, he turned away from the body—and found himself face to face with his miracle.

"Well, that's wonderful . . . ! I'm happy for you . . . " is all Hun can say.

So now Grandpa Sŏ is leaving. He's going to his son's post about 10 *li* away. Hun and Chong, joined by Grandpa Pak and Grandpa Kim, escort him to the main road, where they stand in a line facing the jeep carrying the dazed and speechless Grandpa Sŏ in the back seat.

The captain salutes Hun. "Well then . . . we'll drop by again soon." Chong, who knows nothing about what's going on, hasn't taken his eyes off the magnificent soldier once.

The engine roars to life again as the captain climbs back in next to the driver. Just as the jeep begins to pull away, Grandpa Sŏ thrusts his head out and calls back, "Teacher! You, boy, good-bye! The acorns for the squirrel—on the back hill . . . No, better not go up there! Grandpa Pak! Grandpa Kim . . . !"

The jeep drives on over the hill. Chong turns, feeling in each pocket of his sweater for the caramel boxes filled with real caramels.

* * *

Shades of dusk cover the earth. The lighthouse lamps come on, red on the left, blue on the right, and weave their gleaming colored ribbons of light through the water. Shimmering moon rests on the horizon, directly between the blue and green lamps; and from far, far out it rolls in on gentle gold-crested waves to Hun's breast.

Hun's daughter has found the switch for the radio. The sound of a passing train signals the end to some serial drama.

"That's a train, isn't it?" Chong asks his big sister.

"Sure is."

"Is a train bigger than a ship?"

"Of course, you silly."

"Faster than a ship?"

"Of course."

"Even faster than the ferry?"

"Of course!"

"Even faster than a patrol boat?"

"Of course, dummy."

"Were you ever on a train?"

"Of course," she boasts, as if she actually remembers having ridden the top of that freight car when she was two and they were fleeing the war.

"Oh boy, if I could only get a ride on a train . . . !"

Out on the darkened porch Hun savors the children's talk. "Columbus . . . Yes . . ."

He goes down into the yard. Spot crawls out from under the porch. In that short time the full Harvest Festival moon is already approaching its zenith. A cloud drifts across it. Hun can almost hear the hoarse voice of a saxophone in the air. Gypsy Moon . . .

Hun looks out across the small harbor to town. That light which had always shone so clearly in the tearoom's second floor windows is not there now. From somewhere the notion comes that it may be time for him, too, to be leaving this harbor town.

Hun looks back at the moon. Two gulls pass into view. Where could they be off to now, in the night? But they just push on ahead, winging their way to the moon.

HOUSE OF IDOLS

Ch'oe In-hun

(1960)

The war was over, the capital back in Seoul.

In the battered and forlorn heart of the city was the Arisa Tea Room. We took over the corner where the wall had been blasted out and arranged for ourselves a sort of an alcove there; we gave it the very clever name Venus' Bosom, and passed the time raucously jabbering away one day, staring for hours at the ceiling another day. The house served a rather bungled concoction we called "that stuff like coffee." Even when we couldn't afford to buy a cup we often had the nerve to sit there most of the day without paying the rent, but the people there allowed that we weren't all that undesirable and, rather than making us squirm in our seats with intimidating glares, provided us with a generally friendly, casual service. So we became ensconced in this sanctuary, which we had first chosen simply because of its pleasing name.

K was an established figure in the literary world. When he sat among us many of the prominent literary personalities we revered and envied so would come and go, and it was here that K would handle most requests for his writing. There was also that constant traffic of nameless aspirants to the arts. Among the various types who came to see K was one young man who didn't quite fit into any category. He didn't seem to be into anything special, and there was nothing really worth mentioning in his exchanges with others.

A listless drizzle was falling that afternoon in late August when he first appeared at the tearoom. Something specially depressing that day had gotten me back to that diary I had been neglecting, and now, reading it again, I see that I have recorded the young man's debut in detail, even to the exact date. He walked in, saw K surrounded by us as usual and, without even a nod—the least a man with K's stature could expect—strode directly over to a place a few tables across the room and spread himself out in a chair facing K. The way he entered was more the indifferent, almost disdainful operation of an unfeeling machine than of a human being, and I felt myself clenching in indignation at his impertinence. It bothered me even more when I later heard that he assumed this posture even after not having seen K for quite a while.

K was a rather easygoing type, not prone to exhibit much emotion in any exchange he had with others, so when I was able to catch some minute alteration in his countenance during such an exchange, it wasn't difficult for me to determine how close the relationship was, and how seriously he regarded the relationship. After the person left, I—childishly as it seems now, looking back on it—I would whisper impishly to K what I had determined of their relationship; and he would acknowledge my observation with a patronizing chuckle.

But that day, to my astonishment, this same K of such great composure practically tripped over himself on his way over to the young man, then locked arms and talked with him in an attitude bordering on excitement. Unusual, this. I had thought I knew K better, and now my curiosity was roused.

Who in the world could this person be? He seemed mature beyond his age, which was certainly more than twenty years less than K's; while there was an odd want of circumspection to him, it was clear in his attitude toward K that he did look up to him in his own way and that he did not regard their relationship as one of equals. More than that, though, I could not venture with any confidence. Even as I joined in conversation with my group, my mind was over where those two were sitting, but all my fretting got me nowhere. I found myself blushing at this busy curiosity of mine; it shamed me to be allowing myself to meddle so in others' affairs, and I felt even more ashamed when I saw that my friends were paying no attention to the two.

So I decided to leave off this behavior. Still, there was something the young man exuded from the very beginning that was certainly nothing of an ordinary nature. And considering now all that was to happen, I cannot say that my curiosity was all that unwarranted.

* * *

After that first time the young man would surface now and then at the Arisa. Despite my decision to let him be, I soon found myself back at trying to figure him out. But I couldn't quite put my finger on anything because K would always brush aside my queries with a simple reply like, "Just someone I know." It was weird how, in spite of the way K seemed to be dismissing him as almost a non-entity, as not really having the depths that I was so eager to plumb or, for that matter, not being worth knowing about at all, I came to entertain the idea of his having some mystical persona—I might say I imagined in him some character drawn in a sense similar to Dumas' Count of Monte Cristo. And still, I was confident that I wasn't reading him wrong, that anything in me was distorting my perception. I regarded pretty highly my judgment of people, my intellectual and intuitive eye for reading those subtle nuances in a person's countenance; I believed it right to deal with someone according to how you calculate their worth, for example, giving full attention to one who adds up—after an objective and accurate calculation, of course—as someone of significance. More than this, though, I believed that it is actually a quality befitting the artist, that it is most reasonable for two, in knowing each other, to ensure compatibility of spirit before anything. With such a realistic attitude I would hardly give myself up to some undiscriminating conviction in the mystical quality of this young man. Or who knows—perhaps I am rationalizing and he was actually not all I took him to be. Still, such an inscrutable character cannot be explained away by saying he simply didn't conform to any conventional set of standards we use to judge people, or that he happened to be a composite of a variety of these standards.

He would come into the Arisa, walk to his place across from us, and then K would go over to him—they had it down to a routine. Not once did this young man show any inclination to recognize the presence of the rest of us. I would smolder: "Who the hell . . . ?" And I wanted to give him a stronger dose of his own medicine—until I realized to my chagrin how incongruous it would be, what a real farce. I mean, when by some chance our eyes would meet, his showed a complete detachment from this muddle I had worked myself into. This farce was turning into my own one-man show.

So I vacillated awkwardly and was, in the end, prevented from making any shallow judgment about him. What caused this, and what finally rendered my hostility and revulsion meaningless, I can explain with one small instance. The reader who has been paying any attention up to this point will probably have formed an image of this young man as some person spoiled on the inside, callused on the outside. That is pretty close to the conclusion I was coming to. But I was wrong. He was talking with K one day and then, when they left off talking and his gaze drifted quietly out through the window, the way his lips set . . . instead of the posturing you would see in some of us there, hawking some sophomoric solutions to life's ultimate riddles . . . there was in that countenance nothing of that. Rather, for want of better words, let's say a mind of firm, steady faith in the discipline infused by the orthodox *dessin*—that is what showed so vividly in those lips. With this I began to regard him as the very antithesis of our phony younger literary set, and even more, as someone simply outside my class. Whoever he was, and whatever his relationship with K, it was none of my business. So I stepped aside.

I soon realized that in withdrawing I had wisely put myself in a much better position to observe him. Through humility I had essentially achieved the prerequisite of perceptiveness—the mind that empties itself of its self.

And so now there were only two left on that stage—the young man and K.

* * *

Off the stage and into the audience, I met with yet another surprise. It seemed that, of the two performers, K had the supporting role. In the eyes of society, of course, K was the senior and the young man his junior; but I imagined some subtle current emanating from the depths of the young man's mind, a current that made K bend to its ebb and flow. To my eye, free now of the blinders of involvement, this was a truly intriguing development.

But I had not looked deep enough. I have got to admit, that eye of mine lacked maturity. I had taken only a cursory look at the surface and was incapable of seeing that, in one to whom age comes gracefully, social seniority is more a responsibility to help the young than a chance to dominate. I realize this only now. At that time I had that preconception of the young man's power, and from this angle thought that to be a true spectator of this theater I had to follow every fluctuation in what I took to be a precarious balance of power between the two.

Once, at the Arisa's slowest time of day, K and I were alone together when the young man appeared. He barged right into the cozy cleavage of our Venus' Bosom, where he had never ventured before. He seemed to be on a rather belligerent high, plopping into a seat, reclining with arms and legs akimbo, tapping a light rhythm with his foot, screwing his nose and mouth together into a yawn like a rabbit's . . . it seemed all without any thought of talking with K. But just as soon as he had settled himself he got up, went around in back of K, and clasped his arms around K's chest. He chuckled. "You know, sir, it's really impressive how bright your eyes always shine—a fully grown man like yourself. How about it now, wouldn't you say that's evidence that no female ever fell for them?"

He laughed hard at this. I smelled the distinct stench of something rotten, sensed something perverse about his character.

He didn't appear for about a month after that. Then he showed up one day when K wasn't there; he sat down to wait, but then got up and went over to the window. After staring out a while at the darkening street, he turned, signaled me with his eyes, and was gone. Something inside me shouted, "Follow!" So I got up and went right out after him.

He was standing there in the doorway, vacantly rubbing his chin. I offered my hand, he shook it. There was an awkward moment of silence, but before long it passed, we completed the routine formalities—and became friends right there. I felt a rush of exhilaration, which forced me admit to myself how much I had always wanted to know him. And I realized one more thing, that I was now up on that stage along with him and K.

"Actually . . . well, I feel like we've known each other quite a while now." I felt giddy with elation.

He didn't reply. We walked along side by side and soon found ourselves in the courtyard of the cathedral. We sat down on a bench, and he finally spoke.

"I don't know . . . It seems to me that two who really feel of one mind or heart really ought to do all they can to stop the relationship from falling into friendship, or love, or whatever . . . "

I smiled and asked, jesting, "To avoid the bitter cup of disillusionment?"

"Disillusionment. Who knows? You might call it that . . . "

I explained all that I had felt about him, my impressions, everything about how I had come to regard him as I did now. As he listened, an unconcealable gloom—no, it was too intense, too oppressive for gloom—something like that, anyway, smoldered in his face. It bewildered me.

"I've been cursed," he said. "I'm under some curse to destroy anyone who comes close to me." But there was that flicker of the most serenely stoic smile.

With this, of course, instead of backing off from him, my trust in him rooted itself even deeper. "Well, if the cards hold destruction, there's not much we can do about it, is there?"

This clumsy melodramatic line pleased me, and I savored the sense of utter devotion it conjured. I wanted to believe, anyway, that we were two real live souls communicating in our very own primal vibes through that cacophony of sophisticated but lifeless routine exchanges that bombard us from all sides. Glimpsing the dancing shadows the sun played on his face through the dense grove of trees, I wondered to myself: Of all those I have ever met, how many could respond to life the way he does, with such heart? Back in those days I had this religion, what you might call the worship of Man. To me the essential element in qualifying for my homage, rather than a breast full of medals, or gold trimmings, or a halo there in the background, was to be magnanimous, to have that certain grace or appeal that could be found only in a fully developed human being. I guess that this way of thinking was more a matter of personal preference—a combination of intuition and fancy?—than of any logical theory. A man with a face whose serenity filters the rays issuing from a myriad of qualities, his dark, naked power—no matter how often life trips him up, it can't keep him from struggling up again—this power augmented by intelligence and common sense. Ask me for a portrait of the object of my worship, and this is how I would have painted him.

The young man's entire countenance seemed to embody this ideal, and for this I dared to set out on the road to knowing him fully. Thus, we became friends.

He appeared faithfully at the Arisa every Wednesday between six and seven o'clock. K knew nothing of our relationship. The young man showed nothing he didn't need to, so that K sensed nothing, and he never paid any attention to me when K was present. If he never gave me a look, I never set eyes on him, either—almost, that is. We ignored each other like two sharing the secret of love.

With our special relationship established I discovered something else unusual about him. We used to go out and sit on that bench at the cathedral after meeting at the Arisa, and one day, heading for the path up the hill, I found I was out of cigarettes and went back to buy some. I was back to where I had left him in about three or four minutes, but he wasn't there. I hurried over to the bench; he wasn't there, either. The next time we met, though, I acted as though nothing had happened, and he certainly had nothing to say about it. This is nothing more than one instance, but it made me see something that distinguished him. Far from appearing to me as some flaw, or letting it get to me in any way, I saw it as some eccentricity of the true artist. Here, now, was the real thing!

And then one day he said, with a very serious look on his face, "There's something I think I'd better tell you . . . "

The tone in his voice was so unlike him. "What is it?" was all I could manage in my surprise.

"It'll probably disgust you. I'm asking you to listen to something that could destroy anything you feel for me."

"You're going to break us up? Let's hear it, then, all the gory details, and see how it goes."

He was silent, ignoring my attempt at wit. It seemed he would stand there like that forever, when at last he spoke.

* * *

I'm from W. Yes, on the east coast in the North. When the War broke out I was in my first year of high school. Up to liberation my father operated a private clinic, but then the new government closed it down. So he had to work in the surgery of the provincial hospital.

There was always this gloom hanging over our house; my father must have been bringing it home with him from outside, in his despairing heart. But whatever ideological torment my father seemed to have, it had no direct influence on me, probably because I had problems of my own.

I was at that age when you can fall completely under the spell of the right novel. Well, I fell for Zola's *Nana.* The publishing industry was subject to those moralistic prohibitions you find in totalitarian societies like the North, so there were no books that offered any more knowledge about sex to a budding youth like myself than what you could find in *Nana.* It was really one of its kind, a Japanese translation out of Shinzosha. I came across it in some used bookstore in the market and pestered my mother for the money to buy it. But what they charged even for used books then! At the bookstore I started paging through it and came upon a really thrilling part that turned my face beet red. So I put the book down, ran home for enough money, ran back again and gave the man what he asked without any thought of bargaining him down, grabbed the book and dashed right on home. I devoured that book the same night. Compared to something like *Lady Chatterley's Lover,* of course, the world of Nana is innocence itself, but to me, in those times, even Nana was enough to show me things I'd never imagined. It was overwhelming. The lust and passion of this hussy was more song than sex. You could find everything I knew about sex on a blank sheet of paper; I mean, what hope could there be of having learned anything through books that didn't exist, and with that, no friends to trade even street knowledge? Nana standing there at the mantelpiece, undressed—in front of a man—that was all there was to know anyway. My eyes caressed her every curve in the print the book offered. If I closed my eyes, the woman's entire body would linger there in my mind. She—and everything in her world—possessed me, I was lost in that sublime dream she created. But there wasn't the slightest hint of physical desire in all this. It wasn't these two eyes, it was the eye of my soul, that caressed an image, not a body. Of course, that was the finest way a man could love a woman.

It was at this point in my life that a real Nana appeared to me. I used to take this quiet residential lane to school, and about halfway down this lane, where there was a steep drop on the left—you could see the whole harbor from here at a glance—I would pass a big frame house. One morning I saw a woman leaving that house. I just kept on walking—until, when I got to the next corner, a hot flame burst in my breast and spread until I could feel great clouds billowing up in the back of my head. I turned and looked back to the front door of that house, but she wasn't there. All that remained was her impression, a blossom of the sweet briar, burned there in the retina of my eye. And then—a huge wave of sorrow surged through me and turned my eyes to the sea, where shimmering reflections danced on its surface, and clouds billowed high up into the sky above.

I saw her a few times after that. I think she might have been a little over twenty. Her and Nana's images merged in my imagination till they finally became one and the same person. And suddenly, I was George.

She always looked fresh as a daisy in that light skirt that fluttered so free in the breeze, with the parasol one day or the summer hat with that floppy wide rim the next. Of course, there was nothing in me of any desire to get to know her somehow. I just wanted her to be always in my sight, never to go away. Then one day I saw her walking at the side of some strapping young fellow. She must have thought there was no one around to see, and made a motion of picking a speck of something from his hair, probably more out of affection than for anything really being there to remove. I felt crushed. Betrayed. So I made up my mind not to pass by her house again, and decided to go the longer way to school from then on.

About a week after this the war broke out. Day after day the bombs rained down on us so hard we soon lost the spirit even for a "Look-at-that-one!" And that constant chaos with the refugees milling about on the outskirts of the city . . . Soon our anti-aircraft batteries fell silent, and every day flocks of those big bombers would appear in the sky, casually dump their bombs on us, and then disappear to the south. To watch those silver-gray casings glinting out from between those flimsy cotton wisps of clouds, with drone ever so faint and distant . . . it was like spotting some fish cruising idly about the bottom of a clear pond. There was such beauty in this weary scene. To me, anyway.

And I didn't really dislike this war, by the way—after all, it freed me from school. School was prison to me, with its political indoctrination and the oppressive discipline of the Youth Brigade, all that poppycock so alien to the nature of a child. The war chased just about everyone out of the city, but our family stayed. We couldn't evacuate with the others because my father wouldn't leave all the casualties that were poring in. Suddenly I felt that this city, which school had kept me apart from, was now mine. I could lounge around the yard of the Catholic church to my heart's content, and there was no one around to say anything if I walked about with my arms folded, or slouched, or made faces as my fancy moved me. And it gave me great pleasure to fill all those empty houses, lanes, theaters where real people had lived with my own characters and incidents, to paint them in my imagination with memories glad and sad.

Once I went back to the young woman's neighborhood. An empty round wicker basket was tipped over in front of the main door, which was locked tight in a deep silence. I kept a watch on the house for nearly two hours, but no one went in or out. It was the same the next day. I dragged myself back home, feeling quite dejected.

When I got back my father scolded me. "What are you doing gallivanting around out there at a dangerous time like this? You should be at home, where you can get into the air-raid shelter when you hear the sirens." He scolded my mother for not restraining me, but even a mother is helpless with a child who would run around doing the weird things I did, unless she kept me tied up all day long.

There was a battle the next day, and with it came the biggest air raid yet. The bombers attacked in waves of four, with other planes flying in at low range to fire off their rockets. Until that day the area around our house and her house had been left untouched, but this time we didn't escape. When the attack was over I climbed up out of the shelter and looked over toward her house. Black smoke filled the sky all around it. I dashed off, fists clenched, tears streaming. When I arrived at her house it looked as though about half of the back part of it, around the kitchen, was on fire, but then I saw that it was actually the flames which had enveloped the house next door leaping over to her house. I can't imagine where I got the courage, but I rushed inside, through the front door. The girl was lying there, pinned down at the chest by a large pillar. I saw her face and gasped "NO!"

That ghastly face.

The blood. That gaping mouth. Her hand reaching into the air, reaching out to me . . . reaching out to me . . . I turned and ran home, twice as fast as I had come, and buried myself in my blankets. I lay there till evening, head throbbing, my whole body convulsing in feverish chills.

But then I finally forced myself out of bed and went back to her. Several corpses were being carried out on stretchers. A faint voice drifted over to me.

"Crushed. But we could have saved her if we'd found her in time . . . " And I blacked out on the spot.

* * *

The young man got this far and fell silent, reflecting. I waited . . .

"But then the real problem began. After our family moved to the South, this agony—which I couldn't speak of to anyone—grew day by day. If I had only moved that pillar from the girl's chest, or if I'd run and called for help, she'd be alive now. 'But we could have saved her if we'd found her in time . . . ' Those words became an insistent curse. How I could ever have done such a heartless thing, I don't know even now. But I do know I took someone's life. And I made that life squirm in agony before finally killing it off. Not just some stranger, either—she was my love. She lives here now in my heart, a curse, never letting up, a curse on my cruelty. Look at me—a murderer. I'm a murderer!" He broke down in wrenching sobs, burying his head in his arms over the back of the bench.

And now all my questions were answered.

But what could I say? All I could do was put my hand on his shoulder. In my mind, still stunned from what I had just heard, I sensed that obscuring cloak of enigma falling from him, exposing all. "And he's been carrying this hideous torment with him all this time." An irrepressible wave of pity rushed through me. My grip on his shoulder tightened as I cursed the limitless horror of life.

* * *

Between then and the next time I met him I fretted over how to find a way to console him. For want of any better idea I decided it might be good to take an easy, relaxing trip somewhere together. I suggested this, he thought it over a while, then said fine, I should stop by his place when I was ready.

A few days later I took the map he had drawn for me and, with a suitcase stuffed with everything we would need, set off to find his address. I wandered all around the section of P'il-dong he had indicated on that map. I finally found myself at the address, but then halted in confusion. What he called his house was a brick building with the sign "St. Mary's Clinic of Neuropsychology." I recalled that his father was a doctor.

The gaunt man sitting at the information desk put down the scale he had been holding and looked up at me. I put my suitcase on the couch to the side.

"I've come to see someone."

"Who? Did you want to visit a patient?"

"No, I . . . well . . . "

"Oh, an employee then. What's . . . ?"

"No, you see, the director . . . "

"The director isn't here right now."

"Yes, of course, but it wasn't actually the director I wanted . . ."

Wondering why I had so foolishly been avoiding just coming right out with it, I finally managed to give him my friend's name, telling him I was under the impression that he was the director's son. With that, a smile appeared on the attendant's face.

He laughed. "Well, it looks like he's up to his old tricks again. That young man is a patient here. If you want to meet him you'll have to talk with his doctor first."

He sent me through a door with the sign "Consultation." At the far side of the small room a doctor who appeared to be in his forties raised his eyes from a thick volume he was poring over. In my confusion I finally managed to stammer out what I had come about.

"I'm responsible for the patients while the director is away, so we can settle this here. We authorize travel if it seems appropriate, depending on the patient's condition, of course. But can I ask how you are related to the patient?"

What he was saying sounded reasonable enough, so I told him that I was the patient's friend, and repeated how I thought a trip together might help him with that problem that had been bothering him so badly. "But why all of a sudden did he have to be admitted here?" I asked, and then caught myself, remembering that it was he who had given me the hospital's address. "Or, wait a minute, he's been . . . !"

"Yes, that's right. He's been here three months now."

"Three months?" I gasped. I hadn't even known him for three months.

The doctor sighed, "You must be another one of his victims."

"Victims?!" In my bewilderment, all I could do was startle like a rabbit every time the doctor came out with something new.

"I mean what he said about that girl killed in the bombing raid."

"Yes, of course. You're treating him for it, so it's natural you'd know about that. But . . . "

He laughed. "That's a good one! Seriously though, I should have handled his story purely as clinical data, and I would have been doing my job as his psychiatrist. But I was fooled, too. I'm also one of his victims."

"Doctor . . . " I stalled, trying to get my breath, "what's going on here? There's no way I'm going to understand unless . . . I mean . . . "

The doctor nodded a couple times in sympathy, then offered me a cigarette and lit one up for himself.

"Yes. All right, I'll tell you. First, the main thing . . . This whole story about the girl dying in that fire is a fabrication, start to finish. He's never been north of Seoul. This is his hometown, he was born here and grew up here."

This was a real blow. How could I believe this? The pain in the young man's face when he told me his story, his mastery of all that detail . . . ? And what could be compelling him to tell that same lie to everyone he met, and why would he ever have to create such a torment which, if untrue, would be so abominably maudlin?

"He's got a variety of complexes all wrapped up together in him like a ball of yarn, and I can't really sum up his condition in one word. Exhibitionism. Megalomania, Oedipus complex, hero complex . . . a muddle of these roots all tangled inside of him. It all shows itself in that audacity of his, and he finds some release for his problems in that story he's concocted."

"But I don't see anything wrong with him, other than this story of his."

"That's exactly what has me stymied, that no other symptoms have appeared. His is the most difficult sort to fix."

I learned that K was coming to the hospital from time to time. They had arranged for the patient to visit with K on a regular basis because K, more than anyone else, was such a powerful influence on him.

I just sat there, smoking my cigarette in frustration, falling into a state of vertigo, as if I had been picked up and whirled around and around and then sent flying with a solid kick in the rear by someone I couldn't see.

"Would you like to see him?"

He was so much a part of me now I couldn't decline the doctor's offer. I nodded.

Soon the door opened and he walked in. When he saw me there he was as composed as ever. "So that's it!" I thought to myself. With what I heard today I finally realized how I had mistaken the vain posturing of someone gone wrong for the intriguing poise of a deep character.

He gave me a warm smile. "Hey there, buddy. I guess the doctor here's been giving you his introductory lecture on Freud. Sure, I fabricated that story. So what? It's obviously great sport to sucker someone with phony protestations of love, but a really elaborately worked sport—a really original creation that shows what the war has done to us—that's considered sick, it qualifies me for the mental ward. Do you believe I'm a lunatic? Up until a few days ago, anyway, did I ever do anything that would make you suspect that? And another thing, didn't I tell you the address of this place—did you ever hear of the criminal leading the detective to where he's hiding?"

I was dazed, stumped by his rhetoric, when the doctor abruptly broke in.

"Isn't the very fact that he tells the detective where he's hiding proof that he's not normal?"

Whatever the value of its logic, this intuitive blitz hit home. That sober composure of the young man's face drained away and left it deathly pale, but just as soon his face was blazing with fury. He glared at the doctor. "You cunning fraud, you. Think you can fix people's minds with these piddling scraps from Freud? Discharge me—I want out of this place. And I want my money back. Me crazy! Put me up in front of some university lecture hall and watch me discourse on Hegelian logic for a few hours, you'll see how crazy I am. And you," finally turning his sights on me, "is this what your friendship amounts to? You're going to let your friendship kowtow to these hackneyed formulas of this worthless quack? You pitiful . . . I really pity you. Go on, get out! Who needs the affection or sympathy of some conventional lackey?"

I saw spreading out between us a chasm that could never be crossed. That special bond of ours, which I had believed so strong, evaporated like the morning mist, and we were strangers again. I felt I was really losing my mind. A raging fury coursed through me, which I was sure I could vent only by kicking and smashing something, anything, to bits. I couldn't stay there any longer. I snatched up my suitcase, flung open the door, flew from the room and bounded out of that place, almost running into K on his way in. As his stunned face swept past me, a lofty roar of laughter chased me out the door.

"HA! Will you look at that! Metamorphosis of great intellectual into King Convention! In front of our very eyes! Hey there . . . !"

I ran on, blindly, suitcase flying in tow, as if I had just escaped from that hospital. Then, even as my feet pounded on, on, on . . . an eerie silence filled me. It carried me away, far off to a vast desert, still, utterly lifeless, wafts of parched air stirring up lonesome dervishes of sand, all this desolation expanding without end.

END OF THE ROAD

Ch'oe In-hun

(1966)

The August sun has begun its afternoon descent, but its rays still sizzle on the railroad's iron rails. Straight, still tracks, stretching from one horizon to the other. Silent now, empty, these tracks have nothing to do but shimmer in the sun.

A country highway runs along these tracks, newly paved, not a blemish on its sleek, glistening asphalt surface. Smooth, and it looks even straighter and steadier than those iron tracks. Not much happening here on the highway, either.

Soon though, one vehicle appears off in the distance. It comes closer, closer, riding the road mirages unsteadily, as if it is going to slip off the highway at any moment. An American military compound occupies both sides of a long stretch of this road, but this is no military vehicle, it's civilian, a bus.

Now, in the middle of the week, at this slow time of day, the bus is carrying only a few passengers. Just six. One of these passengers is wearing a dingy yellow shirt without a tie, and his drab out-of-fashion double-breasted suit that used to be blue is draped over an arm of his seat. He's around fifty, looks like one of those who sells black market goods in the village by the American compound. There are two farmers dressed up identically in traditional white ramie long coat and faded fedora, bus ticket stuck in each one's hatband. And then there are two young men, also from the countryside, in summer shirts, hair grimy and uncombed. In the back sits a pale young man holding a college student's school bag in his lap, eyes out the window on the railroad tracks.

The bus comes to a security checkpoint. A military policeman boards halfway, takes a look inside, then gets back off. A regular cop gets on. He checks the ID card of the man with the double-breasted suit. "Job?"

"Merchant."

"What do you sell?"

"Oh, you know, this and that—just small stuff."

The cop ignores the two older farmers, stops at the young men. He sticks out his hand for their ID cards. He checks them and asks, "Coming from your physical, huh?"

"Yes," one answers sullenly. What's the guy bothering us for? They don't draft you if you've got something on your record.

The policeman goes on to the young man in the back seat, examines his ID. "Student?"

"Yes . . . No . . . " His face reddens. "I mean, that's from when I was a student."

"Job?"

"I'm a teacher."

"Where you going now?"

"I'm on my way to my new position."

"Well don't you have anything to show it?"

The young man reaches into his bag and produces a document.

"Just elementary school, huh?"

"Yes," he mumbles. Where do these police get their manners?

Finally the cop is off the bus, and he motions it on. The driver gives him a friendly wave, and soon the bus is rolling again. The young teacher looks back at the empty tracks, which keep following along, mute, shimmering in the relentless sun.

* * *

Just before a bridge the bus comes upon an American military convoy. The guy in the lead jeep is waving the bus off the road. Around here a military convoy is king of the road, so the bus driver grudgingly pulls the bus over. A line of trucks is soon passing, one after another after another, each one with a plank on the front warning "Danger: Explosives" in red letters, and gratuitously, just so there is no mistake, a skull and crossbones. Each truck has a tarpaulin cover. Two soldiers sit in the cab of every one of these slick, shining trucks. Some of the drivers wear sports caps instead of helmets. One darkie gives the bus a raised fist, flashing a cocky grin full of gleaming white teeth. The two youngsters returning from their physical crane their necks to get a good look, and giggle at the strange sight.

Each identical truck is going the same speed, has the same tarpaulin cover, the same two soldiers in the cab, the same "Danger: Explosives" sign, the same glimmering yellow headlights. One after another passing by, no end in sight. Way down the road as far as one can see, around that ridge where the road crosses the tracks, they appear stacked on top of each other, then string out farther apart the closer they get. They just keep coming, one after another, like the pads on a caterpillar track, an inexhaustible supply.

Meanwhile, a long line of vehicles has formed in back of the bus—civilian and military, trucks, jeeps, three-quarters . . . On every face in every vehicle is the same simmering irritation at the incessant wait for this convoy to come to an end.

After an eternity the last truck passes, and the bus starts off again. The teacher turns his eyes back to the railroad. Solitary tracks shimmer in the sweltering rays of the sun . . .

The bus is humming along now, nothing breaking the monotony of the smooth ride. Nothing to relieve the tedium of vacant fields backed by that low ridge.

But then, suddenly, everyone is straining to get a look at the sight ahead. A profusion of colors is coming slowly down the middle of the road, and soon the passengers hear an eerie wail. Again, the bus pulls onto the shoulder of the road. All the passengers bend in one direction to get a better look.

It is a traditional countryside funeral procession, with its myriad banners, baggy white mourning clothes, women in loosened, disheveled tresses. They are all women, in fact, even the pallbearers. A countryside funeral, but their clothes and demeanor show that none of the participants, neither the pallbearers nor the mourners following them, are country people.

The driver, foot propped up on the door handle, elbows resting on the wheel and chin cupped in his hands, takes it all in calmly and explains as if he has seen it a hundred times. "Some GI prostitute. The girls in her guild are seeing her off."

The passengers nod in appreciation. On every banner is a different slogan, but they are all something like, "Good-bye, big sister" and "Susan, don't leave me behind."

The procession bunches up on itself, then strings out, heaves up and back sluggishly, the shaman moans a line of the dirge—"On her way to the Great Void"—followed by the wailing refrain of the marchers, one step forward but the dead one's soul pulling them back, lurch forth and fall back, resisting the relentless pull of fate.

There is no telling how long the bus will be stuck here. From each end of this unruly jumble monopolizing the highway stretches a long line of vehicles. After what seems like hours the head of the procession finally turns into a dirt lane leading off the highway, swinging its long, unwieldy trunk out across the road. But the vehicles still have to wait because the sluggish procession cannot make up its mind, advancing, retreating, staggering from side to side, one step forward and two or three back. What is this, a funeral or a circus? Undulating indigo silk flags and banners in the glaring sun, marchers milling about in almost the same place they were a while ago, showing no concern about the long lines of vehicles—Susan's in no hurry. Not a breath of wind. Hot.

At long last the procession has almost all passed by. Someone at the end of the procession smacks the bus on its rear as she lets out with a verse from their lament.

Free now, the bus jerks forward and gets rolling again. After a while the primary school teacher takes a look back at the procession. It has crossed the tracks, disappearing into the lower ground on the other side. The lone, shimmering railroad tracks catch his eye.

✲ ✲ ✲

Before long the bus comes upon a small settlement. The highway is dotted with these hamlets of shops that line both sides of the road, so close their eaves touch, with signs in English like "Arizona Club," "Sisters of the Lily," "Honey Cats," "Pink Heart." Here and there among these clubs are tarp-roofed makeshift shacks that boast a stock of c-rations and peanut butter and after-shave and the like, quite a bountiful array against the barren highway's barren offering of fields and paddies and the railroad skirting distant low hills. In one shop a young woman is grabbing a black soldier from behind and pounding him on the back; he's shielding his head with both hands. These shops apparently service American soldiers. And behind them are a few makeshift houses. The bus could cover this whole stretch of highway in one breath, but it slows and stops to pick up four more passengers.

Four people get on the bus, and it's off again. The air is charged now with a strange new energy. First on is a young woman; her pink blouse and pink shoes show that she is one of the sisterhood who work in the ghetto the bus has just left. She's carrying a suitcase, most likely foreign-made, with all she owns.

The others are three drunken young men, in old army fatigue jackets. Their hair is slicked back over their ears with oil.

It's not long before one of them addresses the girl in the pink blouse. "Hey! Nice puss you got there. Where you been all this time?"

She says nothing, but the rage seething inside sets her silver earrings trembling. It's true, though—she does have a nice face.

"Something stuck in your ear? Am I talking to you or what?"

"In her ear isn't where you stick what you're thinking of sticking."

A few timid chuckles from the passengers, and the driver's shoulders twinge. She glares at the men teasing her. The young teacher, who happens to be sitting next to them, is singed by her glare. As a matter of fact, he's the only one on the whole bus that didn't laugh.

"Huh? Looking us over? So you stoop to doing Koreans too?"

She turns away and stares hard out the window.

"Hey you, don't stick your nose up at us. Xxxxx!"

The passengers titter uneasily again. But the teacher's face flashes red and he makes to get up . . . then sinks back in his seat. He looks at her, helpless. That face turned so defiantly out the window—beautiful. Fine lips.

The young men keep on with their lewd comments. With each one the man in the double-breasted suit utters a disbelieving gasp of a laugh. The two in their traditional ramie long coats gape in shocked amusement. The two youngsters coming back from their physical are cackling to each other. The teacher's face blushes brilliant crimson, and at every crude joke he sneaks a look over at the girl to see how she is taking it. She just sits there, rigid, glaring out through the window. She has no way of knowing that the teacher is not one of those laughing at her.

One of the bullies makes another remark, and it draws more nervous titter from the passengers.

She springs to her feet.

"Stop the bus—I'm getting off."

The driver looks over his shoulder at her, turns back to the front, says laconically, "It's a long way to the next stop." And truly, all you can see in front and in back is the highway stretching off into those wide open fields.

"Fine. Let me off!"

The driver shrugs, slows down, shifts to neutral and brakes to a stop, revving his engine to keep it alive. The girl has taken her suitcase to the door.

"What's this? Getting off so soon?"

"You sell it on the highway too?"

"See you later. Wash it out and we'll be along soon."

They're keeping up their lewd remarks till the very end. The girl has been pretending to ignore them, but now, on the bottom step, she turns on everyone in the bus and shrieks, "Filthy curs, every last one of you!" And she jumps off—just in time, because the bus has started pulling away.

The Canine Carrier hesitates a couple counts between gears, then the driver throttles it. The drunks are hanging out the window, paws on the sill, barking back at the girl. The whole kennel is hurrying off down the road as if they have been kicked in the balls.

And then it's gone. There's nothing else on this road. All that's left on this empty highway is one girl, a small pink doll.

She stares blankly in the direction the bus has disappeared. Way up ahead the white highway and the shimmering tracks meet and cross, then each continues on its own separate way, out of sight.

There, before that crossing, towers a huge pack of Salem cigarettes as tall as a building. A tall steel frame supports the tilted green pack, and a cigarette juts about a third of the way out, like the barrel of an artillery piece aiming up into the sky. She sets down her bag, stares blankly at the billboard. A few trucks pass, with their GIs shouting their banter. But no bus. Her face is calm, though. She just keeps on staring at that pack of Salems, lost in her thoughts.

The girl stands there in the sizzling rays of the sun for maybe half an hour. Finally, she shrugs, then picks up her bag. She sets to walking again, listlessly, head lowered in thought, and passes on by the Salems.

In a while she has reached the shade provided by the billboard. She sets down her bag. Soon she hears a vehicle approaching from far behind, looks around. A bus. It stops for her. She picks up her bag and gets on.

The door closes and the bus takes off. It disappears into the distance, soon melting into the sleek shimmering highway.

Now on the deserted plain are the empty road and the empty tracks, two lonely travelers with nothing to say. The huge green pack of Salems watches the two, each silently traveling its own way far, far out of sight.

☆ ☆ ☆

At the outskirts of the city, where the highway crosses the border, and just this side of the railroad crossing, a small boy has been waiting. In the midst of this August twilight. In the shade of the tin "Vita-M" sign, bigger than his house. He's been here since noon. Several buses have come and gone, but not the one he is waiting for. It is gradually getting dark, and the railroad tracks in this waning light, like the boy's last hope, glimmer faintly in fading gold.

The boy hears the sound of an engine. He gets up, takes a

step forward. A bus with its headlights on appears on the other side of the tracks. It crosses . . . and passes on by. The boy squats back down on his haunches. The tracks have turned a dull, hard gray.

From out of the deepening dusk a train thunders toward the boy. He gets up and moves back a bit. The engine, angry for some reason, roars on by. Then a passenger car with a big red cross on its side. At each brightly lit window the boy sees faces of Big-Nose men and white-clothed Big-Nose women. One woman in a white cap, head resting against her window, is peering out into the dark, eyes locking on the boy as she passes by. After the passenger car comes a flatcar. A huge artillery piece sprawls on the car's bed, a barrel rammed down its throat, wasted like a dying soldier. The next flatcar carries a tank without its tracks, squat and heavy like a small mountain, bigger than the boy's house. Next, a wheelless truck, its front smashed in. Mute, injured, exhausted travelers. An endless train, an endless march of wrecks of trucks and tanks and artillery which will never, ever pass.

The boy's worried now. If this train doesn't end soon his bus, even if it does come, will never make it across the tracks. Even now it must be there waiting to cross and bring him the one he's waiting for. He makes up his mind to go on waiting, squats back down for no matter how long this thing takes to pass.

Finally, after he has endured what seems an eternity, here comes the last car of this train with its battered passengers. He stands up tall and looks for his bus.

Nothing. Can't even see the road, not even the tracks. They've gotten on the night and gone.

Nothing left, except the ink-black darkness engulfing the boy and his sinking heart.

Where can Sis be?

RIVER

Sŏ Chŏng-in
(1968)

"It's snowing."

On the bus. The window seat. His pallid face is half hidden in his black overcoat. Heavy hair, sides plastered back past the ears, a startled swirl of cowlick up top.

"Hmmm . . . Sleet, anyway," croons a mellow voice from the aisle seat. Then this one shifts focus from the big flakes of dandruff in his companion's hair, through the slush crawling down the window, onto the gloom outside. His dapper appearance suits his voice, white scarf circling his neck and tucking down into his brown leather jacket, sideburns trimmed sharp and clean . . .

"Sleet? Sure is!" The man in the aisle seat behind, very sensible red wool knit cap pulled snugly down over his ears, is leaning across the girl next to him to get a look out the window, as if he can't see without pressing his nose on it. His shoulder presses the girl's breast, but he seems too engrossed in the weather outside to notice.

No matter, she's putting up with it just fine. She has pressed herself back up against the seat to give him some room, and her silky hair sprawls atop the smooth vinyl headrest in the flowing curves of a reclining nude. Plump girl, swarthy face powdered white.

The dapper one is looking back at these two, envying the man's good fortune. But the lucky fellow just keeps on mumbling something like "Yessir, certainly is sleeting," staring so intently out the window, apparently oblivious to anything else, even to the one staring back at him. "Yessir, it certainly is sleeting!"

The one at the window, still sulking down inside his black overcoat, can't stand sleet. It was sleeting the day he arrived at Shinyongsan Station for the train to his basic training unit, so it's no wonder he remembers induction whenever he sees the miserable stuff. In those worn, dyed-over fatigues, the battered boots, toting that cheap vinyl bath kit, thinking it's just a time like this you need a girl and picturing some lovely thing, her eyes brimming over in the grief of parting. . . . But no, the nearest thing that day was that diseased whore he saw coming out of the station plaza's filthy public toilet, matted hair, shuffling along like a crab, finally disappearing into the lane winding back in among the shanties of the red light district. About twenty recruits that day at the station, and nary a soul there to see them off. No band, not one lousy flag. Nothing but that sleet. Each time one of those long whistle blasts rose and dispersed into the sky with the yellow coal smoke lifting sluggishly from the station office chimney, his eyes would drift back to the shacks where the sick whore had disappeared and he'd sigh, "Well, it's good-bye Seoul!" Later, far away from Seoul, the sun about to set, all those extravagant emotions of loss and longing having long since given in to the tedium of waiting and the long train ride . . . some NCO met them at the station and led them off to camp.

"Where was it you went into basic?" he asks his companion glumly.

Without turning from the aggravating scene in back the other just throws an annoyed look at him out of the corner of his eye. "A small town." But then he loves to talk about his army days, rain or shine, sleet or snow, any chance he can get. He chuckles, then opens up, his voice mellow again. "We got smashed together and then, just like that, there I am in the army. Saying good-bye to all of them, you wouldn't believe it, handshakes once, twice, three times around—any hand in sight, who cares—all of them pumping away so hard it's a wonder I still have any teeth. All those heads wagging in sympathy, the good-byes—oh those good-byes, those endless good-byes! And the singing. So many of them there I didn't know who . . . But then I'm finally on the train, still so taken up in the send-off though, and when I come to my senses . . . be damned if it isn't the freight car!"

Their friend in back doesn't feel good about this conversation up front. He's a draft dodger, and gets nervous whenever someone mentions induction or that induction center. He straightens himself up off the girl. Free now, she eases her head down from against the headrest, rearranges herself, looks out the window. He admits there's nothing really wrong with talking about basic training. Everyone he meets has to talk about it, because everyone's been through it, so what better topic is there to get a conversation going? But enough is enough. This one's talk about getting kicked so hard in the rear by the PFC he ends up with his head through the lattice door, another's tale about how it would take a collection of just one army cigarette from each recruit to get on the better side of those NCOs on the rifle range. And the experience every one of them claims of posing to another platoon as one of those special trainees like standard bearer or acting platoon leader, whatever, and organizing a collection of some sort just to poach the proceeds for himself and a few lucky buddies. And then all those parodies of the graphic speech of the regulars stationed on the compound . . . Yes, he knows more about basic training than anyone that's ever been there. But that's just it, he hasn't been there, and this worries him to no end.

"How far you going, Miss?" he asks the girl. After all, there's no reason to let things get you down. You have to get your mind off it.

"I'm going to Kunha-ri." What a blush she can flash—even considering he's a stranger—all the way to her scalp, every blossoming capillary.

"So where did you go for basic training?" The one in the jacket asks his companion. He is miffed at the way his moody friend got him started before and then, right in the middle of his nice monologue, the guy let his attention wander back out the window. But he wants another opening so he can keep on talking.

"Me? Well . . . " But he would rather drop it.

"Oh?" The one with the girl sticks his finger up under his knit cap and scratches his head, edges closer. "Well, isn't that interesting! That's right where we're going!" She looks like she's having a pretty good time. A very easy girl to please—wouldn't take all that much to make her happy.

"What's the problem with this bus anyway?" the smart dresser up front grumbles, glaring at the door. The bus girl isn't even there yet, probably still at lunch.

"Where's this bus for?" A fellow at the door is looking down his nose over his sunglasses, around the bus. No one answers. He cocks his head questioningly a couple times, shrugs, gets off, the door closing behind him, and he is soon disappearing out of the frame provided him by the door's narrow window.

Those sunglasses, does he need them? The draft dodger feels better now with something substantial to occupy his mind. Could be just for looks. With most, these things are just an accessory, a luxury. Luxury? A lot of nerve to call those cheap hundred-*won* variety store things a luxury! After all, he himself has settled for a used pair for a thousand *won* after considering a new pair for two thousand. Right here in his pocket now, ready to pull out and hang on his nose just as soon as there's a little more glare from the snow to justify it.

To the one in the window seat it's a blind man in back of those sunglasses. He remembers that fantasy he worked himself into once, him blind, dark glasses and all, eking out a living as a masseur. A war injury, and he's in the hospital, eyes under layers of bandages. His girl comes to find him, searching through all the chaos of a war hospital. Of course the smallest thing prevents their reunion. He leaves the hospital in his dark glasses. Soon he's wandering the residential streets at night, tapping his way with his cane, announcing his progress with that eerie whistle of the blind masseur. A window opens above him. A woman's voice summons, a voice he's heard before.

"Do you live there?" the girl is asked. Her new friend wants to get his mind off those sunglasses. Plainclothesmen wear them, and plainclothesmen hunt down draft dodgers. Every payday, until he was finally found out and fired, that plainclothesman was waiting there for him, to offer "protection."

"What? Oh, yes. And you, sir?"

"Nope, not since I got my belly buttoned."

"Since you . . . ? Oh!" Tee-hee-hee!

Her giggle shatters that nicely developing fantasy about the blind masseur. You can't imagine yourself in the role of a blind masseur without a strong sense of the poignancy of it all, and just as the story is working its way to its climax the whole thing collapses with this girl's silly giggle. This fat girl. And himself an underfed masseur. But then again, maybe it's not all that bad—massaging a nice, plump woman could be all right, after all. Or try it like this: the one who calls him in is his old girl, of course, and it's the husband that giggles. So he's massaging the husband, and his lost love is at his side assisting. He knows her, but she doesn't know him. He finishes up, she gives him his pittance, he sticks it in his pocket and goes back out on the street. And then again, that lonely whistle in the night.

Up front at the driver's seat there's a loud whack under the window, which turns out to be a door. A gloved hand reaches in and grabs the wheel, hoists up a patchy three-day beard, then a jacket and finally worn corduroys with faded pockets. "So we're going at last?" The driver gets into his seat and twists around for a look in back. The sour look he puts on the passengers says there aren't enough of them, and he swings back around with a disgruntled snort. His right shoulder dips and the engine splutters to life. The passengers, who have been waiting over thirty minutes already, are sheepishly contrite—after all this time, only this paltry few. Maybe if there were a hundred or so crammed into this forty-eight-seat bus, suffocating, crawling over each other . . . who knows the driver might not manage a little regret for the late start?

The rear door opens and the bus girl backs on.

"Well, you think we might get this thing going today?" asks the nice dresser.

"We'll be off in just a second," she says automatically, not even bothering to look at him. She hangs up her cheap plastic mirror, sweeps the steps, counts her tickets, takes out . . .

"Just a second, huh? So what are we doing still here?"

"We'll be off in just a second."

"What are you, a broken record or something?"

Now she looks around at him. "And what would a broken record be doing on a bus?"

"Little girl," he chuckles, "You've got the brains of a little bear."

"Me a bear? Then what are you, sir?"

"Me? Your uncle, honey," with a wink and a wag of his finger. "Better be a good girl."

* * *

The bus is bumping along, and the knit cap can now bounce from side to side, usually to its left. With each contact the girl makes a show of edging away. But not to really put him off, she looks him full in the face and asks, "Why are you going to Kunha-ri?"

"Just a little trip with my friends here."

"You're all together then?"

"Sure are, young lady." He lowers his voice. "That one there next to the window, Kim, he's already been in the army, so he looks a bit old for it but he's in college."

"College! Oh, my!"

"And this one right in front of me is Lee. He's in the tax office. And I was an elementary school teacher, till recently. Name's Pak. So there you have it."

"You certainly look like an interesting group. You're all friends, you say?"

"We live together."

"Goodness, is that so!"

"Sure is. Those two are my boarders."

Kim is dozing against the window, his head bouncing with every bump in the road. It finally registers and he straightens up in his seat.

"This thing can move! For a while there I was thinking it was made for a parking lot."

"It's all thanks to this young conductress's superb navigational skills. Hey there, honey, am I right?" The bus girl is wearing sheeny black synthetic pants. Lee likes the way they show off her substantial buttocks. But she's in a sulk at the kidding she got before, so he takes a pack of gum out of his pocket . . .

Kim is looking out the window. The bus is rolling along now. It relaxes him, settles him all over, and he's feeling a little better with each mile the bus travels.

"You think you can handle one of these?" Lee offers a stick of gum to the girl's back.

She looks around, smiles. "How would a bear know how to chew gum?"

"What's tha . . . ? Ha-ha, very good! You sure got me there! But then we all know how talented a bear can be . . . Go on, try it. It's not going to bite you."

She takes the gum. Lee passes out a stick to Kim at his side, to Pak in back, and to the girl beside Pak. He unwraps one for himself.

Pak and the girl sitting with him are getting along splendidly.

"From Kunha-ri?"

"No, Incheon."

"Oh, you moved?"

"No, I just live there. With my mother and older sister, just the three of us by ourselves."

"In Incheon?"

"No, Kunha-ri."

"So there's no one in Incheon?"

"Oh, of course. There's . . . But whatever makes you so curious about every teeny-weeny little thing?"

"Oh, of course! Now what's got into me!"

What's got into me. Oh, come on, Kim snickers to himself. His eyes are out the window but he's been listening to everything going on there in back of him. He gets a kick out of doing his dumb fox routine. Know it? Play it dumb. Don't know it? Play it dumb just the same. It's great fun, really gets them going. Especially Lee. "Whatever it is, you've got something up your sleeve." Who, me? "Okay, so where were you yesterday between two and five?" But what would you want to ask that for? "Sure. Fine. Try to put something over on me? Pak might fall for that stuff, but not me." Ha!

He sneaks a look at Lee. The guy is no fool, he knows what's what, but he can't pin you down if you just smile all his questions away.

"Sit down a while, will you? Standing's no good for you."

"I'm fine here."

"You're fine now, sure. But what about when it gets time for you to marry? It'll be too late then. It's no good for you."

The bus girl turns red, goes to a nearby seat so Lee will stop it. Lee grins. Sure, it's all nonsense, this chatter he puts on the girls. But what the heck, it's good fun. He tugs at his white scarf to get it nice and snug there up under his ears, leans back, pulls out a cigarette. He sticks it in his mouth but doesn't light it, just looks out the window. A few flakes of snow drift about here and there in the grim sky.

Kim and Lee are silent, each in his own thoughts. In back of them Pak is going on in muffled tones with the girl, and an occasional chuckle or giggle rises above the throbbing of the engine. What could they be talking about back there?

* * *

And so the bus pulls into Kunha-ri. It's just before three.

Our friends, a few others too, get off the bus. The sodden yellow clay road stretches on into the distance. The bus takes off after it.

"Now why didn't they get off too?"

"They probably have no business here."

"Ah, but do consider, it just may be they have something to attend to farther on."

"I do believe you may have something there. Which would

mean, of course, it is not that we had no business back at that last stop—Sofa Rock was it, or Couch Rock . . . ?"

Kim marvels at the profundity of their observation. Up till now he's been wondering about those getting off, but now he knows—it's those still on the bus he ought to be wondering about. Yes, his two perceptive companions may very well have something there.

The girl has gone off up the road a way. Pak catches up with her. The short, chunky couple stand there chatting, a white billboard with "Farmers Cooperative, for a Better Life" providing a backdrop. She giggles and edges some off the dirt road. After another short exchange she sidles crabwise further off, a little further, and then disappears into a building about ten steps off the main road. "Seoul House" is crudely lettered on a flimsy wood panel over the door.

The others join Pak. The street is deserted, except for these three. Everyone must be at home, saving their money for the village's fifth-day market.

The three amble down the town's main street. They pass the drab gray cement warehouse of the farmers' cooperative. After that the county office and the police station, nestling up to each other. And next to them squats the barbershop. A youth, about as rustic as they get, is sticking his head out the window since there is not much else to do here, and you can tell by his short hair it can't be all that long since he got his discharge. A little further on is the drug store, and then the beauty shop which, hick town though this may be, looks like it might actually be able to do brides. From the outsized grocery shop next door a transistor radio airs some scratchy, warmed-over soap opera. Beside this shop is an empty lot, and set back of that is another bleak warehouse type of structure, probably the community hall. This is where a movie ends up when it has absolutely nowhere else to go after having toured every nook and cranny of the country, but they'll come in from miles around to see it.

They turn the corner of the community hall, station themselves at even intervals facing the wall. They unzip, take aim, and fire in unison, shooting strong and steady after having held it so long. They're not the first ones to visit this wall. Pak, at the end, bursts out in a guffaw, and the others zip up and go over to see what is so funny. A pair of scissors is painted on the wall, open and poised to strike.

The three come back out onto the road. Along comes an older gentleman who looks like nothing can happen around the place without his knowing about it.

Pak approaches him. "'Scuse me there, but you wouldn't know of a marriage going on around here? Kim family?"

"Hmm, must mean old man Kim Cha-bang's over in Rocky Hollow."

"Yes, yes, that's it. Stony Hollow, whatever."

"Like I said. Now you just head straight on up this way for a few *li*, and you'll see a little village of about fifty houses. That's Stony Hollow right there."

Finished, with his first step off he brings his thumb up to his nose, blows once left, once right, both with the same thumb. His masterly display leaves them gawking. They recover before long, though, and take off in the direction he's indicated.

* * *

About ten that night the three drunks are leaving the Rocky Hollow celebration behind them in their raucous wake. They bump and stumble abreast of each other along the narrow path in a slowly advancing jumble of arms and legs, each taking his turn to rend the quiet of the country night.

"The bride wasn't that pretty at all."

"Amiably plump is what she is."

"None of our business, anyway . . . "

They come up onto the bus road, where they have room to spread out.

"So what do we do now?"

"Back to Seoul, of course."

"There's no bus."

"Hell, we've got a Seoul House right here."

"You think we don't know that?"

"Then what are we waiting for?"

"What about money?"

"What's that you got from your uncle, thank-you notes?"

"Right! I saw it too."

"What you saw was about a thousand *won* for the bus back."

"That'll do just fine!"

"These tax people like their free booze, don't they?"

"When was the last time you passed up a free drink?"

"How about our student friend here, can you handle a drink or two?"

"Me? Once I get started . . . "

"Guess that settles it then. Let's get to it." And at a pace of two steps forward, one back, they press doggedly ahead for the Seoul House.

It is as dead as when they saw it earlier. What could have driven all the customers off?

They throw open the courtyard gate, expecting a grateful welcome. Nothing. No one is there. The yard is dark, all the darker because there's no electricity in this remote village at night. They bang on an inner door, shouting for some attention.

"How about a drink here!"

"Come and earn your keep!"

"You got guests here!"

A doorway down at the far end of what seems to be a long row of doors creaks open, and a head pops out. "What do you want there?"

"Sell us something to drink. We'll even pay you for it."

"Ha ha! Not here, though. Try next door."

"What are you selling here then?"

"Rooms. This is an inn."

"Well, I'll be . . . ! But what about the sign we saw earlier?"

"What sign?"

"So what's an inn doing without a sign?"

"Who needs a sign to put someone up for the night?"

"Well at least let people know you're in business—leave the gate open or something."

"Nope, no use. There are no guests after the last bus, and that was at nine."

"What do you call us then?"

"Whatever we are, we aren't guests. Not here, anyway, next door."

"Well, I am." The student is already on his way in. "I need to get a wink or two."

"Hey! Hold on a second . . . !" the others call. But he doesn't even look back.

The courtyard is almost invisible in the surrounding darkness. Through the window of a room off in the pitch black of the far side of the yard filters a lantern's light. The door opens and out comes the lantern. Kim strides over, sits down heavily on the low porch. The boy who has just come out hangs the lantern on a post and straightens the room. He's been using this room to study in, but now he has to give it up and join his family in the only other heated room.

"Okay to go in now?" and Kim gets up onto the porch without waiting for an answer. It takes twice as much to haul himself up now as it did for all the walking he's done all day.

Everything is quiet now. The others must be settled in next door already. The boy gathers up his litter of books and comes out. A piece of broken pencil on the floor catches the weak light of the lantern. Kim stoops through the low door and staggers into the cramped room. A putrid stench assaults him. The boy comes back with the lantern and hangs it on a nail in the flimsy wall, clinking the glass shield against its metal guard.

The boy leaves again. Kim sits down on the floor at the wall across from the lantern, leans back and lights up a cigarette. He draws deep on it, lets it out strong and steady. The lantern flickers.

The boy returns with the bedding, lays it out on the floor. When he stands back up a badge shows on his breast. Kim calls him over for a closer look. "Fifth Grade, Class 2" is written across the crudely worked badge, and vertically bisecting that, "Captain."

"Say there, looks like you're quite a student!"

"I got first place last time too."

"Will you look at this little guy, ugly as a toad, and these rags he uses as an excuse for clothes, and he's got the gall to go and place first in his class twice in a row! You living here with your folks?"

"No, this is my uncle's. My family's back in Wŏlch'u-ri, 30 *li* from here . . . "

Penniless college student. Streetcar clattering along the late night street. Tired passengers. Hoarse whistle blast: last stop. The streetcar opens up front and rear, disgorges its load onto the street. Passengers scatter into the darkness. Weak lamps in the windows of the humble street shops fish these forms hunched against the cold out of the darkness, then cast them back into it again. In ones and twos they disappear with their footsteps, up the back lanes and byways.

He gets to his boardinghouse, stands there at the locked gate, glances absently over his shoulder. If he could only bang away, "Open up, Mom!" But he opens his fist, pushes once, twice against the gate, tentatively, apologetically. He rattles it gently again. Slippers slapping along the courtyard, a diffident gait, the maid's. Good—not too late after all.

His heavy eyes slide half open. "You go to school here in this town?" No answer. He makes out the weak glimmer from the lantern the boy has turned down on his way out. Now where'd you run off to? The ondol floor is warm and he's really feeling what he drank back at the wedding. He turns on his side, crouches into a half fetus to get his hands and feet under the warm bedding at his side. Got to loosen this tie . . . and his eyes slide shut again.

Class captain, huh? Best grades—good going! That's right, you study hard. Sure, life is full of opportunity for those who study hard. America, England, France, go study anywhere you please. Money? No problem, the government will foot the bill, somebody will, as long as you show you really want to study. No, no problem about money, scholarships all over the place, all you need is a good head, and keep your nose to it. Study hard. Study hard is what you have to do—and confidence, you've got to have that confidence.

He's mumbling incoherently through clenched teeth, nobody there to hear him anyway. His monologue fades off into a maze of wandering thoughts, but soon out of these appears, step by step, his metamorphosis from genius into mediocrity. First it was, "Bet you're the school genius!" Then "exceptional" in the village middle school, "above average" in high school, then average and now just holding on in college in the big city. All that work it took to fall this far! Should have been satisfied with hamlet genius, and stayed there, who cares if it's miles from anywhere, grubbing in those mountains for a few bundles of firewood to peddle in town. That extravagant stuff about "genius," only those dumb hicks could come up with such nonsense. How their little genius gets thrown up against poverty and ends up near the bottom of his college class, what could they know about that? Nobody can set the Thames on fire, no matter how hard you try. That middle school student trudging all those miles to town and back every morning and night in his faded, ankle-length pants. Lots of sympathy, a little admiration. And now the pale college student shifted off from Cousin's to Aunt's to Aunt's to Uncle's, whoever will take you in. Tightening the belt another notch to quiet that grumbling stomach, lugging that heavy old hand-me-down ox-hide school bag under the arm because the handle's about ready to snap again, how oh how to come up with next term's tuition never allowing a moment's rest or reflection, trudging back from the library late every night. . . . So in the meanwhile what's happened to our little genius? All that's left is this worn out, compromising, egoistic moral dropout. Desperate enough now to do anything he needs to succeed, or at least to keep from sinking any further. Just get your faculty adviser or some professor on your side, that's the most important thing. Latch on to one of them, scrape and slave and grovel, because without his help, you can forget about any study abroad. But once you get your hands on that diploma, there's no stopping you. What you do is get that diploma, forget everything else . . . No. Not anymore. You know now. Diploma or not, it makes no difference now, because succeed or not, success this way could never mean what it used to mean. Poverty has already debased it of everything it could have been. Damn, so much squandered, gone for good!

He's been turning fitfully in his sleep and finally, eyes still shut, sits up, struggles to squirm out of both vest and coat at once. He gives up and sinks back down. Now he's snoring away, deep and fast asleep.

* * *

They're beating their chopsticks on the table in accompaniment to their impromptu version of the song.

"Did you make yourself a beauty?"

"Did I make myself a beast?"

"Nope, it's money that makes you . . . "

"And none that breaks you!"

"Ex-ACTly!"

The teacher is stretched out on the warm floor, propping himself on an elbow. Lee is still sitting up. They're at a table spread with snacks and drink, with the girl between them at the end of the table keeping them entertained and their glasses filled. The teacher exclaims to the ceiling again, "Ex-ACTly!"

And the girl yawns. Lee grabs her at the waist and pulls her to him. She giggles, he's so strong.

"You've had your fun with Mr. Pak, now it's my turn." He pulls her closer into his arms. She wriggles herself free. He grabs at her upper thigh, she yelps and lifts her skirt to inspect the milky white skin there. The lantern sputters and throws dancing shadows on the wall.

Pak is on his back now, staring blankly at the ceiling. Actually, he doesn't like the tax man. He's what they call a charmer, smooth, a smart dresser, good dancer too. There was that one time the guy grabbed Pak's wife around the waist—he'd teach her to dance—and the wife, whom you'd expect to put him off, at least pretend to be offended just a little, only ran out of the room giggling all the way. And then later when he mentioned to his wife, "The guy's a lot of fun," what did she go and say but, "Is he ever!" And she meant it! Quite a jolt that was. But the student, now, he's no problem. Doesn't know how to dress, withdrawing, not much to say at all. Whiling away the whole day sitting in the corner of that miserable room of his, who else of the three could do that? He'd manage somehow to get through a whole day, a whole week at a time without needing anyone.

Pak looks across at Lee, whose hands are busy under the girl's sweater. "You suppose our student really is sleeping?"

"Oh my, that's right! Where is the young gentleman?"

Okay, Lee, I know. You're smooth. You want to think you're such a Casanova, fine. But do you have to advertise it? Isn't he pleased with himself, that smug smile. . . . This nonsense might turn the girls on, but what about the guy who has to sit here and watch it? Disgusting. How can you get so . . . vulgar? No, I'm not jealous, it's not envy or anything like that. But try to find him at home except when he's sleeping, and then when he finally does come back, late of course, it's always, "Score like that, you feel like flying," or "Did I dance Chang's old lady a round or two!" Always something like that. To him, self-esteem is how many husbands you can cuckold. When the student is there to hear this talk of Lee's he blinks it away and finds something on the wall or ceiling to look at. Nothing sanctimonious there, though. Judge people? Not him, he couldn't care less, and that's why they say in the house that he's beyond rules and conventions and all those things. He's okay. You've got to like the fellow.

"Go and fetch our student for us, honey."

"The college student!"

"That's right, the gentleman next to me on the bus always staring outside with who knows what nasty thoughts going on inside. Go on, he's slept enough by now. I don't think he's going to mind all that much getting woke up for a little fun . . . What the heck," leaning his heavy arm on her shoulder, "why not make a night of it!"

She's interested, listening close. Pak has been listening too, but he is getting sleepy himself, his eyelids keep slipping. Then the girl is up like a whisper, before Lee knows it, and he's part of the floor now. The door slides shut and she's gone. The flame in the lantern dances.

She gets a surprise outside. The yard is white, utterly still in the falling snow. She slips into her sandals, descends into the white softness. She throws her head back, this wine-house girl, lifts her face to the heavens swirling with those icy black fluffs. She glories in the cold tingle they yield settling on her skin, and opens her mouth to drink in as much as possible.

A night like this, wouldn't it be just perfect for a new bride! "Snow the first night, riches thereafter." And happiness. The girl blinks once, twice. Swarming snowflakes, there, not there, there again. She tries to imagine her face as a bride, but somehow can't . . . Anyway, all brides would have the same look, wouldn't they? Of happiness, hope, maybe apprehension, why not all together? She looks down into the fresh whiteness of the yard, locks her knees and shuffles off, stride by long stride, laying a set of tracks. The falling snow gathers on her hair.

Then the girl leaves off her ski walk and heads to the outer gate. She opens it a crack and slips through, quiet as a cat.

The snow is deep out on the road, too. Her steps are mute, the whole world still. She looks down at the snow-capped slippers kicking out from beneath her long skirt and feels she could just keep walking like this for a hundred *li*.

When she comes up to the inn next door, though, she stops, works her fingers in through the brushwood side gate and flicks open the catch. Cotton pods of snow float down from the sky and settle, white on white. There is a light in one of the two guest rooms. A slight hesitation, then she goes over and steps up onto the porch. She peeks in through the hole someone's finger has left in the paper of the lattice door. A man is lying there in the faint glimmer of the lamp. She retreats to the darkened room next to his, puts her face close to the door . . .

"Little boy," she whispers. "You in there, honey?"

No answer. She pushes on the door, rattling it softly. Still no answer. She goes back to the guest room, listens, and slides the door open.

He is on his side, curled up like a shrimp, uncovered except for his arms and legs he has stuck under the cover to escape the cold. The girl takes a closer look at his face. Yes, it's him, the one on the bus. College student! She takes him by the shoulders and rolls him gently over on his back. He frowns—tie must be too tight. Look at you, not even getting out of your clothes before you go to bed! Poor thing. Now she is big sister and mom, takes off his tie, pulls back the cover he has dragged with him and slips off his trousers, his shirt, then straightens his mat.

He squirms, about to wake up. Then he slips right back under the mat she has just readied for him to lie on. Behave yourself now! She pulls his arms and legs back out, raises him to her breast and maneuvers him gently onto the mat.

She covers him, then slips the pillow neatly under his head.

She sits back, and looks. Her eyes rest on his face.

College student . . .

The lantern sputters. The girl stands, picks up his scattered clothes, and hangs each, one by one, on its own nail in the wall.

She goes to the lantern, bows over it, puts it out with a gentle puff.

Outside in the courtyard, soft white stillness. The snow deepens, erasing her steps.

FIRST LOVE

Sŏng Sŏk-che

(1995)

Dust from the dirt road blossoming up and out in a big flower. Delivery trucks pouring out of the baking factory. The trucks coming out bulky like the cream-filled Full Moon cakes they carried, and coming back in as thin as rusk toast. Here and there on the street the muted figures of girls in their sky blue uniforms and white kerchiefs tied in back. Old men sleeping like the dead under the shade trees. The same old scene every day. Just like the breads and buns and biscuits pressed exactly the same from the same molds, today like yesterday and tomorrow like today.

And there you were, following me. Following me every day.

And Ch'un-ja's husband was there singing away every day, just like the day before, at the entrance to the market, the old school uniform he wore always mud-caked and tattered, but his shoes always glistening. Every day, chanting his mantra *Have you perchance seen my dear Ch'un-ja? Ch'un-ja my love. Family name Kim, given name Ch'un-ja, oh my love Ch'un-ja.* The denizens of Hell Precinct walking by him with blank faces like boiled eggs. That day, too. And I knew that soon he'd start grabbing the girls one after another and ask the same question and then scream *You're all my Ch'un-ja!* and then laugh to himself *So many Ch'un-jas!* and eventually collapse and twitch and squirm in a dust hollow in the dirt road. His legs would kick and shake and his eyes would roll up inside his head and he would foam at the mouth. When he came to he'd shine his shoes and go back to his chant.

I passed Ch'un-ja's husband and jumped over the sewage ditch with its ash-gray water. Just like the day before and the day before. And you were following me that day, as usual.

The kids' soccer ball got kicked under the number 268 bus. The bus girl called "O-ra-ee!" and slapped the side of the bus *bang-bang!* The bus took off from our Hell for a wider, bigger world somewhere out there, and later it would return to Hell. The ball shot out *Pop!* from under the wheel. And that smoke always rising into the sky, from something burning somewhere. And you were there, like always, in the background, now like the smoke, now like the kids playing, now like the wheel of the bus, now like the ball.

You were taller than me by a hand. You had a big, square, dark face. You gave off an odd, provocative smell. Our teachers said you looked like a bandit—as if they had ever run into a bandit before—but even a bandit wouldn't live in a hell like this, and the teachers didn't live in a hell like this either. They came on the bus from another world and taught us kids and then picked up their lunch boxes and went back to that other world. After these people from the other world took off, all that was left was the darkness and the dust and the noise and the stench and the coal fumes and fat older sisters. And there was one more thing about this place. Something I couldn't stand. That something, that awful something, was all those animals called people. Herds of hordes of people animals. This people zoo. This Hell Zoo.

When I first met you, Hell Junior High senior class 26, like the other twenty-five senior classes, had less than ten students that were native to Hell Precinct, Hell Ward when they started school. And there were about forty students in the class who had moved to Seoul from the countryside. I was one of them. And twenty other sorry souls had moved to Hell Precinct—of all places—from other parts of Seoul. Anyway, you were one of them. Kids from all these different backgrounds scrambled to establish a hierarchy among themselves. From top to tenth were settled within a day, the rest took longer; after a few months all five thousand had found their proper place. The king of them all bragged, "I hang around with senior high guys. And I know some real hoods from the outside world."

You were the one person that this proud king was afraid of. I didn't know why you were respected by this hoodlum who was never defeated by anybody and who would have his knife out at the slightest excuse. Because I was just a new kid from the countryside. I soon realized that you could get killed if you messed with this hoodlum. You had to know stuff like this to survive in Hell Junior High in this ghetto on the outskirts of the city. If you were going to make it out of here to another neighborhood, in that other world, you had to graduate in one piece from this one. But I didn't know that yet. Because I had just transferred here. Within a few days of my arrival the hoodlum ordered me to fetch a roll and soda from the snack bar. I didn't know he had a reputation in Hell Elementary, Hell Junior High, even Hell High, Hell Vocational and Hell Sunday School. Why did this high and mighty hoodlum bestow on this pale, naïve kid just up from the countryside the mission to "Go get me a roll and soda from the snack bar"? Another kid would have clenched his fists in victory and run off thinking "My big chance! What an honor to be sent on an errand by the King! I'd fetch for him even if it cost me my life." But I had no such intention. I didn't know about the world. I didn't know about this hoodlum. I was just a numbskull from the countryside. So I refused to go on his errand. "No."

The hoodlum approached me with a baffled, stupefied, annoyed, uncomprehending look on his face. He grabbed me by the collar and twisted hard, and dragged me from the classroom on the third floor down to the toilets outside. All five thousand students saw what was happening but nobody asked why and nobody tried to stop it. He beat the crap out of me in this isolated, stinking place with all the broken desks and blackboards and lumber stored there. I was being beaten—this was the first time somebody's fist had given me a bloody nose—so I didn't know lunch break was almost over. And it was going to be the first time I'd ever cut class, because I couldn't go back to the classroom in this shape. Poor me. Pitiful me, but I didn't cry. Instead, I changed my life's goal: Even though I got beat up by this hoodlum, even if I got another bloody nose and couldn't go to class, I wouldn't kill myself.

At that moment you approached me. You stood there in front of me, casually buttoning up your fly. "Ho ho ho, what have we here?" you said, and spit a nice clean one—zzzip—through your teeth. "Looks to me like we have another one playing hooky," mimicking one of those student monitors. "Were you in a fight?"

That was no fight. Somebody just beat me up. I got up. I turned my head away. I didn't care who you were, who I was. I just wanted to get out of there. But then you came up to me quick and light as a cat, in no time, and started pushing me back down by the shoulders. Soon I was sitting in the dust and sawdust. At that very moment I changed my life's goal: to survive and escape this Hell. I just glared at you. Because I had just changed my life's goal.

That was a day in spring. Mating season for the rhinoceros in Africa, for the elk in the Siberian tundra. The sky was bruise-blue. In the air of Hell the dust in the air blackening your buggers mingled with the hearty, acerbic smell from the plant steaming a batch of buns. Just like any other day. All of a sudden you were raising my chin with your finger and looking at my face as if you found something intriguing there. Your touch was very soft and artless and felt irresistible to this guy who wanted solace any way he could get it. And you said, "Pretty as a girl!"

I glared and glared and glared and broke into tears. Sobbed like a girl. You looked down at me quite a while. I wasn't crying from grief over the fight or my bloody nose or cutting class. What vexed me so was your "girl" stuff. I felt so sorry for myself just sobbing there and not being able to say anything to stop you that I kept on crying till my head hurt. And then you vanished. But then you came right back with a pail of water. The pail said "Soccer Team." That pail was something nobody dared touch except for the soccer team, which had the fiercest hoodlums in the school on it.

"Wash up."

I totally ignored you. I ignored the soccer team pail and the soccer team. I ignored the whole world. I got up and walked out. I wasn't afraid of you. I was humiliated.

Everyone steered clear of you. And you ignored these kids. But you came closer and closer to me, who disliked you. I wasn't afraid of you. I just disliked you.

For some reason you stopped cutting class like you used to. The teacher said, "Hey, long time no see, Paek Sŭng-ho. How've you been?" You snorted and leaned your chair back and stared at the ceiling. And you made spit bubbles and launched them into the air one by one. The kids around you giggled. Then the teacher blushed and closed the attendance book.

One day after that you came closer. You moved over to the seat behind me. And with your pencil you traced, word by word, "You're dead," like you were writing on the blackboard.

But you didn't scare me. "Cut it out!"

The music teacher, who was writing some music on the blackboard, turned around along with the shorter kids in the front rows, and the kids next to us and the kids in back held their breath. You snatched a notebook from the kid next to you and were pretending to write in it. The teacher asked the kids what was going on but they didn't answer. The teacher knocked me on the head with the attendance book and then went back to the blackboard. You shook your fist at the teacher's back and the kids laughed soundlessly. I had become the first kid in school to ever yell at you. No big deal.

Every day the old same thing. Maybe not every day . . .

That day too a truck loaded with bakery stuff passed by. The kids playing soccer on the street dropped their game and tailed the truck close. These trucks sometimes dropped stuff as they bounced and rattled on down the road. Today, though, unlike other days, I didn't join the kids. But a whole case—not just one or two pieces—jumped out of the truck and landed right in front of my nose.

"There's some!"

Within a second dozens of kids gathered around me. A cloud of dust rose as they scrambled over each other and punched and bit each other to carry off their booty. Since I was closest to the box I grabbed one first but before I could open it somebody knocked my hand and made off with it. I was standing in front of the box, stunned, when from out of the blue, "Put it back, you little shits." Didn't even need to raise your voice. The kids put them all back into the box right away, even the half-eaten ones. I just wanted to get out of there, but you called me. "Hey you, take five."

I ignored you. I hated you. I hated the way you wouldn't leave me alone. "I don't eat that stuff."

I knew how delicious that thing inside the wrapping with the full moon was. But I left it there in that box. I plodded off home. And when I got there you were waiting for me out in front. You took some Full Moons out of your torn cap.

I glared at you. "Why are you doing this to me? I'm no beggar. And I hate those things. And I hate you too."

Your jaw stiffened. Square and firm, like on those Greek sculptures in the art book. You threw the Full Moons on the ground and yelled, "Can't you see *anything*?!"

Then you went and tore up your cap and kicked the front gate hard and stomped off.

"What'd you go and kick the gate for? When the landlord finds out we're in for it!"

I was still glaring at the torn cap and battered Full Moons when big sister came running out.

"Where did all this come from?" She gathered them up.

"Throw them away . . . Go on."

"Dummy, you don't throw away food. And they're not even opened. We can have them for supper."

She ate like a pig that evening. I hated her. And I hated that lunch box she packed for me. So the next day I pretended I forgot all about it and left it at home. After school I was starving so I ran real hard after the bakery truck. But it didn't drop even one bun, let alone a case of them. Not the next day either. Nor the next day. The same thing, day after day. Well, maybe not *every* day.

One day big sister and I began skipping breakfast. The factory couldn't pay her. She cried and went off to the factory every day with swollen eyes. I didn't suffer as bad as she did because I staved my hunger by gorging myself at the faucet at school. That day you were waiting for me in front of the bakery at the school gate. You pulled me into the bakery.

"Here, have some. Bought it for you." You pushed a few steamed buns at me. Then you ordered a bottle of that milk with the big cow on it. I was dizzy from hunger but I didn't eat.

"Try it."

"Why are you doing this?"

"I just wanted to give it to you."

"I'm not one of your gofers."

"Who'd want a gofer like you?!"

Then the fragrance of tempura filled the store. I didn't like tempura because it had too much grease. When you're hungry tempura can give you the trots . . .

"Want some?"

. . . but I nodded. And you went and got some, like the whole place belonged to you. Nobody in the shop said a thing. I pecked at it like a bird. While I ate you watched over me, following every move like a big-hearted dinosaur. I hated you. You packed a few paper bags of tempura and stuck them in my bag. I was letting you do all this only because I was thinking of my sister. On our way out I asked, "Can I take the buns?"

You nodded. You stuffed my bag to bursting with more buns. That evening I ate buns, and big sister ate tempura to bursting. The next day she couldn't go to the factory because she had diarrhea. Then things went back to normal. Same thing day after day. *Almost* every day.

I couldn't figure out why the kids looked up to you so. Not until April anyway, maybe May, when the sycamores in the assembly ground at school were heavy with new leaves, and we were getting our physicals. When we got the test we had to take off our coats, our pants and our undershirts, and revealed bodies that had been scrubbed the day before in the public bath or the kitchen. There were fat bodies like balloons, pale and stocky ones like tofu, and dark skinny bowed ones like mine. The kids sniggered and snickered and tickled each other and left the marks of their claws on each other . . . then all at once everybody fell silent. You had appeared.

You had something that we didn't have, or hardly had. That something was what we sometimes mistook on ourselves for a thread to be pulled out, something budding strange and unfamiliar, with the smell of adulthood. Hair.

You had it in your armpits, and it paraded from your chest to your stomach to your groin under your shorts. Hundreds of eyes fastened on you, then turned away, then came back and stayed there. You pretended to be totally indifferent, but you took your time with every move to let us all get a good look, and it became obvious to me why the students who had already witnessed your show the year before paid you such extravagant respect. It was because of your hair that even the strongest kid in the class didn't dare mess with you.

Were you older than the other kids? I don't know. Were you older than your age? I don't know that either. Anyway, your hair got you respect. You placed that strange hairy body of yours up on the scale. I was right in back of you, my turn next. You glanced at me from up on that scale, "Well, what do you think?" in your eyes. I kept quiet. It had nothing to do with me. You seemed to think it was strange I wasn't impressed by you or your hair. Maybe that's why you tried again with another pose, to make sure I saw what none of us could even dream of having.

I bought a month's pass to the cram hall and spent the summer vacation there studying for the high school qualifying exam. As far as I knew there was only one way to escape Hell and that was by studying. So I studied and studied and even tried a few senior high textbooks. The owner of the cram hall allowed me to study in the senior high students' room, encouraging me with, "You might study harder among the older kids." They *had* to study, because they were preparing for the college entrance exam.

One day you showed up. You bought a ticket for half a month. When that was used up you collected money from the kids in the junior high room and got a ticket for another half month. You didn't do anything like study. I knew why you were there. You were there because I was there. I was with the older kids studying for the college entrance exam, and you were with the kids that were afraid of you. In the junior high room practically all they learned was things like connecting electric lines to metal chopsticks in an old powdered milk can to boil ramyon, and masturbating. In this study hall I wasn't a junior high kid. I had long since graduated from things like that. I had no reason to go back to that. And so it was that day after tedious day I was up on the rooftop at 3:00 in the morning, taking a break. But one day was different. You were there. If I hadn't been up there that day I might have gotten through the whole summer vacation without meeting you.

There was a public bath house on the first floor of the building next to the study center. Until late at night the fragrance of soap and female skin wafted from around the back of our building into the noses of both junior and senior high kids, asses sweating away on their small steamy chairs. Sometimes at dawn on Sundays when we opened the doors of our prison and left for our free day at home, we would pass by young women and housewives with radish-red faces and wet hair carrying their baskets with towels and soap and shampoo. Swollen with contentment from their hot bath, they waggled along body and spirit and giggled constantly so you could almost see bubbles coming out of their mouths.

From our rooftop we could see the neighboring rooftop, which looked exactly like ours. Sitting on that roof was a small room. Behind that room stood an electric pole that looked like a giant stretching out its arms. The dawn moon was long gone past the chimney of the bakery factory. That chimney, belching fumes day and night. Into our sky of Hell, where you could never see a the star. A girl in her early twenties was renting that small room. She had a habit of leaving her light on all night. The only ones who knew this secret about the light were the older guys preparing for their second or third shot at the college entrance exam. Her light was out, though, so it was pitch dark all over.

The supervisor of the center had put a combination lock on the door to the roof. Except for him, the only ones who knew the combination were the older guys. I found out the combination from eavesdropping on them. So after I made sure they were asleep I used to open the lock and go up on the roof. In the study hall I was a senior high student. And in Hell, even a senior high student had to grow up. To grow up you had to sneak a look at the room of a girl who slept with her light on. This girl was a noble princess living in the palace that their imaginations built for her. She worked in a factory and had a habit of singing while she combed her hair, totally naked, before going to bed. Like any princess confined in her Tower of Hell by her mean stepfather. With a few vigorous strokes of my right hand I whacked off a futile salute to that window with no light, all the while cursing that hand. Then the laundry lines netting the rooftop snapped a warning, and I turned. I didn't know when you had come up or how long you'd been watching me. You stood there tall and strong as that electric pole, smoking.

"Long time no see." You flicked your cigarette at me, to hide how tense you were.

"What are you doing here?" I asked as if it were you who had come up first and me who had discovered you doing something embarrassing. You didn't reproach me.

"I came up to see you."

"What for?" I wanted to get out of there. If the older guys found me there they wouldn't let it rest.

"Just got back from a few days outside Seoul. Bumming around on the train. And then I realized I missed you."

You slid the bar shut on the roof door. I was locked in that rooftop prison now, so I had to say something. Besides, I was just a junior high school student who had never been on a train. "Where?"

"Down to Ŭnchŏk. And I got off at every stop on the way there. And I got off at every stop on the way back."

"Jerk. One station's the same as another." There was nothing to laugh at, but I did anyway. You laughed too, awkwardly.

"Who lives in that room there?"

"Who knows?" Back to the cold junior high student again. I was in a hurry. Somebody might come up. If the older guys found out they would beat me half to death and send me back to the junior high room. When I tried to get past you, you had the nerve to grab my arm.

"Just gonna go?"

Your grip was so gentle but so firm and determined it sent chills through me. It was a touch only somebody in love can have. I wasn't some junior high student foolish enough to fall in love with you.

"Right." I coldly brushed your hand away.

But you were on fire. "Hey, let's talk some, will you?"

"What's there to talk about?"

We tussled briefly. Then you whispered, breathing heavily, "You want to see a girl so much?"

"What do you mean?"

"I know why you're up here."

I was ashamed. Indignant. Angry. You were nothing more than a little child who didn't know what sex he was. I knew what sex I was. I swore I would never see you again if you didn't let me go.

"I'll show you a few."

"Forget it."

"Come to the back of the bath house later, when it opens. There's a narrow path between the wall and the building. Meet me there."

"I'm not going."

I knew where he meant. The wall behind the building was too high for me to touch the top, and it looked like it could collapse any time, and there was broken glass embedded in the cement at the top. The wall and that glass on top had the effect of quelling the curiosity of anyone that might be fool enough to try for a look inside by climbing over the wall or perching on top of it.

"Five o'clock." That was all you said, and left.

I washed my hands. Over and over. I swore I wouldn't go. I dozed at my desk. I tried to sleep. I did sleep. I'm sure I slept. But somehow at 5:00, when the steam started coming out of the bathhouse window, I found myself at the base of that rotting wall that was about to collapse.

"You made it."

You were there already. When you saw me, you picked up a wooden plank at the base of the wall, revealing some bricks that you had stored there to help us up.

"Up you go. I'll give you a boost."

You were more than a hand's span taller than me. And you were twice as strong as me. You could give me a boost. You could help me up. The more reliable and trustworthy you appeared, the more embarrassed and humbled I felt. So I came up with an excuse.

"There's glass up there."

The bathhouse's rear window was a bit higher than the wall, so a guy could only see inside from on top of the wall, but on top of the wall was that embedded broken glass. I wasn't going to take the risk of cutting up my butt just to satisfy my curiosity.

"I took care of it."

And you had. You had come a few hours earlier, climbed the wall, and cleared away enough of the glass shards for one person to sit there. I was thinking how careful you must have been to avoid making a noise and getting caught and why you went through so much trouble, when you grabbed my foot and cupped it in your hands and started boosting me up. So I was climbing up the wall before I knew it.

I got to the top and sat there. You called up to me, "See anything?"

Nothing. Inside it was full of steam. In that heavy steam I couldn't tell whether those shadowy forms were humans or just big chunks of meat. And even if they were human I couldn't tell whether they were male or female. And even if I could tell that, I couldn't tell whether they were naked or clothed, or whether they were dressing or undressing. I shook my head, and you came up, frustrated.

You looked at the window, which was belching out a column of steam, and apologized. "It'll be better next time. Just some bad luck today."

I was about to tell you, sitting with your big ass on that sharp glass, that it was okay. And I was going to tell you you didn't have to apologize. And of course I was going to tell you that I would never sit on this wall with you again, side by side like a pair of sparrows. But I didn't have the chance.

"You . . . you . . . you little punks!"

Someone came from inside the bathhouse screaming. Even in the murky light of dawn I could see the hammer he was holding in his hand. I panicked and knocked off one of my shoes.

"My shoe!"

One of the pair my sister had bought me. The only pair I owned. You pushed me off the wall, to the outside, and even after I landed I was shouting "My shoe! My shoe!" You fell down inside the wall and I limped away as fast as I could. You cut your ass on the glass shards, and you got hit in the shin with that guy's hammer. But no, you didn't fall—you jumped. While the owner was holding you around the waist and shouting triumphantly what he was going to do with you, you were looking around for my shoe, and when you found it you just dumped him.

Then you showed up at the front gate of my house with my shoe. And you told me, "Sorry."

Thinking back on it, I never told you I was sorry for anything. "Sorry" was something you did. I took the shoe but didn't even thank you. I could only begrudge you a simple "How about you?"

Without saying anything you rolled up your pant leg to your knee and showed me your leg. Your copiously hairy leg, bruised purple from knee to ankle. I turned away. And

"I'm sorry . . . "

It was *you* said that.

"I'll do better next time."

That also, it was *you* that said it.

2

Yesterday like today, and yesterday's yesterday just the same. Every day at ten in the morning the bakery factory's chimney belched out its steam, carrying the buttery, yeasty smell of bread and buns and biscuits baking. That smell drifted like a kite in the sky around the factory, then just before lunch break wafted into the classroom and taunted the kids' stomachs. We were always so hungry back in those days that at just the sight of a biscuit a kid would go out of his mind getting hold of the cursed thing and gobbling it up in a breath.

"You know that babe in the bakery shop by the front gate?"

That girl in the bakery shop was no babe, as you put it. She was a young woman, helping out in the family business after graduating junior high. There wasn't a kid in our school that didn't know about her. If she'd continued in school she'd be in senior high now, maybe her second year. She was slim, beautiful, had full breasts, and a hot tongue, and loathed it when junior high kids showed interest in her. The only way the kids, even the best fighters, could bask in her presence was to eat one cursed steamed bun after another, eyes firmly on their plates, until they felt their stomach would burst. Oh, that cold stare that she could freeze a kid with at the slightest provocation. That look full of ennui and disdain. That now frosty now scorching hand. But there was nary a one of them who could pass that shop without stopping in. All those stories about her on the toilet walls. All those tales of her beauty, her lust, her cruelty and callousness secretly shared among even the first-year kids like irresistible cream cakes.

"I don't care about girls," is how I answered you.

In those days the type of person I was interested in was the music teacher, who starred in those toilet tales as often as the girl in the bakery shop. The music teacher sure was no girl.

"Well, I did her."

Liar. She exuded chilling fumes like a hunk of dry ice. Whenever the kids lingered around the bakery shop or peeped inside she spewed volcanic blast of foul language. She'd dress it up with a start or ending of "you placenta-smeared rat suckling you." The same every day. Did *that* witch?

It was getting windier as we slipped into autumn. I supposed it was the same in this world of yours and mine as it was in the other world. You were still following me, still hanging around, still apologizing. We came to that empty lot that used to be an orchard, just before my house. The trees there were doomed to be buried soon in the garbage that kept piling higher and higher. A few small, spunky pears hung on the trees that survived.

"You like her?"

I didn't know that girl well. I wasn't jealous either—I couldn't care less. You boasted, "I have no interest in her but she keeps following me. And you know what? She's always got holes in her panties. You want me to bring you a pair next time?" Every time you talked about her like that I let you know how it turned me off.

A bug-eaten pear dropped off the tree. You got anxious when I made to go.

"You want to watch me do her?"

I looked you in the eye. "Whatever."

This stopped you a second. But you persisted. You sidled closer, whispered, "Come to Bear Rock after the test tomorrow?"

I went home and scrubbed my hands and didn't give another thought to what you said. Then what did I go to that Bear Rock for after the test? The rock was in a secluded place on the hill in back of the school and they said it was used by grownup couples from time to time to do whatever it was they did. Anyway, I didn't sleep at all the night before. I had decided to stay up the whole night preparing for the exam, to get back first place in the class, to get my ticket out of Hell. So why did I go to Bear Rock? Well, even though you were a lousy student, and never had any intention of being a good one, you followed this good student around. You, who were kind of like a grownup, gave your affection to me, who was more like a kid. So if I were to show some appreciation for this one quality you had, I'd kind of be paying you back somehow for your blind devotion. And . . . And . . . And . . . no matter where a guy lived—Hell or no Hell—he had to grow up someday. Yes, that's why I went.

When I went to that rock, school bag in hand, you weren't there. And neither was the girl. Lying on that rock I thought about why on earth I had come all the way up there. Scuffing up my only pair of leather shoes, which Sis had bought with her first paycheck. Count on you? I laughed to myself in that autumn sunlight in Hell. Good. Not showing up released me from that silly obligation. Just coming here made us even. I started to leave. Then I heard a low voice. I lay down on my belly, flat. I just knew instinctively I had to make myself invisible. I couldn't tell whether that voice was yours or someone else's. A male's voice, but too low for me to make out anything. Then a female's voice saying "I'm cold." My heart beat furiously, like two hearts were fighting there inside my chest. And then there was a sound that I recognized. Even though it was a sound I'd never heard before.

It was the sound you hear when the tenderest parts of a man's and a woman's bodies come together. A long *smoooch*. A repeating *jjap-jjap*. Something getting pulled, *jooook*. I wrapped my arms around my chest to hold myself in check. Then, the noises stopped. A sour smell of yeasty bread, a foul smell of an open sewer, a provocative smell of the bathhouse all assaulted me. From that rock the school campus looked so quiet. The sycamores stood like stalwart toy soldiers and from somewhere I heard what sounded like singing. I wished those two weren't there behind that rock. If they left, I could too. I wished I could sit in some corner of that empty campus and listen to the music teacher singing and get all choked up again over that strange emotion I felt those other times she sang.

I stuck my head out over the rock. I was going to leave if nobody was there. But something was moving down there. It was somebody's bottom. Was it yours? I never asked you. Just like you never asked me whether I came to that rock that day. At any rate, all I remember is two long, sleek legs stretching out from under those buttocks. Those dazzling white legs were blinding me, but I couldn't take my eyes off them. My feet were being pulled from behind—I had to get out of there—but I struggled against it. And something was pulling me from in front but I fought that, too. I was worried my school cap might fall off so I grabbed it tight. Meanwhile the legs had moved around. Now I could see the face of their owner. It was the girl in the bakery shop, her eyes squeezed shut. That girl, with her hair streaming in disarray. Her legs trembling, the lips over her clenched teeth trembling. A metallic taste rose back in my nose and stars exploded in my eyes.

I'm not sure. Not sure at all when she opened her eyes. And how long had her eyes been squeezed shut like that before they suddenly opened right into mine? Oh, oh, oh, I had knocked a pebble off the rock and startled them, got caught watching them. Without a thought I jumped down between them as they separated, and scampered off down that path that seemed hundreds of meters long, getting all scratched and cut. Her eyes followed me home and into my dreams and into that one day in my twenties when I slept the first time with a woman. They haunt me even now, on occasion. Yes, even now, those eyes . . .

I fell in love that day. With that young woman's eyes. With that look in them, so startled and befuddled, their anger stinging me like bullets. Those eyes drilling me so hard, popping so big I could draw you a detailed map showing every capillary. Those big eyes. Those piercing eyes.

3

From that day on, every day dragged by exactly the same. I stayed away from you, and the bakery shop girl ignored the junior high students—and me. You and me were like distant planets each spinning in its own orbit. You went about your life longing for me and I went about mine yearning for her. You dropped out of school a few weeks before the senior high qualifying exam and I sat through my last exam in Hell. You disappeared, then she disappeared. And when she disappeared, that was the end of my first love.

In February, just before graduation day, we were given a slip of paper with a number on it. That number would tell us which high school we were to attend. The kids who were only going to vocational school or Hell Special District High didn't get that slip. Those who had failed in the exam didn't get it either. So what were you doing there on that special day, at that special place? You had dropped out of school, didn't take the graduation exam, didn't even take the general equivalency diploma exam—in fact, you weren't even interested in vocational school. It was strange indeed that you showed up there.

As soon as I got that slip of paper—my ticket out of Hell—I dashed out of the classroom and ran onto the assembly ground with a sense of liberation that made me feel as strapping as my big sister and as tall as you. Then I saw the bakery shop across the assembly ground, and came to a halt. But soon the words from that song came to mind: " . . . Alas, that's how love goes" and I shrugged and took off again. And stopped again. You were walking toward me, illuminated by the bright sun. You were wearing a long, heavy coat and stylish hat that made you look like some rich guy from the other world, like a train engineer or a deep-sea fishing boat captain, or an astronaut.

"Where you going?"

"How about you?"

We stood there face to face on the assembly ground. Slowly you came closer. How did I get that feeling that this was the last time we'd meet? The golden rays of the sun lighting up your face seemed to be coming from that other better world that I was going to. That sun shining on my back cast toward you a short, distinct shadow.

"How about a hug?"

"Okay."

For the first time, I did what you wanted. You hugged me. Then you swiftly unbuttoned your coat.

"You won't be back here again."

"Right."

You opened your coat wide. I moved inside.

"I love you." You hugged me tight.

"Me too."

We got a few dubious looks from some kids passing by. But that day in Hell, when the trucks poured from the bakery factory, and when in that other world whales breached in the sea, on that day I realized that I had become a man.

WHAT'S TO BE DONE

Kong Chi-yŏng

(1992)

Walking, walking . . . and suddenly it's twilight. This sidewalk along the old palace wall is almost empty, but in the street the cars in the lanes heading for the Hyehwa roundabout are lined up bumper to bumper. Twilight cuts distinct outlines, and the edges of the centuries-old palace's stone wall, even the grain in the moss-coated tiles at the top, stand out in sharp relief. Above the wall, skinny barren branches tremble delicately against the washed-out evening sky. At one time a heavy foliage sprouted from these branches but then the autumn winds came and shook them, and their big leaves fell and left the branches to shiver in the slightest breeze. I shift my bag and keep on walking.

I left the publishing company that my senior in the movement owns, then canceled my appointments for the evening. But now I'm left with nowhere really to go, and feel abandoned, even by these streets I've walked so often, by the bus stop I pass every day.

Trying not to think of him—but I can't get him off my mind. Someone at the publisher's mentioned he was getting married. If they hadn't told me that, I'd probably be at that celebration for Professor Kim's new book right now, and complimenting the gentleman on his work even though I don't really think much of it. I'd be making small talk during that buffet meal, trading useless jokes, drinking a full-headed beer . . .

He . . . is . . . getting—married.

The light at this deserted crosswalk is red. Across the stalled line of cars I see a woman. Might be a little over twenty. She's wearing a shabby parka that looks like she just grabbed any old thing from a bin in the market, and a pair of pants with bulging knees. Looking from across the street at the crosswalk light on my side. She seems quite anxious about something. As soon as I get that idea, I get the feeling that this woman facing me is someone else. Another woman with that same expression comes to mind, a woman in her early twenties standing there at the other side of this same crosswalk, with short-cropped hair, a parka that looked like "any old thing" grabbed out of a bin in a market, a pair of pants with bulging knees. Watching the crosswalk light, waiting for the green, just like this one.

Just me and this woman standing across the street. Only the two of us in this world with that big street between us, all those cars lined up waiting. But again the woman in my memories takes her place. The pages of the calendar start flipping back in my head, back to the winter of 1986.

Her face was pallid, her big eyes limpid, nervous. Her whole body was clenched, trembling now and then. When the light changed she walked quickly across the street and up toward the Hyehwa roundabout.

When she finally arrived at the entrance of an old building she paused, took a deep breath, then went in. The stairs leading up to the second floor squeaked with every step of her worn sneakers. She stopped halfway up and wondered: a bad omen?

Then she climbed on up to the top of the stairs and tentatively pushed open the door to the dingy tearoom. The hour was still too early for customers. She warily took a seat at a table off to the side, by a window. She felt in her pockets, desperate for a cigarette, but out of her pocket came only the sad click of a few bus tokens.

After a short while he came in. Her face, which had been nervously staring at the entrance, blushed with a rush of elation. He wore a navy blue plaid halfcoat with artificial wool collar and lapel. At the sight of that halfcoat she bent her head a bit. It wasn't to hide the tears that halfcoat drew from her—with all they had between them what was there to hide?—it was her heart sinking at the thought that this was the last time.

He came over and sat down across from her. Slowly she raised her head. Was that anguish that she saw in his eyes, or was she just imagining it? He looked at her with the same intensity that she was looking at him. At the thought she felt something tear inside her breast. As she lowered her eyes to the old table, away from his gaze, her hand went on its own to her breast, where she could feel each drop of blood dripping from her breaking heart. But she lifted her eyes again to meet his, and forced a smile. She decided to ignore the fact that this was the last time, and that this meeting was forbidden. After all, last time or not, it's good—he's here, I'm here, together for now.

Apparently he thought he knew what the smile was for. "Must have had one too many last night, you and me both."

Her smile froze. She should have known he would come up with something like that. But she hadn't.

She realized they were breaking the rules. Right now it was morning seminar time. Everyone must be wondering why he hadn't shown up, why she had left the house without saying anything. The looks and the criticism they'd pour on her . . . She was already feeling their stinging stares. But before she even came here she had psyched herself against the criticism they would soon wound her with. That gave her even more courage than the fact that this was the last time. The last time, and she had nothing to lose.

So she spoke. "Too much to drink? You know that's not it. I'd commit my life to this."

Their eyes met in challenge, the eyes that said it was because of alcohol and the eyes that said she could commit her life to this love. He was going to respond, but then, with a rueful smile, let it go. She dropped her eyes.

She had done the same that day she decided to leave graduate school, to leave home and join the movement, and asked her parents for their understanding. After all, they were her parents. Men, though, she had always looked straight in the eye. But this talk about "one too many" was going too far, and she couldn't help but look away.

"Coward."

He didn't say anything. He searched his pockets for his cigarettes, pulled them out and offered her one. She took the cigarette, thinking back on the night before, that night that had come upon them so suddenly. No, though, it wasn't so sudden after all . . .

One fall day, back in 1983, that's when she first saw him. The students were demonstrating again, after several co-eds had been raped by the plainclothes police in the woods at the back of the campus. All that autumn girls had been falling like autumn leaves to the brutal lust of those thugs, who would casually despoil their prey, zip up and be gone even before she could pull her skirt back down. Now, peeking around the student center building, the undergrad bit her fist in horror as she watched that girl, her senior, who'd been passing out flyers in the building across from the library, jump out the window when the plainclothesmen got too close.

And she saw him there, too, hanging out the window of the library. He was shouting, "Survivors, onward! Survivors, forward!" and then got dragged off by the police.

One year later she entered graduate school, but then quit and left home to join the movement. It was natural, since there was only one road for survivors to follow, and she was one of those survivors. And she wanted to follow that road to jail, the road that thousands of other young people—survivors like her—

had taken. It was a time when conscience made being outside jail more tormenting than being in jail.

Before being dispatched to a factory, where she would inspire the laborers to organize, she had to go through indoctrination and training. It was the harshest study she'd had in her whole life. And of course she'd never experienced such privation. She and her fellow trainees got a meager daily ration of food and a huge daily ration of work. The cheap Ŭnhasu cigarettes were also rationed. She threw herself into her study. It was hard, but satisfying.

But that plain "easy to manage" hair style, the secondhand clothes, meatless diet, communal allowance, all that anxiety about the future—in fact, many comrades got arrested when they were found in one of these training groups—started to get to her. She started feeling anxious about the choice she had made to become a laborer, one of the proletariat. She had tasted the pleasures that material things can give. Still, she wouldn't let anyone see how difficult it was for her. Then winter came and found her wavering in her commitment, still wrestling with herself, with no idea what she should do.

And then one day he came to their group.

He came to replace the instructor who had been arrested. Of course, he was also on the wanted list and might also be dragged off at any time. He couldn't remember her, nor did he know she was his junior from the same university. But she remembered him. She still remembered that autumn day when, as he was being dragged off by the plainclothes police, he shouted "Survivors, onward!" To some that slogan was getting old, but the memory that it stirred still pierced her heart like a dagger.

"My name is Kim Chŏng-sŏk," was the simple introduction he gave his new students. Of course that wasn't his real name. She introduced herself with her alias too. And that was how they came to know each other. From time to time during breaks from study, he picked up his worn-out guitar and plucked out a song. The girls, weary from studying, gathered around him in a circle and sang along. Looking at him playing the guitar and singing, she remembered him from three years ago hanging out that library window. At that time he certainly didn't look like someone who would strum a guitar with such a gentle touch. When he fired up the others, when he was dragged away shouting—could this man with such a sonorous base voice be the same person? That first time he sang her heart ached at hearing his voice soft as a whistle as it wrapped her in its power, something a heroic rallying cry could never do.

She needed to talk about her problems in the movement. Whenever the situation permitted a few personal words, she discreetly approached him and got him to speak with her. It seemed that if he had a voice that could fire her up and a voice that could soothe her, he would have what it took to help her. A voice strong enough to rally hundreds of students, a voice soft enough to beguile her—he would surely be able to succor her in her confusion. He would encourage, he would comfort. He would temper her like steel. And that's what he did.

For security there was a strict taboo against talking about a comrade's past, but once when he was not around she learned more about him from the group's gossip.

"Remember that demonstration in our junior year? And that older sister that fell from the fourth floor of the library when she was running away from those thugs? Well, he's marrying her. That fall paralyzed her below the waist but you wouldn't believe how hard she's working now. They look so good together. And you know how they got started? They wrote letters to each other in jail, behind the guards' back. Isn't that the sweetest thing?!"

And a few days after that he showed up wearing a new sweater, vivid spring green, hand-knit. She envisioned the fingers of that woman in the wheelchair, the round ball of spring green yarn slowly, patiently getting smaller and smaller. Of course, when it came to knitting she also had confidence, just look at those smart hooded cardigan sweaters she'd done for her younger brothers. She didn't have the time for such things now, though. Moreover, it wouldn't be proper for her to knit something for him. She couldn't give him anything, and she realized for the first time that worse than not getting something from that one you love is not being able to give something to him. And with this realization, she then wondered why on earth she was thinking such silly thoughts.

She felt herself falling into a bottomless pit. She struggled with all her might to uproot this jealousy, this feeling of desolation. After all, she didn't quit graduate school and leave home just to be bombarded by such emotions. Wasn't she that dignified young woman who hadn't given in even when her father slapped her in the face and forbade her to leave home? Now, up before dawn to wash some rags in the icy water, she turned on the faucet full blast to flush away these thoughts. But what came out of that faucet was a torrent of absurd emotions that bewildered her. She broke down in tears.

The gossip had once told her, "You wouldn't believe how strict he is with himself. Even when his sweetheart is sick in bed, if it's time to go to one of his groups he just gets up and leaves her. Always smiling like that but as strong as steel inside. Never anything but correct and proper. So everyone calls him Chŏngsŏk. Get it? *Chŏng* for proper, and *sŏk* for place; everything in properly its place, principled. If it isn't, he's not going to have anything to do with it.

That was so. And while he always kept his dignity, he was never imperious. He always spoke in a lower octave, and even when he had something to emphasize, his voice never went over middle C. Except, of course, when he needed to for a song. If there was a perfect example of how they should behave to achieve their goals, he was it. From economics and philosophy to history and literature, from English and German to Japanese and Spanish . . . he'd mastered them all. The girls looked up to him and he inspired in them a passion for the movement. He was the guiding light for the group, especially for this woman who was withdrawing more and more into the shadows as she wore herself out from her all-out war with her feelings.

She never dared to hope for a special smile from him. But once he did smile at her. One night, in the middle of a seminar that had been going on for a few days and nights straight, he fainted. It was the flu. The girls helped him sit up, holding their emotions inside for fear of attracting attention and getting caught. His pale face frowned and he waved his hand lightly, dismissing it all as nothing serious. He listened to the rest of the seminar lying down.

Needless to say, the seminar that night didn't go too well. It was her turn to present, but from the time he collapsed she was too agitated to do anything but sneak looks at his pale face. When they adjourned the seminar at dawn one of the girls went out to the deserted streets to buy some medicine for him. And she went to the kitchen, because that day was her turn to cook. Then she remembered the leek root tea that her grandmother used to boil for her whenever she a bad flu. She cut off the white roots of the leeks that someone had brought from the market the day before, scrubbed them nice and clean, put them in a pot, poured in a cup of water, and boiled them. The student who had gone out to buy medicine came back empty-handed. Now she and her leek root tea were all that could help him.

She gave him the tea, excited at the thought that finally there was something she could give him. Even more exciting was that deliberate though brief look he gave her and the smile that followed. It was such a radiant smile that she didn't see, until he finished up the tea, the stares that all five students in the room fixed on her. She took the empty bowl that he handed her and hurried into the kitchen, trying to calm herself. Those stares were filled with suspicion. Those days there was already an occasional complaint that she was thinking of herself before the group. Some time before, for instance, when a student was sick in bed, she had been slow to go out in the middle of the night to get her some medicine. And she didn't even think of the leeks that they always had in the kitchen.

Now she was busying herself in the kitchen when another trainee, the oldest in the group, came in. The trainee looked straight at her and said in a composed voice,

"Nice going. Looks like Chŏng-sŏk will be feeling better soon. Now, if you could spread some of that comradely devotion around to the rest of the group . . . "

In reply, she forced her trembling lips into a smile that was supposed to say that, of course, she wouldn't have it any other way. But both she and the other student knew differently.

Then the punishment started. Maybe not actual punishment—no, it was more like segregation. Like when a couple of the trainees got to go out to accept delivery of some books from another group, she was excluded, because sometimes he was the one who delivered them. Her day was arranged for her in a way that made it impossible for her to see him, except for when the five other students were around. And he stopped giving her compliments about her "outstanding imagination" or that she "led that seminar well," and the like. When the other five girls were sleeping, she lay awake, staring at the wall. And she thought again, "What on earth are you trying to do? Why are you letting your emotions distract everybody when we should be putting everything into training for our mission? Sooner or later we're going to get our assignment, and we've got to be ready. Didn't everybody swear to give up love when they came here? Every girl here has someone she longs to be with, but she's holding back her tears because she's dedicated herself to the slim hope that she might be able to change history. But you . . ."

With this thought she quietly accepted the group's treatment. When the next comrade caught the flu she went out herself to get leeks and gave her the leek root tea. The others smiled at her, but that night, she thought to herself, "Phony. Did you really do it for her . . . ?"

Over the next few months, little by little, the group eased up on her. He still avoided speaking to her, but when their eyes met for a very brief moment she could feel something special in that look. That brief but lasting moment was one that only people in love could feel. But this scared her: Soon they would be working in the factory. She had to avoid causing any problems. And just as soon, she wondered, "Am I just dreaming?" Was it really something there when their eyes joined—in that way his pupils darkened and expanded and came closer and closer toward her? But just as soon, she lowered her eyes back to *Das Kapital,* the most difficult of all subjects, and tried to lose herself in it.

One day he came in with a beaming smile on his face. He announced he had come across some money and was going to treat the group to a nice meal. For the last few months they had been subsisting on vegetables and cheap fishcake; they screamed in excitement, and the house sang with a jubilant mood. Soon fatty slices of pork were broiling and a few bottles of soju appeared. For the first time in a long time they got out their worn-out guitar and talked about things not related to the cause.

It was the first time she had ever seen him drink. In the traditional way, he gave one of the girls a bowl, filled it with soju, she handed it back to him, and he did the same in turn for every girl sitting in the circle. He listened closely to the burdens that each girl was struggling with in this difficult and dangerous life, giving each his full attention. Though he was a man of few words, on that day he said some very funny things, often breaking up these girls who had been living such a life of difficulty and stress. She also had a lot of good laughs for the first time in a long time, and she was happy. It was all she needed. Here were people with the same goals, who could definitely change history together, and here in their midst was a man who lived a glorious and exemplary life every day.

The night deepened, and one by one the students, who weren't big drinkers, went back to their room to sleep. It must have been past three in the morning when she suddenly realized that they were the only ones there in the main room. Their eyes met, and neither he nor she let go.

Keeping his gaze on her, he asked, "I'm supposed to meet somebody on Chongno tomorrow, but I'm afraid I won't be able to make it. Would you go there for me and tell him I'll contact him later?" Her eyes lit up with joy. She hadn't been able to take a trip downtown for almost a month. This meant that she had served her sentence. He took out a piece of paper and carefully drew a map to guide her to the tearoom. She moved close to him and leaned forward to get a better look, and her lowered head brushed his forehead. "Somebody will probably call you there."

She gazed at him like a devoted student attending to every word. Then he suddenly reached out and grabbed her arm and pulled her to him. But wasn't it she that had already made the first move? In their awkward embrace she thought to herself, "Oh boy, now I've gone and done it."

She buried her head in his spring green sweater, feeling the heat of his body. But bliss wasn't the only emotion that she felt. The sweater they said the woman in the wheelchair knitted—she felt his hand slowly coming to her back—was it okay to be doing this? Then, gently, he held her away and took her face in both of his hands. He gazed into her eyes for a long time.

It was about that time that she broke into tears. "I'm sorry. In fact . . . actually . . . I think I'm in love with you."

He hugged her again, this time stronger. He said, "I've known that all along . . . "

She nuzzled her tear-bathed face in his shoulder. That spring green sweater, his woman in the wheelchair . . . But neither he nor she drew apart from the other. How long did they stay in that embrace? Finally, though, she felt his shoulder twitch and stiffen. He slowly pushed her off, this time not looking at her, got up, and quietly left the house. She had no idea where he could be going. Without stopping to think, she followed him outside. He was standing in the dark, both hands stuck in his pockets.

"I'm sorry . . . I was trying to avoid this . . . " he said.

She shook her head and said, "Meet me just one more time. Not with the group. I just want to see you. Ten o'clock tomorrow morning at the tearoom out in front."

He stood there looking at her, chewing his lip. Had he heard her?

She left him in the dark and came back to the house. In that room with the lights off she quietly lay down, covered herself with her blanket, and turned to the wall as always. The oldest one, still awake, let out a long sigh . . .

Two cups of coffee were brought to this table that separated the man and the woman.

"Must have had one too many last night. You and me both . . . "

"I could commit my life to this."

A rueful smile, and he lowered his eyes. He offered her a cigarette. She took it from him.

"Go on, say it, whatever . . ." he said.

He was trying to avoid eye contact with her, but their eyes drew each other's like a magnet. She sat there stiffly with her hand at her breast, feeling her heart bleeding drop by drop. He offered her a light. She accepted it demurely.

"Coward."

Dragging himself from his thoughts, he nodded.

"It wasn't the alcohol."

This time he didn't nod.

She stared at him, biting her fist like she did in the fall a few years ago when she saw him dangling from the library window and then finally get dragged off by the police. She looked at his spring green sweater under his navy blue plaid half coat with the artificial wool trim. He and his woman in the wheelchair had been together a long time. . . . They had been together in that demonstration when she got paralyzed, they had nurtured their love as comrades in jail, secretly exchanging letters. And now she was still knitting him things . . . Well, I can knit a pretty good sweater myself. Yes, but you can't knit it for him . . . The last time now. It hit hard. She had been feeling that, even though it was the last time, just being together would be enough. No, it wasn't enough. This was it. This was the last time, it didn't matter who was ending it.

She had to find out. She dropped the fist that she had been pressing to her lips to suppress her tears. She wanted to know the meaning of that look he had sometimes given her, wanted to know what was in those pupils that expanded as they gathered her in.

"Give me just one thing then. Your real name. I won't ask for any more." If he were willing to break the rules for her, then he must . . .

" . . . Kim. Chŏng. Sŏk," he finally said, deliberately. Tears of resentment welled in her eyes.

"What's the use of knowing my real name? I'm just the guy

you know as Kim Chŏng-sŏk. Our job is to put everything we've got into doing our duty—there's no room for anything else. Now, there's no reason to meet each other like this again. But if we serve the cause heart and soul we *will* be meeting each other. . . . Do you understand what I'm telling you?"

She shook her head. "It's not the party line I need to hear now. All I want is to know your name, and not just your party name . . . "

Before she even finished his eyes flashed red. But he didn't take his eyes off her. He tenaciously held her eyes as if he were resolved to convey a certain truth through them that couldn't be conveyed with the lips. She returned his gaze, as if she intended to soak up like a sponge everything that he could not utter.

"I'm wrong. I'm sorry," she said. And they left the tearoom.

He started walking toward the bus stop. Then the realization that this was the last time came to her again. She forced herself to call him once more. He turned and looked back. There they stood, a few steps apart.

"I'll go to that tearoom downtown and tell him you can't come," she said, remembering the promise she had made before they embraced.

He rubbed his face with his bony fingers and stood there quietly for a while, then said, "No, that's not necessary. Go on back now—everyone will be waiting. We should be thinking of them."

He turned and started walking again. She knew that she shouldn't grab him, but this time she called his name in an even louder voice, that name Chŏng-sŏk that he persisted to the end in calling himself. He kept walking, faster now, his shoulders hunched. Then he broke into a run, and hopped on the bus that had just come along. The bus coughed its white exhaust into the winter air. And that was the last time she saw him.

She returned to the group. They welcomed her with icy

stares, this woman that had disappeared without a word. She sat facing them, returning their stares. A heavy silence descended.

"Now, don't you think what you did was childish?" the short-tempered one scolded. "What were you thinking?" No one said anything more and the morning passed in that frigid atmosphere.

A few days later a new senior in the movement arrived to teach the group. He told them simply that the person they called Kim Chŏng-sŏk could no longer teach the group because of his personal situation, and he opened his book. The girls all stared at her in unison. Her eyes were fixed on her book, her body trembling. He didn't have to go this far. She wasn't going to ask him to take her into his arms, she wasn't going to tell him that she loved him fearlessly, she wasn't going to disappear again from study period. It was all right if he didn't tell her his name.

She completed training, but wasn't dispatched with the other girls. On the day each went to her assigned factory and joined the ranks of labor, she had to go to another house, where there was a group of new girls. They told her that she had to take the course again. But she didn't really concentrate on her study. One day she announced that she was going out to buy fixings for supper, left the house, and didn't come back.

She returned home like the prodigal child, and a few days later she went to her aunt's in Kangnŭng. She wandered the beach all day and only at night did she go back to her aunt's to sleep. On the beach even during the winter, people strolled in pairs, in groups . . . She was the only one walking that beach by herself.

One day she had walked till she was exhausted, then collapsed on the sand. She wanted to talk, anybody would do. So she talked to herself. She mumbled, "Once I said I could commit myself to the cause. Yes, I did say that, and I was able to commit my whole life. It was my daily life I couldn't commit. Dedicating my every trivial day was harder than dedicating my whole life. My future, my youth . . . your youth, that's your future. But every day? That goes on and on till who knows when. Dying for the cause would have been easier . . . But would it? Could I really . . . ?"

A young man approached her. He jumped right into his introduction: graduate student from Seoul, here to get some fresh air. If he hadn't gone and claimed to be from her school she might have believed him.

The two drank together on the beach. He bought a dish of sashimi and they had soju with it. Before long he tentatively took her hand in his, and when she didn't resist he started pulling her off to an inn. She followed, like a zombie. Inside, he pulled her to him even before they turned out the light. She buried her face in his shoulder. And she remembered that spring green sweater. She pushed violently away from him, like some wounded animal, but the bewildered man started pulling her back. She grabbed her coat and put it on. He slapped her cheek a couple times. Rubbing her hot cheek, she said, "I'm sorry. I just—well, I was going to do myself in—and I thought spending the night with a strange man wouldn't matter if I was going to be dead the next day. But now I've got to live. So I want to go now. Please let me go." He looked at her for a couple seconds, dumbfounded, then started hurling curses at her. She ran out. When she got to the beach, she slowed, and started walking. To her aunt's house. It was cold and she tightened the scarf she had thrown on. The sound of the waves showing their white teeth splashed in her ears. She walked, wiping her tears.

A twenty-four-year-old woman loved a twenty-five-year-old guy. What—something wrong with that? No, normal as can be. Wrong? Okay, then, how's this: enjoying some meat after months of fishcake? Is that wrong too? And how about wanting to wear a pretty skirt instead of a shabby parka and pants with bulging knees? Or when you're with people on the wanted list, shaking in fear that you'll get dragged off and be tortured, raped—are you such a coward if you're afraid? How on earth can any of this be so bad? Or when I asked you to tell me your real name once, not that phony name, not your organization name, but your real name . . . How on earth, how in heaven could that be such a crime? . . . I already knew your real name. In fact, I've known since that day you were hanging out of the library building and got dragged off.

She should have told him that. Stupid. Really stupid—should have challenged him. Then she realized her mistake. She reversed herself. From out of nowhere came this vision of herself telling that phony student that wanted to sleep with her: But there are standards, standards you have to keep. It may seem silly in your eyes, you might think we're obsessed with our strict rules . . . but they're the only weapon we've got. Without those standards, how can we—no money, no power, hounded like we are—what else do we have to confront this, this force—with its roots dug down so deep in the past—this force that's distorted everything, the truth, all our values. . . . Who dares criticize the one who takes the right path, even at the cost of abandoning any hope for real love?

At the end of that winter she returned to her home, and went back to graduate school, which a few months ago her conscience had made her regard as more odious than going to jail. In 1987 she saw his name—his real name—on a list of those who had been given amnesty. In grad school she kept herself awake through sleepy seminars, visited the homes of her teachers on lunar new year's day and offered the new year's bow, finished her classes, wrote her master's dissertation, got her master's degree, and enrolled in the doctorate course. During those years the first cracks in the wall of the Eastern Bloc appeared, along with the occasional account of one or another former comrade getting found out and hauled off to jail. She saw the Soviet Union declare its own dissolution, and she heard that Chŏng-sŏk was suffering from second-stage tuberculosis and had gone down to his hometown to convalesce.

It was his junior in the organization, just released from jail, who told her this. He had set up a milk distributor's shop in the neighborhood. His wife, now the size of a small mountain in her late pregnancy, was there to help while away the hours that she had no desire to spend on her studies. They talked about life as they sipped on carton after carton of milk.

One day his junior asked her, "Chŏng-hwa, you didn't happen to know a guy by the name of Chŏng-sŏk, by any chance?" She choked on the milk she was sipping. "What . . . ? Well anyway, after he got off the wanted list—that was back in '87—he dropped by. He mentioned once that he saw you on the street right out in front here and asked about you, and I kind of joked you were one of my neighborhood girls. Told him you liked to drop by now and then. So after that he started coming by pretty often . . . er wait, come to think of it, it's strange you never ran into each other while he was here. Anyway, once my wife and I went out to a movie and had a drink and came back after midnight, and we found him sitting in front of our shop, which was all closed up, of course. He was drunk. Smashed. And he says, 'Just followed my footsteps from Chongno to here.' Pitiful. Tuberculosis, the organization in shambles . . . I'd been telling him over and over to stop drinking like that but he never listened. Well, eventually he had to go to his hometown because he couldn't take care of himself anymore. I heard his cousin was running some golf shop, and Chŏng-sŏk was going to help him out there . . . His family's always been poor . . . and now they say his father's passed away . . . " He paused and stared into the empty air. "That Chŏng-sŏk, he was really something. But it's just the clever ones that survived."

She couldn't picture him working in a golf shop. Maybe because she'd never been in one. A customer drives up in his posh sedan, saunters in and selects a few golf balls, tests a couple clubs . . . she couldn't imagine the expression that would appear on the former dissident's face as he regarded this kind of person.

But the image of him sitting on the sidewalk in front of that shuttered shop in the middle of the night, dawn still far off—this image was quite vivid. Why this image, though, more than all those others . . . ?

And now the pages of the calendar in my head flip me forward to 1992.

The young woman in her any-old-parka and pants with bulging knees is still there at the light, and we're still facing each other across the street. I'm still watching that red light across the street in the midst of the angry din and the noxious smell of exhaust from those lined-up cars. This woman in my memories would think no matter how long it took, no matter how hard she shivered in the winter's dusk, soon the light will turn green and make all the cars stop and let her cross safely from her side of the street to my side. But that same woman these days doesn't believe in anything. The cause had died, and the establishment had won. The green light might never come and that woman across the street will have to stand there forever.

I give up on crossing. After all, I've got nowhere really to go. The trembling branches on those trees have already lost their verdant foliage of spring and summer. Will the leaves return to these trees when spring comes again? Who knows? Will spring itself even come? I don't know. Like my prehistoric ancestor dreading what the night will bring and that it may not bring the morning.

Anyway. He . . . is . . . getting . . . married.

With the woman who decided to place her fate in the hands of gravity rather than the plainclothesmen chasing her . . . With that woman who chose to fall without wings, who, ever since that day, could not stand on her own two feet . . . Still knitting for him?

"Old Chŏng-sŏk, he was one really fine fellow. Did he ever get over his TB? Well, the two of them are both getting on in years . . . That old boy, wasn't it in 1987—before he got taken off the wanted list—saying something about breaking up with her . . . ? But now he ends up marrying her . . . How about you, Chŏng-hwa, you're going to be there of course? And by the way, isn't it about time you got married?" He handed me his name card with gold-leaf print that announced "Director, Planning" for a conglomerate. And I told him that I had finished my dissertation on "Socialist Realism in the Fiction of the 1930s"—used what I learned in the movement—and was going to get a doctorate with that dissertation and had already been offered a full-time instructor's position in the university.

Nobody showed any surprise at how we had all changed, these comrades of the old days gathered there at that publishing company sheepishly exchanging our name cards and talking about the era that dinosaurs roamed the earth. "So the mammoths crash to the ground, and they become encased in ice. And even after tens of thousands of years they're still perfectly preserved—frozen blue—sharp round ivory tusks, eyes fixed on empty space, everything still the same, even their frozen red blood. And the poachers find the mammoth and take the ivory—just the ivory, because ivory is money—and sell it. So only the mammoth's eyes fixed on empty space and its frozen red blood stay underground forever. Without their valuable ivory

. . ." An older one who had spent thirteen years in jail overheard that and burst out laughing. "No, let me finish . . ."

The senior stood up, getting ready to leave. This one, a dozen years our senior in the dissident movement, felt uncomfortable meeting with us. Once we grabbed him when he wanted to leave, and he sheepishly smiled and said, "I'm supposed to be your senior and here I'm letting you treat me. I should be treating you. But look at me—I'm broke. Please forgive me."

I stood there watching him leave. His back was already bent.

I walk slowly, trying to find that tearoom from 1986. That tearoom in the narrow alley that was twenty paces away from the end of Ch'ang-gyŏng Palace's stone wall. Now it's a karaoke room, with a crude neon sign throbbing purple and yellow.

I stand there speechless. Not because the tearoom has become a karaoke room—that happens so often these days it no longer hurts that much. What stops me are the lights I remember, very different from neon lights. The one that got TB and became an employee at a golf shop; the woman who knit for that light, spending her life in a wheelchair; one who did jail time for the cause, running a milk distributor's shop now; a glorious warrior for democracy, juniors watching this stooped figure with no money to buy them dinner . . . And we gather and all we can do is exchange name cards with titles in glittery gold and talk about mammoths preserved forever. I can see in front of me the fixed gaze of the mammoth stuck in ice. I can see the red blood, once warm but now frozen, and it seems I hear that voice. "But it's just the clever ones that survived."

I look up at early winter's darkening sky. Still waiting here at winter's door.

THE FACE

O Chŏng-hŭi

(1999)

The kite mounted the updraft, danced with it a bit, then took off high into the sky. Its line pulled so taut the boy worried it would snap. He didn't want to lose this kite. He struggled with the reel to pull the kite back, but it was no use. Instead, the boy found himself being dragged by some scary force that pulled him scrambling along after that kite soaring off further and further. His uncle must have put his magic in it when he painted those dragons on it, with the magic pearl in their mouths. You watch now, boy—this kite's going to ride the skies till there's no sky left, free as a bird. Just like I'm going to one day.

Uncle had quite a reputation for being good with his hands. Anything you can see or touch he could make just as good, and people said he could ply his brush or knife as easy as you can snap a finger. The family said he was good with his hands because he was of low birth. He was born of a concubine.

The boy was the only one in the neighborhood who owned a kite with both a blue and a gold dragon on it. And no other kid could ever cut the line that his uncle had coated with that ground glass-and-glue concoction.

The boy raced with his kite across a plain howling with a fierce wind that pushed him along at his back, his feet hardly touching the ground. It pushed him over a low rise, and down there he saw kites crashed in the middle of the frozen paddies, kites hanging torn and dirty in the skeletal branches of trees.

Any boy knows his kite like he knows his own kin, and can

identify his kite wherever it falls. But once its line has broken and flown off, he'll give up on it. And he'll surely give up on that kite when the line snaps and it wings its way out of his village—keep on chasing it and you're likely to end up lost. No matter how much hard work and devotion go into making that kite, once the line breaks it's all over. Any boy knows that a kite lost to the wind never returns, and no matter how hard the kite struggles to stay up there, in the end, sooner or later, it will fall and finish its life in a sorry pile of torn paper. Even if one day later he happens upon his lost kite, it's no longer that kite he launched and it has nothing to do with him.

How far had he come already? He'd been looking up into the sky as he ran, and now when he finally came to a stop he found himself standing in the middle of a vast crimson mirror, a solidly frozen reservoir, glowing disk in the rays of the setting sun. The darkening silhouette of that mountain ridge, that distant village sinking in the purple twilight–where was he? In this anxious instant he let the last of his line spin off the reel; the kite became a distant spot and was soon gone from his sight. It was then that he discovered that face in the ice. A white face with black hair snaking out in all directions peered up at him through the clear ice. It looked startled at seeing him, eyes and mouth frozen wide open, as if fixed in its shock of horror at this strange world it had fallen into. Distant voices rode the wind from across the empty fields, mothers calling home children too absorbed in what they were doing to see it was getting dark.

Something is nudging him awake. His wife is bending over him, putting her arms around his shoulders to lift him. He stares, startled, at this close, big face, this face he's known for fifty years.

Another dream? she responds casually to his look of surprise, in a coarse voice, the husky rasp of a goose. He remembers she started talking a lot less when she injured her vocal chords, but now that he's lost his speech she doesn't hold back anymore. And he can't talk so she talks louder. Or it could be she's so loud because she's losing her hearing.

He's reassured by the familiar sound of her labored breathing and her sour breath. Good, it was only a dream. Those disturbing things, whatever they are, that are creeping more and more now through the cracks between sleep and dream and memory, he prefers to regard them simply as dreams, nothing more.

But how did he finally find his way home from that strange village? All he knows is that from the instant he saw that face he lost the ability to speak, through the whole spring till the end of the summer.

His wife's way of lifting him says oh my, how heavy. Now and then she complains it's beyond her how he can be getting heavier and heavier the more he wastes away to nothing. It's because she's getting fat. And isn't it just as hard for him every time she jostles him or her heavy body bumps against him when she turns him over or sits him up?

Through the window he sees the vapor trail a jet has left in the sky. Maybe the wind he heard in his dream was just the sound of that plane overhead. Their house is in the airport's flight path, and since it isn't that far away they hear countless takeoffs and landings every day. *I'm sure this house is collapsing bit by bit; that noise shakes the house and it's causing cracks.* Whenever he hears that he silently replies that the house is wearing out because *they* are. . . . *And you remember when they wanted to knock down the house next door, the one that the owner built with his own hands, just like this house, all they had to do for the whole roof to fall in was give it a few whacks with a sledge hammer? How could that place that people occupied for decades have become so feeble?* Well, maybe she's right; might not be all that wrong after all to say it's getting bruised and battered from the noise of those planes, who knows? In the few moments he's been watching, the sharp vapor highway has blurred, and now it's gone.

Every day as they get deeper into fall the rays of the sun are creeping a hand's span deeper into this room with its southern exposure.

With a grunt his wife sits him up against the wall, props him up straight with a thick cushion on each side, and, frowning at the odor in the room, opens the window. *My, that smell—something rotting. Can't figure out where it could be coming from. . . . You can't smell it? I guess the nose of a man who never leaves his room would have to go bad sooner or later.*

She's been going on about that odor for a few days now. When the breath of fresh air comes in through the window he realizes he's been smelling it all along. That funny sour smell. Might be some rotten fish or meat she bought and left in some out-of-the-way place and forgot about, or some ferocious mold that's grown on snacks she's left around and hasn't thrown away. Always eating, always forgetting everything. There are even times she'll spend a few hours getting home because she got lost in the labyrinth of the neighborhood market she goes to all the time. Their bedroom too is littered with the fruits and snacks she's munching on all the time and forgets to put away. Now and then he'll open his eyes in the middle of the night to see her sitting there by herself in the harshness of that florescent light that keeps getting dimmer and dimmer all the time, all absorbed in crunching away on puffed corn or peeling a raw radish or the like. That rotund body all by itself there, so alone. Sad. Says all those rats are scuttling about behind those walls because the house is decaying. No, it's turning into this dump because she can't stop eating. And she's absentminded.

Here she comes with his medicine. One is to lower blood pressure, the other is to loosen up his bowels. He stares blankly at these little white pills with the same blank look he'd give a cryptograph. Supposed to regulate the flow of blood and make his intestines work better, but . . . She gestures come on and open up, deposits them on his tongue, then puts a glass of water to his mouth. Some water runs out of the paralyzed right side, down his chin and onto his collar. Lying there like a knocked-over cup.

She leans him back and starts getting ready to go out. For quite a while after she got that phone call she'd been walking around in a daze. *And all along we were thinking she was dead. Kyŏng-ja, I mean. You remember—of course you do, with that dark skin and we called her Blackie—well, she phoned. She's alive! How she found our phone number, though . . . Blind now—so she can't leave the house—says she wants to see me once more before she dies. The way we'd all been thinking she died so long ago. Felt like I was talking with a ghost.*

She's already said this a few times. Remember Kyŏng-ja? Of course, why not? Kyŏng-ja, the one she swore sisterhood with, slightly older. The one they said died in the big fire in that International Market in Pusan after the war, when she was selling pilfered relief goods. The two girls made their oath before he and his wife married. When this Kyŏng-ja was young she made you think of some Spanish woman with her swarthy face and heavy eyebrows and thick bones. The vivid greenish-black mark like an old tattoo from when they eternalized their oath in their skin was still there on his wife's forearm, and still quite noticeable.

Kyŏng-ja got her on the phone, then switched the phone to her niece to give instructions on how to get to her place. The wife wrote down every detail, and now she's on her way. Going out. Hardly ever leaves the house. She used to go once a month to her primary school alumni meeting, but that ended several years ago. *A few dead, a few sick in bed, got so that hardly any of them showed up anymore—we're too old to hear so much upsetting news, so we just stopped meeting.* Hardly anyone even phones anymore. Every once in a while she'll be talking about one of these old friends and then *But she's probably dead now,* she'll end with a sigh.

She opens the wardrobe's door wide, letting out a faint smell of mothballs and musty old clothes. *These old rags—what am I going to do with them all?* After rummaging a while she pulls out one of his suits and turns to him. The instant he sees it a strong emotion assails him. That outfit carries the memory of the last time he wore it. They still have these old clothes because who would've thought then that he wouldn't be able to wear them again, and since then there's been no special reason to throw them out they've finally just forgot about them, leaving them there to slowly decay and disintegrate all by themselves.

If he could get a better look at it, it would have bulging elbows and baggy knees his habits had formed over a long time, and probably the creases and a faint spot or two from the last time he wore it. A wave of sadness sweeps through him. Since she threw out nothing, no matter what, his shoes are probably in the shoe cabinet at the front door, the heels molded to his habitual walk and worn away almost to nothing on the insides, and the top bunched up and wrinkled. These things he wore could tell a person how he lived.

She has turned from the open wardrobe and is looking out the window. Must be checking the weather to decide what to wear. He looks past her rounded, thick shoulder to the tree in the corner of the yard. That tree fills more than half the sky. It was already old when they moved into this house but is still producing those berries the size of Indian beans; they appear every autumn after the tree sheds its leaves and stay through the winter. He still doesn't know what they call this tree . . . Leaves so still, must be a fine autumn day out there.

She pulls out the chartreuse *hanbok* he remembers she wore for someone's wedding, holds it up against her, sighs, wraps it up again and puts it back in the wardrobe. She takes out a pair of black pants and a brown jacket, puts them back. Then she takes out a long gray pleated skirt and a purple blouse and a white sweater, and starts changing into them.

Before taking off the old house skirt she drops her panties to her ankles, kicks them over toward the corner. She takes off her skirt, puts on new panties, her thigh-length underwear, then white cotton socks. She's not shy about dressing in front of him, going about it like that as if no one were there to see her. Heavy pouches of doughy flesh at her armpits, curiously large waist and buttocks, sagging folds of flesh at her thighs—the vestiges of time, shaped by the daily labor and production of every day of her fifty years of marriage and all those things that slowly, steadfastly worked on her from the day she was born.

As she dresses she looks at the open door to their room, and suddenly utters a threatening *Shoo!* A shaggy black dog is looking into the room. The startled dog scampers a few steps off, but soon comes back, not realizing it's showing in the mirror. She stamps her feet and curses. Its tail slips between its legs and it disappears. He looks out the door. In the film of dust on the floor he sees the tangle of his wife's and the dog's footprints. Fumbling with her poky hands to tie the ties on her blouse, she's oblivious now to the dog, but he sees it hiding there behind the door, looking in through the crack between the door and the wall.

He summons all his strength to extend that one part of him that isn't paralyzed, lifts his hand, points and complains, "The—dog—behind—the—door." But these words are just unintelligible grunts to her, and she turns to him, and says, like she's trying to placate a whining child, *Someone we thought all along was dead is alive all of a sudden. I can't pretend I don't know. I'll be back soon.*

Once on a TV talent show he saw someone twirling himself in the air on one hand. Turn that TV upside down and you could even think he was twirling the world. But all this bedridden man can do with this one living hand is uselessly wave it in frustration and pique, or press the buttons on the TV's remote control, or shake the bell to call his wife when he's done with the bedpan. When she first put the bell in his hand and told him to ring it if he needed anything he hit her on the forehead with it and drew blood. Another time, when she had removed the bedpan and was putting on a new diaper, he threw the bedpan with its contents at her. Because he hated her? Or was it because life had betrayed him, because of his impotent resentment at an existence in which he is supposed to accept the fact that he can speak no more, move no more?

A few days ago his wife put her finger to her lips and told him, in a hushed voice, that a dog had come into their house. *I left the door open when I went out for just a second to the shop down the street. I come back and a dog is there, right inside our house. Never seen him before. Black all over, standing there staring me in the eye. Gave me goose bumps! So I chased him out, closed the door, and then a good while later I thought to myself he must be gone now, so I open the door again—and there he is. Been sitting there all that time, not moving a muscle. And then he came right on in as if he owned the place. What on earth could it have meant? They say you'll be sorry if you go driving out any living creature that's come into your house, and I guess he'll go when he's good and ready.*

It isn't only for her superstitious fear that she's let the dog stay. From time to time he can hear her talking with this Blackie, as she calls him. Here, try this, or stop chewing on that shoe, or she'll even whine about her troubles one after another, feet hurt, back hurts, can't keep anything straight anymore, looks like I'm not long for this world anymore, all in that cloying undertone. But then just the day before yesterday she said, with a face full of dark foreboding, *just going to have to send that dog away the way he keeps on digging holes in front of the porch, and that ominous howling now and then. You remember don't you what they say when the fam-*

ily dog starts digging in the yard or howls, that there's going to be a death in the family?

Finished putting her clothes on now, she sits at the dressing table to comb her hair, then applies a light dusting of powder and a bit of rouge. She's always said the older you get the more you need to be touching up. That new face in the mirror with its hidden wrinkles and age spots looks at him. It sparks a memory of that feeling he used to have when they were young and now and then somebody would see them standing there together and greet them as Mr. and Mrs. Kim, that peculiar forlorn feeling at realizing that he would be spending the rest of his life with this person. That emotion had nothing to do with happiness or unhappiness or disappointment, nothing to do with this woman in the mirror. He'd have felt the same no matter who he was going to share the rest of his life with. Maybe this sense of emptiness came from looking back at the past that he could never return to, or ahead at the future he was locked into, or just the whole business of being human.

I'll be back before dark. Watch TV if you get bored. She puts the remote control where he can reach it, and goes. She remembers to leave the door open a bit, knowing that he's afraid of being in a closed room, that he fears the dark.

His eyes follow the head of frizzy ball of white hair, the gray skirt and white sweater out the door. He often has the premonition he's feeling now, that this image of his wife will stay there in his mind's eye, that he'll never forget this inconsequential, very ordinary figure before him today, her sound and her smell. But now it strikes him—she's a lot shorter than he remembers.

His ears track the wife he can't see now. *You good-for-nothing mutt, digging holes again!* Her sharp outburst makes the dog yelp as if it's been kicked in the ribs.

The closing front door, then a few steps on the flagstone in the yard, then the front gate. When he hears the front gate click shut he feels something close inside him.

Don't go.

He tries with all his might to form the words, but before he can get them up out of his throat the consonants and vowels entangle themselves and the whole thing falls to pieces.

The rays of the setting sun, which had reached the top of his blanket, have retreated and are now playing softly at the top of the dressing table mirror and the wall above that. His eyes shift from one familiar item to another, from the clothes she's left on the floor by her sleeping mat at the other end of the room, to the hollow her head has formed in the white napping pillow beside the clothes, to her blue sleeve caught in the wardrobe's door, to the wall clock telling three-thirty, and settle on the landscape painting done in black ink, next to the clock.

A path, white—is it a bright moonlit night? Or is it snow? A dark grove in one corner. The path stretches on up, narrowing itself out as it climbs, probably to show that those two halfway up the path are on a long trip.

Twenty years ago, after he'd quit his job and he and a couple colleagues set up a small company, someone came from the Association for Rehabilitation of the Handicapped and wangled him into buying this painting. The visitor said it was the work of a deaf mute. He could have bought a painting of a cascading waterfall, or a copy of "Winter Scene," with that pine tree in it that expressed a message of steadfast integrity through a long life of hardship and travail. But he ended up buying the one hanging here on the wall because its abiding sense of seclusion had captured his heart. What also attracted him to this painting was the fact that it was painted by someone living in quiet solitude, closed off from the noise of life.

Where would those travelers be going? Carrying nothing on their backs, no poles even for fishing, they seem to be saying that life is not something that you live, just something you pass through, like this. When Grandfather died, the family wouldn't allow Uncle to participate in the family's mourning because he was Grandfather's love-child; so one day that traveling mask dance troupe came, and a few days later Uncle was with them when they left. Gone, just like that. No one in his family, none of his neighbors, has ever seen or heard about Uncle since then. Probably passed on long ago.

Footsteps padding on the floor, and then that black dog sticks its head in through the open door. It sizes up the situation, decides it's safe, then walks in with a confident gait, glancing casually at the man on the sleeping mat gesturing angrily at it to get back out. Wife apparently forgot to close the side door.

The dog, feeling comfortable enough and in no hurry about anything, saunters around the room. When it comes upon her clothes it digs its nose in deep and sniffs greedily.

Probably on the subway now. Said it's two transfers, then the neighborhood bus for just one stop and Kyŏng-ja's apartment is right there—wouldn't be difficult to find. He sees his wife, this old woman in her gray pleated skirt and white sweater, on her way to meet her sworn sister, forty years now after hearing she died. Walking down that neighborhood lane to the subway, that old lane that passes the cleaner's and the butcher's and the beauty parlor, and the drugstore he always stopped at late at night on the way home for something to fend off a hangover after he's had a few drinks. The little girl there with the blue lips looking at the baby green turtles in her palm, asking *Mama, why did you make me born*? Must be a young lady by now. Her mother, the young pharmacist, told him quite matter-of-factly *She's a blue baby, can't even go to school her heart's so bad.* On his way home one night he bought her a cheap teddy bear and promised next time he would bring her the doll house that his daughter had used when she was her age. But he never kept that promise. One morning before he could give her the doll house, while he was brushing his teeth, that blood vessel in his brain burst.

The lengthening rays of the sun are thinning. The clock sounds clearer, deeper. It's quiet. Must have dozed off again. He hears a persistent scratching, busy scurrying back and forth. The dog is scrambling round the wardrobe in a frenzy, sticking its snout in at the bottom and clawing away there with paws stretched wide open. Then it's around back, trying to squeeze its way in between the wardrobe and the wall. Seems he's trying to get something out of there.

Those leaves, as motionless as objects in a still painting, are stirring now. Must be the wind, it's still too early in the day for the birds to be back. These birds, which don't build nests, come to rest in this tree at twilight, and at dawn on a summer's day he can see a big flock of them flying off the tree, ruffling its luxuriant foliage, darkening the sky. They were vulnerable. At night, alley cats would climb the branches and kill the sleeping birds. Or a storm—when he was well he used to go out and tend the early morning garden, getting his cuffs wet with dew, and if there had been a storm the night before he might come upon a dead bird looking like some rotted fallen fruit, and throw it on the weed pile.

Finally the dog has succeeded in getting its head into the space between the wardrobe and wall, then soon pulls back out, face now dusted white, holding something in its mouth. He squints to make out what it is, imagines something like a rolled up pair of socks.

The dog drops his find in the middle of the room and sniffs it thoroughly, then picks it up again and tosses it like a ball. He pounces on it, then tosses it again. Fancies himself the consummate hunter. Every time the soft thing lands it lets out a dull thud. It ends up on the floor right next to the man's face and he gasps when he sees what it is. A rat. The dog hears the man, and picks up the rat and trots off a few steps, then turns back around. The man fumbles for the remote control and throws it at the dog, but the dog dodges it. Then he hunkers down in the middle of the room and starts chewing away at the rat. Soon he's settled down, fully absorbed in dismembering it. Now they'll be rid of that sour smell in the room.

Finished eating the rat, the dog languidly stretches all four limbs and prostrates itself in the thinning sunlight. Warmed by the sun on its back, it loses all interest and concern with the rest of the world. Each time a plane comes by overhead its ears twitch and it gets up almost half-way, then just drops back down and falls back to sleep. Watchful but at the same time indifferent, almost aloof, this dog seems very old and wise.

Looks like it's having a bad dream. From time to time its body quivers and it issues a startled yelp or an anguished moan. What nightmare could be haunting that thing's gray matter? In a bad dream you're imprisoned in an airtight glass case, or in ice, where your cries have no voice. Pitiful thing it is, a creature having a bad dream.

His thoughts return to that instant he lost his speech. A shocking wave of nausea thrust up his throat and his whole being rebelled. He remembers the vertigo spinning him like a top when that inexorable force rushed up from his depths. Then he saw again in the vast, fathomless abyss inside him that face captured in ice. His speech was taken from him when he saw this face like an infant unable to articulate the secrets of the world it has left.

It's getting dark outside. As the sunlight lingering in the windows retreats, the black hues in the landscape painting intensify. In this twilight that path extends even further into the remote distance.

She's not back yet. Must be difficult to say good-bye to one she had sworn sisterhood with and would never see again in this life.

The fragrances of simmering bean paste soup and fish on the grill float over from a neighbor's house. The clock rings six. His stomach is conditioned to respond, and he feels a sharp pang of hunger.

The dog lazily stretches out all the way, then looks around warily. Its eyes halt at the dusk gathering in the sky, and it mouths a couple mute barks.

She's hurrying home now, of course?

She told him once about her mother. She was about thirty then, same age as her mother in the story. She lost her natural mother when she was two years old, not the way you think, though. People said later she had been falsely accused of adultery, and she was locked up in a storeroom but then climbed the wall and took off in nothing but her bloomers. In the autumn of the year that the girl turned fifteen a total stranger offered to arrange for her to meet her mother. Following instructions to be at such a day and time at such a place she left in the darkness of the night, crossed the ridge and a stream into the next valley, where there was a village she had never been to before. She said the reason she braved this journey at night, all by herself—*just a young girl, mind you*—was simply that she wanted to know what her mother looked like, not that she missed this woman she had never really seen before. They had arranged for them to meet in somebody's home, in a separate one-room structure out back. It was nicely cleaned, and someone had provided a newly washed quilt and pillow, an attractive table of special rice cakes and molasses-sweetened water kimchi. But no mother. She spent the whole night there without seeing the owner or anyone else. There was probably some sort of relationship between her mother and whoever lived in this house, and the clothes on the rack could even have been her mother's. She sat up all night waiting for her mother, and then left the house at dawn. The fog was thick on the early morning road. As she walked she thought over and over about the night before, and when she finally looked up from her thoughts she realized that she had lost her way, recognized nothing on the road she had just walked, *and to this day couldn't for the life of me tell you where that place was.*

When she turned 40 she drank down a bottle of lye. Like any other day she was up before dawn to fix breakfast, prepared five lunches for the five kids, ironed his shirt and the girls' school clothes and got them all dressed, sent them off, and then, while she was boiling the underwear, she drank down the lye she was going to use for bleaching. She lost her voice but survived. For a long time she wore a bandage around her neck. He still doesn't know what made her go and do something like that.

Looks like the wind is picking up—a strong, chilling draft comes in through the room's open door. As soon as he feels it, the door closes, silently, as if someone has pushed it shut. The occasional sound of a car, of people passing by outside the garden wall gradually fades. And then, the room is suddenly filled with an eerie hush.

With the door closed the room is even darker. The black dog has disintegrated into the thick darkness. It starts scratching at the door, spooked at something, whining in a voice edged with fear.

She's not coming. This thing about Kyŏng-ja calling may be nothing more than a story.

A cold draft like a drifting spirit brushes him, scattering his dreams and memories to oblivion.

Stumbling Across a Language Barrier
Notes on the translation of a Korean short story into English

"Translation is sin."
—*Grant Showerman*

" . . . a good translation [can be] a work with intrinsic interest in its own right— . . . a true work of art . . . "
—*Maynard Mack*

Literary translation is regarded by some as a crime of vandalism, by others an act of creation. True to the nature of the translator, I offer a compromise. The translator does not destroy, but he does alter; and he does not create, but he is creative in the process of translation. To get a better idea of the various problems involved in this, share with me some of the issues of literary translation which I encountered in the translation of "River," a short story by Sŏ Chŏng-in, which is included in this book.

The issues considered here range from technical problems, such as treatment of a verb affix, to basic principles, such as "improvement" on the original. For your reference and entertainment, relevant opinions of writers and critics, from Cicero in the first century BC to Tamplin in our times, are presented here in juxtaposition to my opinion. This is not intended as a "How to" guide offering the "right" way, but rather as a record of a few issues and problems and solutions—right or wrong—involved in translation of Korean literature.

I will narrate the story and discuss each issue as it presents itself in the story's development. But let us begin with a synopsis of the story before we recount it in more detail. The story (written in 1968) begins with three men—an older college student, a tax man, and a former elementary school teacher in whose house the other two are renting rooms—engaged in idle conversation as they wait for their bus to leave the depot in Seoul. They are going to a small countryside village to attend the wedding of a relative of one of the three. During their ride down into the countryside, each character is partially developed through the conversation, individual reverie, and non-events typical of a long-distance bus ride. When they arrive at their destination, a small village, the girl goes off into Seoul House, a humble place which serves food and wine—and probably herself—and the men go off to find the house outside the village where they are to attend the wedding.

The next we meet them is on their way back to the village. The two older men go to Seoul House for a drink, and the student goes off to the inn to sleep. At Seoul House the men are served and entertained by the young woman they met on the bus; after a while they send her to the inn to wake the student and bring him back to join them. She goes to his room at the inn, and . . . but let's save the good part for later.

Enhance the Title?

> "Not even a thoroughly prepared French reader, looking at the title of Stendhal's novel [*Chartreuse de Parme*], gets all its implications in a single charge; if one thinks of reading a book as a progress not only horizontally from beginning to end, but vertically from the surface to the subtler implications of the text, it seems arguable that one might want to with-

> hold some of one's overflowing insights into the title till such later passages in the novel as might be expected to reinforce them." —*Robert Adams*

The first translation issue is encountered even before we get into the story, in the title. The title of the original is the Chinese character for river. The question, "Why 'river'?" comes to mind, but the answer does not come soon—in fact, I wonder if I ever did find the right answer. The author may have wanted to establish in the reader's subconsciousness a feeling of flow, so that he could more effectively present the four people's journey as one short stretch in the river of life, which goes on and on with varying bends and speeds but is basically the same ever-flowing river. If that was his reason, it was best to translate the title directly. So I entitled it "River." The English title is not all that seductive, but then neither is the original title. Better not tamper. (The issue of "improving" on the original is discussed in greater detail later.)

Another question concerning the title is why the author used the Chinese logogram instead of its equivalent in the phonetic Korean script. Was this deliberate, or did he do it unconsciously, as a result of habit? If he did it deliberately, why? Did he think that the visual effect of the Chinese logogram (which includes an element denoting water) would better convey to the Korean reader the idea of river, of flow? If so, would the English title, offering no more graphically than the Korean script, have to be padded somehow to say more than "river"?

I surveyed the titles of Mr. Sŏ's other short stories and found that more than half of them are in Chinese characters. Those that are not are in Korean words which cannot be or are ordinarily not written in Chinese. Looking further at the titles of other Korean authors' works, I found this to be common practice. The main reason is probably that Chinese characters were used much more often before the 1980s. In addition, when a Korean word derived from Chinese is representable in a Chinese character there are usually homonyms for that character, which might confuse the reader; a title stands alone and offers no context to help the reader to distinguish between homonyms. In English the word river has no homonym, so we do not have this problem. I concluded that the author had no special reason for putting the title in Chinese, other than that it was a convention at that time. So I entitled it simply "River."

Which Tense?

And now let's get into the story . . .

We are on the bus, waiting to leave the depot. The author uses a very prosaic conversation to introduce the three male characters. "It's snowing"—lengthy description of the grumpy one who says this—"Hmm . . . Sleet, anyway"—lengthy description of this dandy—"Sleet? Sure is!"—which introduces a description of the one sitting next to the young woman.

Description and the entire narrative are in the present tense, and I have to decide whether the translation should be in the same tense. If I am right about the author's intention in his choice of title—and his theme—it is best to go with the present tense, to convey the idea that this story is just one of many scenes in the river of life, which, no matter how it changes, is always there, always flowing. And the author might have decided to employ the present tense in order to better create a feeling of presence. Whatever the reason, there is certainly no problem in using the present tense in English.

The principle in this case: When following the original presents no problem to the reader's understanding or the literary quality of the English, do not tamper.

Rendering the Effect of Grammar Elements

> "[The translator's] version must produce upon the English reader the effect which the original has produced upon himself." —*J. A. K. Thomson*, 1915

The Korean verb *chu-da* (*-da* indicates the citation form of a verb) can also be used as a "processive" auxiliary (Martin). As an auxiliary it is affixed to verbs to express that the subject of the verb is helping to accomplish something. The scarf of the second character not only wraps around his neck, it "does the favor of" wrapping around his neck, connoting that it is helping to make the neck warm. (The verb used to describe what the scarf does for him, without the *chu-* auxiliary, is actually a compound verb of wrap (*kamssa*) and put into (*nŏt'a*); if we affix the auxiliary the result is *kam-ssa nŏh-ŏ-chuda.*)

Should this element be included expressly in the translation? The principle here is concerned with what ultimate effect this element has on the reader of the original. Ideally, that is what must be conveyed to the reader of the translation. The verb by itself expresses only the idea that the scarf is wrapped around the man's neck. I could have added the word snugly after tucking to convey the effect of *chu-da,* but the word tuck—with the connotation of security and warmth it gives—seems sufficient.

His dapper appearance suits his voice, white scarf circling his neck and tucking down into his brown leather jacket, sideburns trimmed sharp and clean . . .

Shall We Rearrange, Just a Bit?

> "[A] proper literary translation does not simply convey to us the elements of the original . . . but

> conveys them to us in something of the same order and structure of relatedness as the original. One might as well have puzzles which begin with the answer or jokes which begin with the punch line, as translations . . . which diffuse explanations long before the problems to which they represent triumphant solution have made themselves felt . . . In short, there is often an artistic question whether a translation or edition is being prepared for a first reader or a rereader—and, the translator being generally the latter, it is an extra act of the imagination for him to put himself in the position of the former." —*Robert Adams*

Conversation continues among the three, and then one of them takes up a conversation with the young woman sitting next to him. The author uses three very effective devices to convey the sense of anonymity among the passengers on a public bus, thus reinforcing the feeling of presence which he initiated with the use of the present tense.

One device is the omission of names, which would help the reader hang a tag on each character for easy identification. Instead, the author describes them in such terms as "the one in the brown jacket," or "the one in the window seat," which do not facilitate reference.

Another device is unidentified dialog. Something is said, and then the reader must figure out through general context and linguistic hints in the ensuing paragraph(s) who actually said it. At times, in fact, the hints are not there at all.

At one point in their pre-departure conversation, one asks his companion where he went into the army. It seems impossible to know who is asking and who is being asked, even after reading the next very long paragraph and then seeing the questioned one answer peevishly ("A small town, okay?"). But the one who asked the question prefaced it with *hyŏng* (elder brother), which would ordinarily be a good hint for finding out who asked the question. It is not that easy, though. For one thing, no relationships have been established by this point in the story. Another obfuscating element is the wide range of relationships which *hyŏng* can signify. In Korean, common nouns which denote a person's age and rank and sex—something like the Western common nouns such as father and aunt, which designate a person's place in a family—are used to or about a person more frequently than the name of the person. A younger brother would almost never call his elder brother by his name; he would address him with *hyŏng*. This word is also used in an informal setting, to address someone who is not an elder brother but within the age range of an elder brother. A freshman in college, for instance, could use *hyŏng* to address someone senior to him in his department or extracurricular activity. If one suffixes the word with the honorific *nim* or *ssi*, it can be extended in an attempt to establish a closer relationship between two males who have just met—even when the one being addressed this way is obviously younger.

In this story, should the translation of the question about where the man went into the army somehow convey the "elder brother" relationship? If so, which relationship—blood or social—should it express? The principle involved here is that the reader of the translation should know no more and no less than the reader of the original. So the translator must determine how much the reader of the original is able to know at this point with the evidence available. Up to this point in the story, there was little if any evidence as to the identity of either the questioner or the one questioned.

A survey was conducted of ten native speakers of Korean to find out how much the reader of the original would know about the relationship. The question in the original (*hyŏng-ŭn ŏdisŏ ipdae hasiŏsso?* "Elder brother, where was it you went into basic?") was shown to the surveyed, and the surveyed were asked to guess both (1) the general age of the questioner and (2) the relationship between the questioner and the one questioned.

In broad terms, the Korean inflection of a verb includes elements which show two dimensions of a relationship. One element (presence or absence of the honorific *si*) will express the attitude of the speaker toward the person spoken to or about; the final element (the presence or absence of a formality marker such as *yo*) expresses the attitude of the speaker toward the person he is talking to. The "sentence-final endings . . . differ according to six types of social relationship between the person speaking and the person spoken to . . . FORMAL, POLITE, INTIMATE, FAMILIAR, AUTHORITATIVE, and PLAIN styles" (Martin). In the question's verb (*ipdae hasiŏsso*), the honorific *si* is present but *o* is a marker which does not show formality or politeness. This combination of register markers should tell the reader of the original generally the speaker's attitude about the relationship the two have—and the translation of the question should thus show this.

The survey, however, revealed that only four of the ten surveyed were able to define the relationship between the two. I suspected that I may have deprived the reader of sufficient contextual information by not letting him read the story up to the point of the question, so I asked three of the surveyed to read the story from the beginning. One changed his answer to the correct answer, and the others changed their answers to incorrect answers. So the original, after all, did not indicate to the reader that the two characters' relationship was.

The third device the author used to induce the feeling of presence on the bus is the way the conversation jumps abruptly from one pair of interlocutors to another. In the example below, conversation starts off with the man and woman in back and switches with no transition (at "So where . . . ?") to the two in front.

> "How far you going, Miss?" he asks the girl. After all, there's no reason to let things get you down. You have to get your mind off it.
>
> "I'm going to Kunha-ri." What a blush she can flash—even considering he's a stranger—all the way to her scalp, every blossoming capillary.
>
> "So where did you go for basic training?" The one in the jacket asks his companion. He is miffed . . .

There is a potential problem with this combination of very effective devices the author uses to make the reader feel he is on a long-distance bus: it is difficult for the reader to follow along comfortably. (In fact, in trying to help me figure out who said what, my Korean informants had a couple of heated discussions among themselves.) The reader has to backtrack too often. Many authors, of course, do not concern themselves primarily with the reader's comfort—ultimately, effect is the author's primary consideration, and the reader is expected to cooperate in achieving the intended effect by putting in a little effort. By moving a few sentences around and adding a few hints the translator could make it much easier for his reader, and the reader might enjoy the story more with less annoying backtracking.

The principle here too is that the translator must determine how much more he, the non-native reader, had to work than the native reader, and then render to the reader of the English translation what the native reader of the original experienced. And another principle is involved: to rearrange would preclude strict correspondence with the original. Moreover, it might after all defeat the author's purpose in using these devices—to give a feeling of presence on a long-distance bus.

But how much does any reader actually concern himself with

who is saying what? How, indeed, do readers read? Is the reader actually annoyed at not knowing who is speaking, or at disjointed conversation? That depends on the nature and the function of the dialog. Thinking back to the first time I read the story, I did not concern myself about who was speaking, because I was involved more in the general flow. And I realize that it was only when I began to read the story with the idea of translating it that I consciously concerned myself with who was who.

After all, I did make one or two concessions in this respect to facilitate the reader's task in following the story. These concessions, though, did not interfere with the author's basic purpose of establishing the sense of scattered bits of conversation and anonymity one experiences on a long-distance bus.

Still, the doubt nags. Were even these one or two minor adjustments necessary? Maybe the reader did not need them. And, even if necessary, did they make it easier for the reader of the translation than it was for the reader of the original? If so, these adjustments should not have been made.

Monetary Values

> "[T]he nonspecialist reader would be well advised not to worry about [the values of different currencies in fourteenth-century Europe], because the names of coins and currency mean nothing anyway, except in terms of purchasing power . . . "
> —*Barbara Tuchman, 1978*

As our friends are waiting for their bus to leave the depot a man with sunglasses gets on the bus and causes each of the companions in turn to muse on his personal association with sunglasses. Here is the reverie of one of them.

> Those sunglasses, does he need them? The draft dodger feels better now with something substantial to occupy his mind. Could be just for looks. With most, these things are just an accessory, a luxury. Luxury? A lot of nerve to call those cheap hundred-won variety store things a luxury. After all, he himself has settled for a used pair for a thousand won after considering a new pair for two thousand. Right here in his pocket now, ready to pull out and hang on his nose just as soon as there's a little more glare from the snow to justify it.

How is the translator to convey the value of a hundred won or a thousand won in terms the reader can understand? Should he not translate the amount in terms of dollars? The principle here: precise value is not important; only relative value is required for the reader to get the author's point.

In a literary work, even if it is important for the reader to know precise value, the translator should not give the amount in dollars; it will reduce the reader's feeling of Korean presence, and it will at any rate be American English (discussed later in more detail). Rather plant one or more clues somewhere in the passage to convey a practical sense of the item's value. Instead of leaving the first amount at 100 won, I added the phrase *variety store*, expecting the reader to use personal experience in establishing a fairly precise value, and then extend this formula to calculate a precise value of 1,000 won. (In the initial translation I used "dime store," neglecting to consider whether this was not an Americanism which a British or Australian reader would be unable to relate to. In the umpteenth revision "variety store" presented itself as a term internationally acceptable—its important features intuited fully by an Australian I tested, though the term is not used in Australia—and it even possesses a Korean flavor.)

Even Contractions Can Serve the Translator

> "There are some long passages of . . . dialog in *The Sound and the Fury*, where a reader cannot be sure whether Caddy or Quentin Campson is speaking; that confusion (sometimes +Mo+mentary, sometimes extended, occasionally permanent) is part of the author's main intent. But Japanese, by requiring that male and female speakers use quite different inflectional forms, forces the narrative voice to commit itself unequivocally, publicly, in advance."
>
> —*Robert Adams*

In the original story, there is often no clear distinction between the author's narrative and a character's private thoughts. The author's purpose in this, of course, is to help the reader enter the mind of the character and thus provide for more effective character development.

Narration and thoughts are conventionally blended in English without marking the thoughts with quotation marks. But in this story there is a much more gradual and subtle transition from event to thought, and, before the reader knows it (but more often without the reader's knowing it), the one having the thought has sneaked into the narration and taken it over. So I thought that contractions would help render the same effect—I rendered narration of events without contractions, and reverie with contractions.

Let us look at the thoughts of another companion when he sees the man with the sunglasses. His thoughts begin with "He remembers . . . " Note that I did not make a contraction of "it is" in the preceding sentence.

> To the one in the window seat it is a blind man in back of those sunglasses. He remembers that fantasy he worked

> himself into once, him blind, dark glasses and all, eking out a living as a masseur. A war injury, and he's in the hospital, eyes under layers of bandages. His girl comes to find him, searching through all the chaos of a war hospital. Of course the smallest thing prevents their reunion. He leaves the hospital in his dark glasses. Soon he's wandering the residential streets at night, tapping his way with his cane, announcing his progress with that eerie whistle of the blind masseur. A window opens above him. A woman's voice summons, a voice he's heard before.

Looking back over the years, it is highly questionable whether the switch from not using contractions to using contractions is of any help in indicating the change from speech to reflection. A key word, like "remembers" in the transitional (second) sentence may be much more effective.

Rendering Onomatopoeia

> "In first-rate poetry the sound exists, not for its own sake, not for mere decoration, but as a medium of meaning."—*Laurence Perrine*

The principle involved here is that English cannot express many of the sounds and images which Korean onomatopoeia (and phonetic intensives) express, because these sounds and images in Korean culture do not exist in an English speaking culture. Moreover, only a person whose genes and experience are of the Korean culture can accurately associate a Korean onomatopoeia with its corresponding sound. One conclusion of those who hold this theory is that it is useless to try to render Korean onomatopoeia in English.

But why does a writer use onomatopoeia in the first place?

He uses onomatopoeia (1) to trigger a memory, a replay of the sound, in the reader, which (2) evokes a sense of presence, which in turn contributes to (3) conveying and then enhancing the author's point. The author's purpose, unless he is one of those tiresome verbal acrobats who describe for the sake of description, is not the sound or the image in itself. Nevertheless, a major element in literature is style, and, as in any of the arts, the meaning's vehicle of conveyance itself should be enjoyable. "[B]y combining onomatopoeia with other devices that help convey meaning, the poet can achieve subtle and beautiful effects whose recognition is one of the keenest pleasures in reading poetry." Perrine speaks here of poetry, but a well-written story is poetry in the format of prose.

So the translator wants to both convey meaning and provide an aesthetic experience. The theory presented at the beginning of this section claims that the wide divergence between the Korean culture and English speaking cultures prevents this. I believe that the translator can almost always render the meaning which the onomatopoeia in the original conveys to its reader. But can he render its aesthetic experience? In most cases the translator can provide his reader with one that is equivalent if not identical to that which the reader of the original work experiences. The translator and his reader already have the general context of the original, and the translator can exploit this with deft use of his devices; his reader will consciously or unconsciously associate the context and the translator's enhancement of it with what he has heard or seen or felt in a similar context in his own experience (in applied linguistics, "schema").

The original uses *kkung* to express the snort the driver of the bus makes when he finally gets on and sees there are only a few passengers. This onomatopoeia (1) causes the reader to recall his own experience of a snort of dissatisfaction, thus (2) evoking an image of the driver, and thereby (3) helping him feel what the bus driver feels. To achieve the same effect in my reader, I could have used the English "Hmph!" But I thought that "Hmph!" would indicate more indignation than I sensed in the original.

I used "snort," and supported this noun with an enhanced context (by adding "sour look") to elicit a response from my reader similar to that which the author got from his reader.

> The driver gets into his seat and twists around for a look in back. The sour look he puts on the passengers says there aren't enough of them, and he turns back around with a disgruntled snort.

Snort is not all that "subtle and beautiful," but then neither is *kkung*.

But This Concept Doesn't Exist in English!

> "[I]t is words and their associations which are untranslatable, not ideas; there is no idea . . . which cannot be adequately produced as idea in English words." —Sidney Lanier, 1897

The bus driver is here. Now all we need is the bus girl. "Bus girl"?

> The rear door opens and the bus girl backs on.
>
> "Well, you think we might get this thing going today?" asks the smart dresser.
>
> "We'll be off in just a second," she says automatically, not even bothering to look at him. She hangs up her cheap plastic mirror, sweeps the steps, counts her tickets, takes out . . .

"Just a second, huh? So what are we doing still here?"
"We'll be off in just a second."
"What are you, a broken record or something?"

This passage introduces another major issue in literary translation. In the original the man asked the girl, "Where do you think this is anyway, a Chinese restaurant?" instead of "What are you, a broken record . . . ?" In a Chinese restaurant in Korea you can ask the busy waiters twenty times, "Where's my noodles?" and you will get the same automatic response twenty times: "Coming right up!" An English-speaking audience would not be able to appreciate this metaphor, which is alien to their culture.

I searched for weeks to find a substitute which would be familiar to the reader from a Western culture. Then one day I mentioned the problem to an old friend, and in the blink of an eye he suggested the broken record metaphor. (That is when I began to realize that the one who translates is not necessarily the one who should be translating.)

The bus girl is another example of a concept alien to Americans, and probably most other Westerners. (Now the concept is alien also to a lot of younger urban Koreans, because automatic doors and coin receptacles and card readers have taken the bus girl's place.) In the exchange above we see that she is young, and in the narration which I embedded in the exchange we get some idea of her duties: "She hangs up her cheap plastic mirror, sweeps the steps, counts her tickets . . . " In the continuation of the conversation, below, we find that she can be saucy. And in a later bit of dialog ("It's all thanks to this young conductress's skilled navigation") is a clue that she helps the driver in some way with other traffic.

The principle: Concepts alien to the reader of the translation can be conveyed by other metaphors recognizable to the reader, enhancement of the original's context with the addition of elements (which must not interfere with the tone or flow of the story), and other devices which a creative or lucky translator will eventually happen upon.

Speech Register: Korean Inflections Into English Words

> "[A]ny work of literature read in translation . . . cannot escape the linguistic characteristics of the language into which it is turned: the grammatical, syntactical, lexical, and phonetic boundaries which constitute collectively the individuality or 'genius' of that language."—*Maynard Mack*

The repartee between the bus girl and our traveler continues.

> "What are you, a broken record or something?"
>
> Now she looks around at him. "And what would a broken record be doing on a bus?
>
> "Little girl," he chuckles, "You've got the brains of a little bear."
>
> "Me a bear? Then what are you, sir?"
>
> "Me? Your uncle, honey," with a wink and a wag of his finger. "Better be a good girl."

The inflection of Korean verbs shows not only tense but also the relationship between interlocutors. One or more register elements combine with time and aspect and mood elements to determine a verb's inflection. In addition to inflection, words can denote register (e.g., *pap* for neutral register and *chinji* for formal or polite). The language also has a delightful way of showing all the subtle aspects of a relationship between two people; it can combine one, two, or three of its several levels of register to precisely indicate the most complex attitude of one speaker toward his relationship with the listener. An honorific element, for example, can combine with an informal element to denote an older house maid's intimacy with her master's younger son. In my boardinghouse years ago, the landlady used to ask me "*Chinji chapsusiŏssŏ?*" (Have you eaten?) using the polite *chinji* and *chapsu* with the intimate *ŏ*.

Mack says a translation "cannot escape the characteristics" of its own language. But then, do we really need it to? The translator can use a combination of several aspects of the collective "individuality or genius" of the language to express most of what other languages express. The same intricate combinations of social attitudes which Korean expresses through verb inflection can be expressed in English through words.

In the translation the bus girl in this repartee shows respect by saying "sir," a Korean equivalent of which was not in the original. (The girl's sauciness is rendered in the content of her speech.) In the original the inflection of the verb spoken by the one who addressed her—a male who is also older—expresses a mix of non-respect (not *dis*respect) and friendly informality; in the translation he expresses the attitude of non-respect with words I added—"honey" and "be a good girl now"—and friendly informality with "uncle" and a phrase I added, "a wink and a wag of his finger."

In a previous conversation between this same man and the young woman he is sitting next to, previous to this, the verb inflection was a combination of a formal-honorific element (*si*) with an informal non-respect element (*o*). In the original his inflection of the verb connotes to her that he renders her due respect but is not going to let that interfere with the casual friendliness he feels toward her. (She would not be able to speak the same way to him, since he is a male and older than she.)

The translator can handle this register mix with both local attention and global distribution. Locally the translator can omit such words as subject pronouns and auxiliary verbs to show informality and familiarity; he can use the more colloquial of two candidate synonyms ("Sure are"). He can add an honorific title ("young lady") to show due respect. He can render the register of one verb's inflection also by global distribution, planting preparative words or phrases at strategic points prior to the occurrence of the inflection, sometimes even from the very beginning of the story.

Shall We "Improve" on the Original?

> "[I]t is the first grand duty of an interpreter to give his author entire and unmaimed."—*The Preface to* The Iliad, *by Alexander Pope,* 1715

> "A translator is to be like his author; it is not his business to excel him." —*Samuel Johnson,* 1779

The bus finally arrives at a small town and the three, along with the young woman, get off the bus. The two older men strike up a playful sophistic analysis about why the others on the bus did not get off too.

> Our friends, a few others too, get off the bus. The sodden yellow clay road stretches on into the distance. The bus takes off after it.
>
> "Now why didn't they get off too?"
>
> "They probably have no business here."
>
> "Ah, but do consider. It just may be they have something to attend to farther on."

> "I do believe you may have something there. Which would mean, of course, it is not that we had no business back at that last stop—Sofa Rock was it, or Couch Rock . . . ?"

According to my reading (and my consultants') the humor is not funny, and the conversation is, as a consequence, annoying. Did the author intend this? Maybe he created this conversation to realistically indicate something about the poverty of common people's sense of humor. Or maybe the author was simply attempting some comic relief. If this explanation—a failed attempt at some comic relief—is correct, would it not make the story better if I just left out this annoying little wart?

Such a temptation to "improve" on the original strikes often. Who knows whether the temptation might originate in the translator's conscious or unconscious fear that he may be held accountable for the author's shortcomings, directly or indirectly? Or he might simply want nothing to mar the work. Or he might have Adams' attitude: "[I]t is not only legitimate but inevitable that [the translator] will select those qualities for emphasis which appeal to his own taste and the taste of his readers, while minimizing those which make the original seem . . . ludicrous or contemptible."

A basic principle is involved here. Modification of the original is justifiable only when the translation's reader will not be able to understand what the reader of the original is able to. An example of this would be the Chinese restaurant metaphor previously mentioned. Adjustment is one thing, "improvement" another. The translator, no matter how much literary prowess he might presume himself to have, ought not tamper with the original any more than is necessary for understanding. Even the literary quality of the English rendering, which I consider to be of ultimate importance, does not warrant willful tampering. If the translator were to be allowed to modify according to his tastes, no writer could feel secure from the idiosyncratic values and tastes of the translator.

Does the Translator Have the Same Liberty as the Reader?

> "[P]oems exist to be interpreted and . . . they subsume their interpretations giving up new substance to different times and people . . . We might adapt E. H. Carr's idea that 'when we take up a work of history, our first concern should be not with the facts which it contains but with the historian who wrote it' to the question of translation."
>
> —*Ronald Tamplin*

Maybe there was a special reason for including the humor passage that my Korean informants and I thought the story would do better without. Should I have tried to read something into them, and present my conclusion to the reader? Here a rather frustrating situation presents itself. Poets and fiction writers will often decline clarification of elements in their works; they will leave clarification to the reader, coincidentally giving a greater depth or breadth of meaning to these elements and endowing them with more value than the author intended. But what is the translator to do in this case? One of his primary responsibilities is accuracy in conveying the author's intentions. Is the translator allowed to take—and convey to his reader—this liberty which the author gives to the reader of the original? That would deprive the reader of *his* liberty, it would risk inaccurate rendering of the author's intended meaning if he had one, and it would violate the author's right to pregnant ambiguity.

Is This English or "American"?

> "Regional dialects are notoriously inseparable from the character of the regions and social circumstances in which they grow up. Not long ago an adventurous translator tried to render into American slang some of the sonnets of G. G. Belli, the nineteenth-century Italian poet who wrote his greatest work in the popular dialect of a lower-class district of Rome . . . But it was only a limited success . . . There is no reason why such a scene couldn't be made comprehensible in any dialect the translator wanted to use, but no organic reason why he should use a dialect at all . . . Above all, it is difficult to deform usage in a second tongue to correspond with deformations in a first tongue, without giving the impression of intolerable artifice."
> —*Robert Adams*

In "River" some of the dialog is quite coarse. If the audience of the translation were limited to Americans, such dialog would be easy enough to translate. In my first attempt at translation of a Korean short story I used American slang. This rankled an Irish critic, who rightly objected that an English translation belongs to all native speakers of the language. The translator into English must be careful to avoid the idioms of any one English dialect.

One way in which coarse or very casual speech can be expressed is with reduction. In the story one of our friends gets the attention of a villager he does not know with the vocative of address, "Uncle." The Korean for uncle, *ajŏssi,* is reduced in the original work to *assi.* I tried to render this reduction, not because I was concerned about word-for-word equivalence, but because the reduction helps to convey the register of speech and general tone of the dialog. Since in English we usually do not address as "Uncle" one who is not an uncle, I added "Excuse me" and relocated the reduction to "excuse."

Our friends are now outside the village, trying to find out how to get to the house where the wedding is being celebrated.

> The three come back out onto the road. Along comes an older gentleman who looks like nothing can happen around the place without his knowing about it.
>
> Pak approaches him. "'Scuse me there, but you wouldn't know of a marriage going on around here? Kim family?"

Technically, the reduction of "excuse" may have worked to render casual speech, but now I wonder if "'Scuse me" might not also be an Americanism.

This tells us that one who translates into English has more to learn about his language than one who translates into another European language. The translator of English must be familiar with the whole world's major dialects of English so that he knows what is palatable to the general English reader. Extensive reading of British, Canadian, Australian, New Zealand, and South African literature would accomplish this; for reference, language usage books (such as *Oxford's Modern American Usage*) from these countries are helpful. Even with this knowledge, the translator would do well to ask the speaker of another dialect to check questionable dialog.

We encounter another aspect of this issue with this village man in the rendering of his slow Ch'ungch'ŏng Province dialect. Shall I render it in an American's southern drawl? There you go again! To avoid another Americanism, how about a Cornwall accent, or an Irish brogue? None of these would do, because a rendering in any English dialect would yank the reader out of whatever Korean presence the translation has managed to establish.

If one or another English dialect is out, we can at least give the man's speech some rustic flavor by employing phrases that convey a general sense of rusticity.

> Pak approaches him. "'Scuse me there, but you wouldn't know of a marriage going on around here? Kim family?"
>
> "Hmm, must mean old man Kim Cha-bang's over in Rocky Hollow."
>
> "Yes, yes, that's it. Stony Hollow, whatever."
>
> "Like I said. Now you just head straight on up this way for a few *li*, and you'll see a little village of about fifty houses. That's Stony Hollow right there."

These phrases and patterns were added in the translation (after it was published): "chews his cud," "drawls," "old man," "you just," "straight on up." I asked a British friend to read this passage and tell me whether the man was speaking in dialect or not. He guessed correctly. Then I asked which of the passage's linguistic elements, if any, made him feel that the man was speaking a dialect. He selected only three of those listed above: chews his cud, drawls, and straight on up. The others had no effect. (He also remarked that I might replace the word house with dwelling, which a rustic in Cornwall would be more likely to use; but I felt that dwelling to Americans has an academic tone to it.)

The Translator Can't Do It By Himself

> "[We must have] teamwork in translating such violently different languages as English and Japanese."
> —*K. I. Ishikawa*, 1955

At some points the translator may become so involved in his English that he loses contact with the original and unconsciously adds an element or a flavor of his own which the author never intended.

Arriving back in town from the wedding, the three men are looking for a place to stay. They approach the outer gate of what appears to be an inn . . .

> It is as dead as when they saw it earlier. What could have driven all the customers off?
>
> They throw open the courtyard gate, expecting a grateful welcome. Nothing. No one is there. The yard is dark, all the darker because there's no electricity in this remote village at night. They bang on an inner door, shouting for some attention.
>
> "How about a drink here!"
>
> "Come and earn your keep!"
>
> "You got guests here!"
>
> A doorway down at the far end of what seems to be a long row of doors creaks open, and a head pops out. "What do you want there?"
>
> "Sell us something to drink. We'll even pay you for it."
>
> "Ha ha! Not here, though. Try next door."
>
> "What are you selling here then?"
>
> "Rooms. This is an inn."
>
> "Well, I'll be . . . ! But what about the sign we saw earlier?"
>
> "What sign?"
>
> "So what's an inn doing without a sign?"

In the translation of this dialog, the owner of the inn enjoys a repartee with the three men. I was mortified to find, however, with a recent reading of the original, that the owner's replies were not clever but quite prosaic. I had let my imagination run off with me. This probably happened around the fifth or sixth revision, when I was completely engrossed in the literary quality of the English. At this point the translator feels such intimacy with the story that he may take his memory of the details for granted and, with each revision for style, stray a bit more from what was intended in the original.

This spotlights the importance of teamwork in a translation. Periodic checks of the developing translation by a native speaker of the original's language (preferably a different one each time) will ensure some objectivity and pull the translator back to his senses when his involvement in English style waylays him.

Korean's "Exclusive" System of Modifiers

> "It were as wise to cast a violet into a crucible, that you might discover the formal principle of its color and odor, as seek to transfuse from one language into another the creations of a poet." —*Percy Bysshe Shelley*

One hackneyed contention of pop sociologists and high school military drill teachers and others who do not know English is that English is not as well equipped with adverbs and adjectives of perception as Korean is. The example used often is Korean's standard system of color description, a systematic yin-yang vowel harmony system, in which *a* and *o* express bright colors and *ŏ* and *u* express dark and obscure colors (*ŭ* and *i* are neutral and can be used either way). The principles of this color system are generally applicable to other Korean phonetic intensives and onomatopoeia.

The fact is that English does have a system for its onomatopoeia (for sounds) and phonetic intensives (for visual and other meaning). "An initial *gl-* . . . frequently accompanies the idea of light, usually unmoving, as in glare, gleam, glint, glow, glisten. . . . Short *-i-* often goes with the idea of smallness . . . some [consonants] are fairly mellifluous . . . " (Perrine). In English, as in Korean, we can convey colors with similes—like "willow yellow" (coined by a Korean student in my college class)—and metaphors, as in the cliché "pearly white teeth."

With phonetic intensives, as with onomatopoeia, enhanced or simply well-rendered context is often enough to compensate for the absence of a single appropriate phrase, because the reader will use memory of personal experience. In the following example, the Korean adverb (*hŭikkŭmŭre-hake*) that is used to describe the light in the courtyard somehow seems to me more powerful in itself than the English equivalent in this case. But I also feel that the English adverb combined with the context render the equivalent in both meaning and feeling to me and my reader as Westerners as the Korean does to its readers as Koreans.

> The courtyard shows dimly in the surrounding darkness. Through the window of a room off in the pitch black of the far side of the yard filters a lantern's light. The door opens and out comes the lantern.

Linguistic Correspondence and Literary Style: Must We Make A Choice?

> "Nor will you as faithful translator render word for word." —*Horace*, 20(?), BC

> "I did not translate them as an interpreter but as an orator . . . not . . . word for word, but I preserved the general style and force of the language." –*Cicero*, 46 BC

> "The clumsiest literal translation is a thousand times more useful than the prettiest paraphrase."
> —*Vladimir Nabokov,* 1955

The student gets settled in his room, and his companions are drinking at Seoul House.

> "'You think you turned you into someone?'"
> "'You think I turned me into no one?'"
> "'It's money makes you, it's none that breaks you.'"
> "EX-actly!"
>
> The teacher is stretched out on the warm floor, propping himself on an elbow. Lee is still sitting up. They are at a table spread with snacks and drink, with the girl between them at the end of the table keeping them entertained and their glasses filled. The teacher exclaims to the ceiling again, "EX-actly!"

The first three lines of the new scene are extemporized verse sung in a traditional song form unlike any song form I have heard in the West.

This awkward first-publication translation of the song raises another issue in literary translation, the perennial tug-of-war between exact linguistic correspondence with the original and the literary quality of the translation. When the original's language has no equivalent in English some will sacrifice literary style of the English for linguistic conformity to the original, and others will go the other way.

A song is a good example of what this issue entails. The elements of a song, besides melody, are idea content, evocative lexicals, and metered rhythm (and sometimes rhyme). Of course, the translator wants to render all of these with complete fidelity to the original. To accomplish this would require that all the song's elements in the original language fit together the same way in the target language. It is impossible to do this, because each word in a song is selected not only for its expressiveness but also for its function in maintaining the song's meter; syllabic structure and stress on the words in the song's original language will never be identical to that of the target language, much less combine identically.

I am interested in close linguistic correspondence not only for the abstract ideal of fidelity but also because I want to introduce to my reader interesting cultural features of the original. For example, if in my translation the person who asked the question about induction into the army were to address the other as "elder brother," the translation would be more linguistically faithful to the original. And if I were somehow to show, in addition, that the person was not his real brother, the translation would inform the reader of one convention used in direct address in Korean society. But it would be awkward English, and awkward English does not make for good literature.

In literature, both ideas and style are essential. Often, though, elements not essential to sufficient understanding of the idea, such as "elder brother," will be hung on the idea. On the rare occasion that this element does not have an equivalent in English and we cannot render it with other devices, we must sacrifice it in the interest of the literary quality of the English. When push comes to shove, strict linguistic correspondence must give way.

If the translator accepts this principle he has to attend to another consideration. How does he determine what in the original can and should be saved and what must be sacrificed—what is essential, and what is dispensable? I have read translations in which what I regarded as minor but essential elements were regarded as extraneous, and discarded in the interest of style.

Here is my sixth and most recent revision of the song above.

> "Did you make yourself a beauty?"
> "Did I make myself a beast?"
> "Nope, it's money that makes you . . . "
> "And none that breaks you!"

This attempt is some improvement over the clumsy initial attempt. Interestingly, the images of beauty and beast, the phrasal arrangement, and the meter correspond with the original. If, before submitting it for that first publication, I had let the last revision of the translation cool a while and then returned to it for one more try I would have come up with something better. And this means that the translator must, at the same time he is prepared *in extremis* to sacrifice strict fidelity for style, try and try again, and then again, for the achievement of both. In the end he may not achieve an ideal blend, but his efforts will usually result in something better than the product of a radical bias toward style.

Ambiguous Ambiguity

> "[T]he translator on his own responsibility may be required to make up his author's mind on points that he never so much as contemplated." —*Robert Adams*

We have already discussed the issue of how to treat ambiguity, but the subject is still kicking. Rendering intended ambiguity is difficult enough, but what does one do with the other kind?

While the men are having their drink the student is encouraging the innkeeper's middle-school nephew to keep on studying hard; the boy leaves, and the college student falls into that hypnogogic state between waking and sleep, where he continues in the conventional pitch about studying hard. Gradually his monolog turns to himself, also tops in middle school, but now losing the financial and academic struggle to complete his education.

> What you do is get that diploma, and it's all easy street from there . . . No. Not anymore. You know now. Diploma or not, it makes no difference now, because succeed or not, success this way could never mean what it used to mean. Poverty has sapped it of everything it could have been. Damn, so much squandered, gone for good!
>
> He has been turning fitfully in his sleep and finally, eyes still shut, sits up, struggles to squirm out of both vest and coat at once. He gives up and sinks back down. Now he is snoring away, deep and fast asleep.

At about this point his two companions ask the wine house girl to fetch the student for a drink. She leaves the wine house for the inn. Here now is the end of the story (with some deleted).

> She gets a surprise outside. The yard is white, utterly still in the falling snow. She slips into her sandals, descends into the white softness. She throws her head back, this wine-house girl, lifts her face to the heavens swirling with those icy black fluffs. She glories in the cold tingle they yield settling on her skin, and opens her mouth to drink in as much as possible.
>
> A night like this, wouldn't it be just perfect for a new bride! "Snow the first night, riches thereafter." And happiness. The girl blinks once, twice. Swarming snowflakes,

there, not there, there again. She tries to imagine her face as a bride, but somehow can't. . . . Anyway, all brides would have the same look, wouldn't they? Of happiness, hope, maybe apprehension, why not all together? She looks down into the fresh whiteness of the yard, locks her knees and shuffles off, stride by long stride, laying a set of tracks. The falling snow gathers on her hair.

Then the girl leaves off her ski walk and heads to the outer gate. She opens it a crack and slips through, quiet as a cat.

The snow is deep out on the road, too. Her steps are mute, the whole world still. She looks down at the snow-capped slippers kicking out from beneath her long skirt and feels she could just keep walking like this for a hundred *li*.

When she comes up to the inn next door, though, she stops, works her fingers in through the brushwood side gate and flicks open the catch. Cotton pods of snow float down from the sky and settle, white on white. There is a light in one of the two guest rooms. A slight hesitation, then she goes over and steps up onto the porch. She peeks in through the hole someone's finger has left in the paper of the lattice door. A man is lying there in the faint glimmer of the lamp. She retreats to the darkened room next to his, puts her face close to the door. . . .

"Little boy," she whispers. "You in there, honey?"

No answer. She pushes on the door, rattling it softly. Still no answer. She goes back to the guest room, listens, and slides the door open.

He is on his side, curled up like a shrimp, uncovered except for his arms and legs he has stuck under the cover to escape the cold. The girl takes a closer look at his face. Yes, it's him, the one on the bus. College student! She takes him by the shoulders and rolls him gently over on his back. He frowns—tie must be too tight. Look at you, not even getting out of your clothes before you go to bed! Poor thing. Now she is big sister and mom, takes off his tie, pulls back the cover he has dragged with him and slips off his trousers, his shirt, then straightens his mat.

He squirms, about to wake up. Then he slips right back under the mat she has just readied for him to lie on. Behave yourself now! She pulls his arms and legs back out, raises him to her breast and maneuvers him gently onto the mat.

She covers him, then slips the pillow neatly under his head.

She sits back, and looks. Her eyes rest on his face.

College student . . .

The lantern sputters. The girl stands, picks up his scattered clothes, and hangs each, one by one, on its own nail in the wall.

She goes to the lantern, bows over it, puts it out with a gentle puff.

Outside in the courtyard, soft white stillness. The snow deepens, erasing her steps.

The last two sentences of this story were especially difficult to translate. I did not know for certain whether the girl stayed in the room or left it. Since an accurate translation requires the translator first to be accurate in his interpretation, I had discussions with several Koreans on whether the girl stayed or left. They disagreed among themselves.

If the readers of the original do not know, does the translator have to know? Should his readers know more than the readers of the original? I decided to render it just as ambiguously as I had found it in the original. Later, in the preparation of this paper (after the first publication of the translation), I surveyed sixteen Koreans and one American with native-speaker ability in Korean. Twelve, including university students, a university English professor, and a professional writer, said she stayed; four, including two not yet in college, one college student, and the American, said she left; and one college student could not commit himself.

This survey confirmed the fact that the original passage is ambiguous, and that it should be translated that way.

Now, for the conclusion to our deliberation on how to render the last two sentences, the author himself will tell us. Before that, though, please read the passage again and make your own guess as to whether the girl stayed or left.

Recently the author was contacted and asked whether the girl stayed in the room or left. "What a question! Anyone can see she left!"

So we will have to work a little harder for our conclusion. The author had not intended ambiguity—he thought "anyone can see" that she left. But three quarters of those surveyed did not see it.

Some basic principles are involved here. One is that the translator should present his reader no more and no less than the author gave his reader. Another is that the translator must not "improve" on the original. And the last is that the writer's message must be conveyed. We will disregard the third principle because it applies only when the author has actually conveyed his message. Adhering to the first two principles would require that I deliberately mislead the reader in my conclusion in order to effect a similar ratio of misreadings among the audience of my translation. To follow this reasoning to its logical ludicrous conclusion I would have to conduct a survey on every potentially ambiguous point in the original story, whether I felt I understood it correctly or not, to determine the ratio of different interpretations among readers of the original; and then, of course, I would have to conduct an identical survey among readers of a draft of the translation to determine whether my rendering of the passage was successful in achieving the same ratio. (With an imagination like this, maybe I should switch from translating to writing.)

So here, finally, patient reader, is the conclusive conclusion. Most of the readers of the passage in the original interpreted the passage differently from how the author intended. I detected nothing in their explanations or the explanations of those who interpreted correctly that would indicate that the author had presented information which would lead the reader to interpret one way instead of the other. Generally, the clues on which some based their interpretation were the basis for the opposite interpretation. This tells me that the author had not actually presented any misleading pieces of information—the totality was neutrally ambiguous.

And this, in turn, tells me that the original's readers must have read their own experience and values into the information which the author presented them. We can probably count on the reader of the translation to do the same, given the same neutral ambiguity. And so the ambiguous rendering—as opposed to a deliberately misleading one—should be provided the reader of the translation.

Would this be perfectly obvious to you without all the false conclusions it took us to get to this point? It very well might be, unless of course you are a translator.

And Finally . . .

I was going to end this article by comparing the translator to an artist, who alters life in a creative way and thus gives joy by truly rendering the facets and thus the spirit of his object. But the translator, contrary to what some think, does not have such freedom. No writer in his right mind would entrust his creation to a translator who has the hubris of a creator.

So it is the destiny of the translator to grope and stumble, sometimes bungle, altering as little as humanly possible as creatively as humanly possible, in his attempt "to render truly the facets and thus the spirit" of another's creation.

The Stories' Background

Introduction

> To Our good and loyal subjects: After pondering deeply the general trends of the world and the actual conditions obtaining to Our Empire today, We have decided to effect a settlement of the present situation by resorting to an extraordinary measure.
>
> We have ordered Our Government to communicate to the Governments of the United States, Great Britain, China and the Soviet Union that Our Empire accepts the provisions of their Joint Declaration . . .
>
> 14th day of the 8th month of the 20th year of Showa.

With these words Hirohito, Emperor of Japan, surrendered to the allied powers. On that summer day in 1945, Korea, which Japan had ruled as a colony for forty years, became free. Now the Korean people would be able to run their own lives again. But this time it would be *all* the people—peasants, laborers, small merchants—not just the King and his aristocracy, who had ruled the land until the Japanese colon-ized it.

A month later, the Americans came and, to the dismay of the Koreans, abolished the provisional government that the Koreans had established. And then, to the Koreans' utter despair, the Americans and Soviets divided the country in two. But three years later despair again turned to hope when the Koreans in the

South declared the establishment of a government run solely by Koreans. Within three years, though, war all but destroyed the country.

Things would go on like this for four more decades in a turbulent cycle of hope and despair. Liberation in 1945 initiated a period of dramatic change in government, belief systems, human relationships and quality of life that culminated, in the Seoul Summer Olympics of 1988, in the nation's initiation to membership in the league of modern societies. Korea's modernization, which had begun in the late nineteenth century, was still in its infancy in 1945; this four-decade period, from a little before Liberation to a little after the 1988 Seoul Olympics, brought modernization from infancy to maturity. The short stories in this book tell of this transition; here follows the story behind our stories.

State and the People

During its transition to modernity Korea took the painful but irreversible steps that led to full democracy. Before Liberation the country was run by totalitarian systems of government; within a few years of the Olympics, truly democratic government was established for good.

For two thousand years Koreans had lived under absolute monarchies. More of what we see in modern Korea comes from those centuries of inner development than from the most recent century (the twentieth century) of influence from the outside. Up till Korea's last king abdicated in 1910, monarchs more or less shared power with an aristocracy. Together, they exercised absolute power over the other classes, and except for infrequent localized outbursts and a major uprising in the waning years of the last dynasty (Chosŏn, 1398–1910), the lower classes submitted completely. Compared with other countries, Korea had a very stable society, with every successive national dynasty lasting several hundred years. It was all the more stable because, until the end of the nineteenth century, it had pretty much isolated itself from the rest of the world.[3]

It was then, in the second half of the nineteenth century, that the society that hadn't changed in any basic way in almost two millennia began to change in a big way. Peasants in one province revolted against the caste system and misrule by the decaying dynasty, and the revolt spread for the next several years. Not only the peasants were stirring—students who had returned from abroad, a few aristocrats, and "noncommissioned" aristocrats (*chungin*, or those with technical and bureaucratic skills, of the caste between aristocrats and peasants) were already pushing for reform.

Outside forces were also causing change. The Japanese forced the Hermit Kingdom to open its doors in 1876 with the Treaty of Kanghwa; in the next few years diplomats and businessmen from Japan and the West opened offices in Korea, and Christian missionaries opened their churches and schools and medical centers. There was a strong movement for reform and a more responsible and efficient government, but meddling foreign powers and fractious Koreans caused the country to end up in the hands of another autocratic government, Japan. With the Annexation Treaty of 1910, which Japan forced the king to accept, Korea was right back in the hands of autocracy, where it had been twenty years before.

This people who had ruled themselves ever since they first populated the peninsula were now ruled by a foreign emperor.

3. Exceptions to this isolation were Korea's suzerain relationship with China, invasions by the Mongols in the thirteenth century and Japan's Hideyoshi in the sixteenth century, and an occasional diplomatic mission to Japan.

They first lost economic and political control. No Korean held a position of substantial authority in the colonial government. The government did have a committee of Koreans, called the Central Council, but this Council had no authority. Even if it had had a voice, it would probably not have been of real service to the people, since the committee's members were remnants from the old regime who had helped Japan take over the country, and those who had common business interests with the Japanese. Eckert presents some telling figures:

> [In 1937] the bureaucracy employed . . . 52,270 Japanese and 35,282 Koreans . . . If a broader calculation of all public and private positions important to the colony is made, the totals for 1937 would be 246,000 Japanese and 63,000 Koreans. These numbers are even more significant when a comparison is made with Western colonies. In 1937 the French in Vietnam ruled a colony of roughly 17 million with 2,920 administrative personnel, 10,776 regular troops, and about 38,000 indigenous personnel.

In the last decade of occupation, the government-general went further than exploiting the country economically and politically; it implemented a cultural assimilation program that enforced policies like prohibition of the use of Korean in any public function (such as education) and replacement of Korean names with Japanese names.[4] Kim Tong-ni's "The Shaman Painting" (1936) and "Loess Valley" (1939) describe the sense of fatalism and nihilism that hung heavy over the nation as Japan attempted to Japanize the Korean soul.[5]

4. For a deeper understanding of this period, read Richard Kim's *Lost Names: Scenes from a Korean Boyhood.*

5. Since the 1960s the Japanese occupation has been almost unexceptionally described as Korea's blackest hour, but for many who lived through

Even before the Japanese took control of the country there had been deep political rifts among the Koreans, but the autocratic colonial government prevented their differences from playing themselves out, unintentionally by providing a common nationalistic cause and intentionally by suppressing dissent. When the two sides fought the Japanese, they were able to work effectively together. In 1919, for instance, in a coordinated operation at over a hundred locations throughout the country, they issued a declaration of independence. Generally, however, there was opposition between the poor and the wealthy, and this antipathy was galvanized with the establishment of the Communist Party in 1925. Then, "The wartime mobilization between 1938 and 1945 had sharpened the differences between the two sides and brought their animosity to a new height. By the end of the war . . . Korea was already an ideologically bifurcated society, held together by the power of the colonial state."

Liberation from Japan came in 1945, with its defeat in the Pacific War. For these "people who had recently escaped from under the oppressive boot of Japanese fascism and were now masters of their own history . . . an abundant sense of potential and promise brightened their future." But they had lived under Japanese rule for forty years and were not yet liberated psychologically. In an interview conducted for this background study,[6] two elderly gentlemen who were young villagers at that time reported that the people had been so effectively condi-

the occupation, life in many ways went on more or less as usual. Not all Koreans looked back on the period as a time when things were horrible. Testimony to this effect can be found in Kang, Hildi.

6. Chongmyo, the shrine that holds the memorial tablets of the Chosŏn dynasty kings, is a popular gathering place for (mostly male) senior citizens. Every weekend, on a stage in the park in front of Chongmyo, musicians entertain hundreds of seniors with popular music from the past. Most of these seniors grew up in the provinces outside of Seoul.

tioned by forty years of Japan's oppressive rule that, when the defeated Japanese left their village, the residents, afraid to show their real feelings, gave them a very polite sendoff. There were others who felt sympathy.[7]

Those who were more in tune with what was going on had already been preparing for Korea to be run by Koreans, and for a few weeks it appeared that they would be successful. A Committee for the Preparation of Korean Independence was established to govern the country. This Committee leaned to the left but included rightist elements—it even elected the rightist Syngman Rhee as chairman of the new state (the Korea People's Republic). It "proceeded to dismantle the colonial administration at every level and to expel those judged as collaborators from positions of political power and influence," so it enjoyed strong popular support.

On August 15, though, "Koreans regained a country that had been lost to Japanese rule only to lose it again to Russian and American influence." The two superpowers established a trusteeship with the rationale that these people who had been ruled by an outside power for forty years would not be able to rule themselves. (Actually, the Koreans could boast one of the most stable string of governments in world history, having ruled themselves for nearly two millennia.) They decided that the

7. One elderly Chongmyo informant, thirteen years old when the Japanese departed, remembered that, at the sad image of Japanese departing with their possessions strapped to their backs, he felt only sympathy, and did not remember any display of hostility from other Koreans. He recalled one occasion when his father, a journalist, entered a neighborhood police station on his way home from drinking and, in a rage of pent-up anger and frustration at the Japanese occupiers, broke some furniture; the Japanese police escorted him home, and the next day the young commander of the police station visited his home to apologize that the Japanese had made him feel bad enough to behave as he did.

Russians would take control of the North. Even as late as 1947, Roger Baldwin, director of the American Civil Liberties Union, observed that "Japan, the former enemy, was like a 'liberated country,' while Korea had all the earmarks of a conquered country."

The American occupation government thought that the country was being run by Soviet sympathizers and promptly disbanded and outlawed the government that the Koreans had established. In their occupation government the Americans reinstalled reactionary elements from the former aristocracy and others—including those who had collaborated with the Japanese—who had struck it rich during colonial days. People naturally started thinking that Liberation was doing nothing about liberating the ordinary Korean from the rule of the privileged class—this new government consisted of those who wanted to preserve the status quo; it was "old wine in new bottles."[8] And so the political discord and frustration that had begun during the Japanese occupation and then abated for a few weeks returned. The resulting milieu of suspicion compels the precipitate judgment and unwarranted death of the street waif in "The Game Beaters."

The uninformed and inexperienced U.S. occupation forces

8. Cumings, p. 215. *Time*, Sept. 24, 1945: "Hodge retained the Japs, including the notorious General Nobuyuki Abe, ex-Governor of Korea, whom he thanked publicly for making the U.S. occupation 'simple and easy.' Hodge also kept the Japanese police, holding that Koreans were 'too excited' to perform police duty and that they were 'the same breed of cat as the Japanese.' Koreans roared and rioted (Japanese soldiers machine-gunned one throng, killed two, wounded ten.)" *Time*, Oct. 14, 1946, adds: " . . . the U.S. is still trying to live down initial errors: the bad feeling created by retaining Japanese police, however briefly, as a temporary control force (the Soviets booted them quickly and efficiently in the north); a willingness to string along with doddering Korean oldsters, instead of young, competent and popular leaders . . . "

were unable to maintain order, and fighting between left and right increased; throughout the country they battled it out, with tens and hundreds dying in daily riots and skirmishes. Elderly informants tell of their youth in the country villages, when they did not know the first thing about ideology and found themselves in the ranks of whatever gang happened to dragoon them first.[9] It began to seem that the country could not hold together. Things were so bad after Liberation, one informant recounted, that there were not a few who looked back with nostalgia on the relatively stable times of the Japanese occupation.

Somehow, though, things held together until, in May of 1948, Korea held its first democratic election, for the National Assembly. Ninety-two percent of South Koreans who were registered to vote actually cast ballots; the one damper on the festive occasion was a boycott by the communists. In the same year, however, the firmly entrenched conservatives (who had managed to jump from the U.S. occupation administration into the Assembly) adopted a constitution that was superficially democratic but essentially Confucian.

> [According to Confucian principles] the authority relationship between the ruler and the ruled ought to be hierarchical. It was the state that should educate and by so doing transform the behavior of the ruled. Not the other way around . . . From 1948 through the early 1960s, Japanese codes of the colonial era remained intact and were in force.

The Assembly elected Syngman Rhee, and he was inaugurated president on August 15, 1948, the same day that the Republic of

9. Interview, July 6, 2005. Kim Chong-un supports this informant: "A people with practically no ideological knowledge . . . was suddenly thrown into the vortex of a chaotic war of ideas."

Korea was formally declared. An ultra-rightist who, in his autocratic tendencies, has been compared to Chosŏn dynasty monarchs, within a few years Rhee turned out to be too despotic[10] even for the Americans who had supported his election to the presidency.

Student demonstrations in 1960 led to a general uprising throughout Seoul, and ended in Rhee's resignation and the demise of his regime. A liberal government took over, but its very openness invited political chaos. When the Assembly began to take on a leftist cast, General Park Chung Hee deposed that government in a military coup.

Park turned out to be as despotic as Rhee. In 1979, after holding power for nineteen years and when he seemed to be getting dangerously paranoid of dissident elements, he was assassinated by his director of intelligence. Almost immediately another general, Chun Du-hwan, took power in another coup. Years later, as a result of a massive popular uprising against his and his regime's financial and political corruption, he was forced (in 1987) to agree to fair elections. These elections marked the final major step in the country's transition from autocracy to a real democracy.

The Struggle against Oppression

For a better understanding of the general social milieu underlying several of our stories—and, in particular, the 1980s setting in "What's To Be Done?"—we ought to closely examine the battle between the period's opposing political forces. The determining political aspect of the transition period was the battle

10. Cumings, p. 342. "American policy makers played several times during the war with the idea of replacing Rhee . . . [and] actual planning for a coup against Rhee materialized in 1953."

between the establishment (state, military and industry) and the people, or opposition. The opposition was a number of weak and fractious opposition groups of politicians and students.

> Since 1948 and until only very recently the politics of South Korea have been characterized by two expanding and opposing forces. Controlling the society at the top has been an increasingly oppressive and systematic authoritarian coalition of political, bureaucratic, economic, and security groups, dominated by a single dictatorial leader. Confronting this massif of power has been a growing and ever more diverse and sophisticated collection of opposition groups, both within and outside the formal political structure.

Except for the toppling of Syngman Rhee in 1960 and Chun Du-hwan in 1987, establishment forces were generally in control.

During the transition period, students provided stronger opposition to autocracy than politicians did. Throughout most of Syngman Rhee's regime, the opposition was comprised mostly of politicians; students joined the opposition later, and it was their resistance that caused the regime's collapse.

Park Chung Hee got on the wrong side of the students right from the beginning by ousting a comparatively popular (left-leaning) government. When he took power after Rhee's downfall, he purged the government and media and academia of what his regime regarded as "corrupt" and "destabilizing" elements, many of whom also happened to be in the opposition. Then he proceeded to overhaul the economy with a plan that focused on industrialization and exports. Millions came up from the impoverished countryside to fill the newly available jobs. The nation entered the sweatshop phase of its industrial transition, which continued till the end of the 1980s: "[L]ong hours, minimal attention to worker safety, and suppression of labor organizations kept unit labor costs down and economic growth up." At the end of the 1960s the economy appeared headed for boom times.

The boom came in the 1970s. It was obvious, however, that the laborers, who had made the stunning economic progress possible, were not being allowed to share in its fruits. Government and corporate management tried to persuade the public that what benefited industry benefited the country—and, by extension, the individual citizen—and that, in the long run, it would benefit the workers to think of the nation before they thought of themselves. Sociologist Kim Kyong-Dong warned at that time that

> it is indeed questionable whether industrial workers will continue to accept the argument that they should endure sacrifices for the supreme national interest of uninterrupted economic growth. They might even feel that successful economic progress is irrelevant to them unless its benefits are widely and fairly shared by them on the basis of social justice and political democracy.

The general public was not convinced by the establishment's line of reasoning; even the middle class,[11] who were obviously benefiting from the government's policy of favoring industry

11. My definition of middle class is what is popularly regarded these days as the upper middle class: the economic sector that includes people who live well by working the capital that they possess, and people who have high salaries that allow them to accumulate substantial capital. Professionals, owners of small businesses, corporate executives, are members of the economic middle class. People who do not own enough capital to live off of its income are members of the working class.

over its workers, showed strong sentiment for the workers. Sentiment, however, can be fickle, and it does not always result in determined action. It is the view of some historians and sociologists that the tendency of the middle class during the transition period was, as Kim continued, to

> behave progressively only so far as they feel assured that the economic system is not in jeopardy. When they sense a serious threat to economic order, the Korean middle classes would quickly change their minds and turn to the side of order and stability. [Choi] argues that this is actually what happened in 1972 and 1980 when Park and Chun crushed popular resistance and installed their repressive regimes.

There is the undeniable fact that the middle class participated in the mass demonstrations that defeated Rhee and Chun, but in the later stages of the regimes few if any thought that Rhee and Chun were good for the economy and many imagined themselves economically better off without these corrupt regimes.

In addition to the argument "What's good for Samsung is good for the country," Park used another tactic to convince the public to support his policies. He exploited nightmarish memories of the recent cataclysmic collision with communist North Korea. In fact, every regime from the U.S. occupation government to Chun Du-hwan relentlessly raised the specter of the threat of communism, painted dissidents as communists, and clothed its own repressive policies as measures essential to securing the nation against the threat of communism.

Establishment's suppression of labor was so effective that organized labor accounted for only 20 percent of all industrial workers in the 1970s and 15 percent in the 1980s. "By the 1970s,

FKTU [Federation of Korean Trade Unions] was tightly controlled by the government and staffed at the highest levels partly by government bureaucrats. . . . The government's objective was to control the unions and minimize the growth of any base for political opposition." The Federation of Korean Trade Unions, which all unions were legally required to join, was controlled by the government; labor laws favored management. Chun's regime was even harder on labor than Park's. In 1979, the year that Chun took power, the number of labor unions that existed during Park's regime dropped from around 4,000 to 2,635. In the treatment of labor by Park's and Chun's regimes, one could only wonder what the difference was between them and the Japanese colonial administrators—it seemed to many that, in most respects, the only thing that Liberation had changed was the names of those in the government.

The Student Movement

College students and intellectuals were usually the initiators of meaningful dissident activity. A few opposition politicians,[12] of course, objected to the exploitation of labor and suppression of the people's rights, but it was mostly the students who were able to exert influence on the state of affairs. These "watchdogs of political morality" and "conscience of the nation and incarnation of the sovereign people" now led the struggle against the Park and Chun regimes. They regarded themselves as descendants of the highly principled, self-sacrificing literati of the Chosŏn dynasty. Kong Chi-yŏng's "What's To Be Done?" in its description of the male protagonist provides a sense of this

12. One of the most active was Kim Dae-jung, who survived torture and a death sentence to later become president. Many "opposition" politicians were co-opted by the regimes.

self-image: "You wouldn't believe how strict he is with himself. Even when his sweetheart is sick in bed, if it's time to go to one of his groups he just gets up and leaves her. Always smiling like that but as strong as steel inside. Never anything but correct and proper." James Wade, who wrote a column for the *Korea Times* during much of the transition period, offers a description of the student in 1960s Korean society:

> The student occupies a very special and sacrosanct position in Korean society. Always in the forefront of resistance to Japan during the 1910–1945 occupation, students also took the initiative in the demonstrations that toppled tyrannical old Syngman Rhee's Liberal Party government in 1960. Deluded by popular adulation, the students suddenly found themselves in a position of real political influence, and grabbed at the chance to become arbiters of policy. Their immature idealism was readily exploited by dissident opposition politicians and, to some extent at least, by infiltrating Red agents from the north, bent on encouraging anarchy.[13]

Throughout the sixties and seventies and eighties, students fomented the campus riots, street demonstrations, jammed traffic and the sting of tear gas that were a common occurrence in the major cities. The public, in spite of these inconvenienc-

13. Wade, L. L., p. 42. Steinberg (1989, p. 79) says that, back in the Chosŏn dynasty, "Students, as the nascent literati, were often the watchdogs of political morality. Student demonstrations, against what they regarded as undue Buddhist influences or unorthodox Confucian behavior, may be traced to the fifteenth century and were sporadic thereafter. Students today continue to regard themselves as the political conscience of the country, although on occasion that role is disputed by elements of the society at large."

es and some concern about communist infiltration in the ranks of the activists, had a basic admiration for the students and expressed general sympathy for their struggle.

Except for when they joined the massive uprising that ousted Syngman Rhee from office, secondary school students, like the kids in "First Love" (set in the 1970s), did not participate in the student anti-government activities. It was only between 5 and 10 percent of college students—like the heroine in "What's To Be Done?"—that planned and habitually participated in the demonstrations; most college students were occasional participants. Students in their first two years of college, freed from the oppressive demands of preparing for the college entrance exam, were much more likely to join demonstrations than were upperclassmen, who had to concern themselves with getting a job. Like our student in "River" (1968), almost no graduate students had anything to do with dissident activity.

In the 1960s and 1970s, student opposition hardly ever challenged the basic foundations of society. They might attempt the overthrow of a regime, but they were basically of a conservative middle class mentality obeying the genes inherited from their agricultural society's forbears, and did not want a total change in the system. They demonstrated for justice in the operation of government, but they did not fight for the overthrow of capitalism. Political science professor Oh Byung-hun described them in 1975: "Traditional bonds still restrain them both individually and collectively and prevent total acceptance of radicalism. . . . If there are students sympathetic to a drastic change in the social system, their number and influence have been negligible."

In the 1970s an underground culture formed around the students' dissident movement. Literary works and songs supporting the movement's ideas and heroes circulated in spite of laws that often landed performers, and even their audience, in jail. In

"What's To Be Done?" when the police raided a campus, one activist leader (the male protagonist) rallied the other students with the cry, "Survivors, onward!" This comes from the demonstration song "March for the Martyrs." The lyrics were put to music for a publicly staged shamanist rite during the 1980 Kwangju uprising; this rite was conducted to send the souls of two "martyrs of the movement" on their journey to the next world. Here's the last verse:

> Friends, be steadfast till that new day comes,
> rise again like the wind-bowed reed
> and go on shouting our battle cry.
> Up, rise up!
> Shout the bloodied battle cry.
> Our martyrs lead us forward, so
> Onward, survivors! Onward!

While student activism in the 1960s and 1970s struggled for the correction of government misbehavior and occasionally even called for replacement of the government, many in the student movement in the 1980s went much further, attempting to change the basic system.

> [President] Chun had to face a more radical and determined student movement than his predecessors [did]. . . . The gradual absorption of Western neo-Marxist and dependency literature . . . , and the failure to achieve reform in the 1979-80 period [between Park's assassination and Chun's coup d'etat] pushed student leaders much further to the left than ever before. . . . For the new student leaders, liberal democracy was no longer a sufficient goal, either in itself or as a necessary step toward unification of the peninsula. They regarded South Korea's major politi-

> cal and social ills, including the national division, as structural problems embedded in the country's sociopolitical system or in its "neocolonialist" relationship with the United States—impervious, in either case, to reform at the top. The logical task, from the students' perspective, was revolution against these two evils, usually seen as interconnected.

According to the author of "What's To Be Done," in the 1970s there was little talk of socialism among students, but in the 1980s, Marxism-Leninism provided a theoretical foundation and methods for their struggle.[14] In fact, the title of Kong's short story is borrowed from a utopian novel written by Nikolai Chernyshevsky (1828–1889), a Russian revolutionary socialist who agitated for establishment of a socialist society and was a strong influence on Lenin. His novel, along with the likes of E. H. Carr's *What Is History?* and Marx's *Das Kapital,* was "required" reading in Korea's student movement in the 1980s and early 1990s.

The two main schools of dissident activity in the 1980s were the National Liberation Movement ("NL"; *minjok haebang undong*) and the People's Democracy Movement ("PD"; *minjung minju undong*). Other groups existed—church groups, for example, that espoused the cause of liberation theology—but they were smaller and not as conspicuous. The NL focused on expulsion of American forces and on unification with the North

14. Walhain, p. 193: "Until the late 1970s, discussions on Marxist, communist, or socialist theories were almost inexistent. . . . Indeed, students from the 1980s believed their predecessors from the . . . 1970s were 'romantic' and 'sensitive' but had failed to propose a thought-out solution to the Korean problem. In contrast, the 1980s students began introducing radical concepts and ideologies which included dependency theory and class struggle, as they moved beyond anti-communist principles."

to regain full sovereignty over the peninsula for Koreans, and admired the "self-reliance" doctrine of North Korea. The PD focused more on cleaning up domestic politics, on labor rights, and aimed for proletarian revolution; they did not admire North Korea. The dissident cell portrayed in "What's To Be Done?" belonged to the PD.[15] These groups did not actually publicize their most radical goals; they knew that if they did, the public would not support their moderate activities (demonstrations condemning corruption, fixed elections, torture of political prisoners, etc.); nor would the public oppose their imprisonment. Even inside the organization there were many who did not espouse complete eradication of capitalist democracy, so the radical clique kept their ultimate goals to themselves.

Kong says that the government was also responsible for radicalization in the 1980s: while the Park regime of the 1960s and 1970s had at least a minimum of moral standards and could be influenced somewhat by the death of just one dissident, the massacre of hundreds in the 1980 Kwangju uprising showed that the Chun regime in the 1980s had few if any moral compunctions.[16]

15. Walhain, p. 192: "[T]hey resorted to guerrilla-type tactics, organizing quick and small-scale protests, involving only a few students at a time, but more frequently. They also organised ideology discussion groups, searching for the appropriate political, economic and social system for Korea." Pp. 194–195: "During the 1980s, a fair number of students sacrificed their studies, and sometimes put their future in jeopardy, to go work in factories as 'undercover' student-workers. They helped workers learn about their rights, and establish labour union structures. Students also denounced the appalling conditions in which homeless people lived in the outskirts of urban areas"

16. WSCF: "During the 18 years of the Park Chung Hee regime, nearly 700 students were expelled from their schools as a result of their opposition to the anti-democratic, violent dictatorship. In comparison, in the three years after the May 17, 1980, tragedy [of Chun's coup], more than

A change in the nature of financial corruption was another major factor in the increasingly radical posture of the student dissidents. Corruption was endemic during the transition period, as it had been for centuries before. In the era of monarchy, those who held public office helped themselves from the public purse—and were expected to do so, within reason. Many exploited their authority to fleece the people under their jurisdiction. After Liberation, Syngman Rhee's cohorts preserved this tradition. Park Chung Hee did little if anything to prevent the exchange of money and favors between businesses and government officials during this time of tremendous growth in the government-supported manufacturing/export industry. "River" (1968, during Park's tenure) hints, with its reference to the tax man's avarice, at the ubiquitous nature of corruption. While Rhee and Park themselves were clean, Chun Du-hwan was notorious for his avarice. He and his cohorts extorted huge "contributions" from industry, and Chun and his wife personally appropriated hundreds of millions of dollars of this booty[17]; his brother embezzled millions from the New Community Movement.

By 1987, Chun had gone too far. In the face of overwhelming public protests (initiated, as usual, by students, but now supported by ordinary citizens who also turned out in great num-

1400 students were expelled and 500 others were forcibly and summarily conscripted into the military. At least 6 conscripted students have died while in the army and many student activists face the prospect of death or injury in the military and on the campuses."

17. Kang Ku-yŏl: As of 2005, eighteen years after Chun was deposed, he has paid around $50 million of the $200 million assessment levied on him for bribes that he was convicted of having taken during his tenure. His claim in 2005 of having a total of $300 in personal assets infuriated the public and propelled the prosecutor's office to renewed efforts to locate the rest of his hidden assets.

bers), Chun anointed Roh Tae Woo (an army general, Chun's coup partner) to succeed him, and Roh immediately promised open, direct elections—just in time for the 1988 Seoul Olympics. This soon made possible the government by the people that Koreans had thought they were getting at Liberation, thirty years before.

The presidential election in December 1987, which Roh Tae Woo won, was only the first step in the establishment of government that was truly responsive to the needs of all the people; it was not until several years later that democracy really took root. In spite of this, Chun's fall took much of the steam out of the student dissident movement, since many supporters inside and outside the movement now sensed the inevitability of full-fledged democracy. However, because there were still issues that drew many students' concern (labor exploitation, redevelopment projects that deprived the poor of their homes, and so on), and the radicals still sought to replace the capitalist system with a socialist or communist one, the movement made its voice heard now and then into the 1990s and dissidents were still being thrown into jail.[18]

How this changing political situation affected the dissidents is the theme of "What's To Be Done?" Literary critic Son Kyŏng-muk tells us how, after democratization looked assured, the movement lost its passion as many of its members dispersed

18. Former general Roh Tae Woo was inaugurated as president in 1987, after the first relatively fair election in many years. Most people, however, were not convinced that democracy was firmly established until Kim Young-sam's "civilian government" took office in 1993; even then there was doubt, because former dissident Kim, to achieve victory in the election, had made a deal with Roh's ruling party. It was not until another longtime dissident, Kim Dae-jung, won the 1997 election for president on the opposition party ticket that all Koreans believed that democracy was firmly entrenched.

into all walks of life, adopting the spirit of materialism and pursuing the values of the establishment that they had tried to eradicate in the 1980s.[19] (You might recognize a parallel here with the "flower power" generation of the 1960s and 1970s in the West.)

With less support now from the students, labor had to go it pretty much alone; they continued fighting, but increasingly for what many of the public thought were excessive demands. Within six months of Chun's departure, the number of labor unions rebounded from around 2,700 to over 4,000. They made their numbers felt: labor disputes increased tenfold from 1986 to 1987, and more strikes occurred in July and August 1987 than in the previous twenty-five years combined.

Belief Systems

A society's belief systems have varying degrees of influence on its members, consciously or unconsciously, and when a society's belief systems change, so will its members' behavior. During Korea's transition period, the speed of that change was remarkable. The characters in the stories in this book evolved from a uniquely Korean mix of shamanism, Taoism, Buddhism, Confucianism, Christianity and such "new religions" as Ch'ŏndokyo. Between Liberation and the Olympics, the once dominant Confucianism loosened its hold a bit on Koreans, shamanism and Buddhism returned from obscurity, and Christianity became mainstream.

Except for "The Shaman Painting," the stories in this collection do not directly address or even mention belief systems, but these systems no less affect stories' development and the behav-

19. Son, Gyŏng-muk, p. 325. Kong, 1995: Kong's short story "Human Decency" (Ingan-e daehan yeŭi), presents a detailed description of how the former dissidents fared. Also see Fulton, 1997.

ior of their characters. When people behave in a certain way, they are usually not conscious of the systems that form the foundation of their relationship with the world. Even a Western atheist is influenced by his Judeo-Christian past.

The old peasant in "The Visit" did not ponder, for example, "Confucianism says that the relationship between father and only son is more important than anything, so I'll visit my son even though I'm sick and even though I have to go into debt to do it." Confucian values were "taken not so much as 'Confucian' as [they were taken to be] the most valid and natural social order." The farmer borrowed the money because he felt that subliminal impulse arising from the social order which had evolved from the Confucian belief system that had influenced Korean thought and behavior for almost two millennia.

These systems came first form within, and then from farther and farther outside. Shamanism is Korea's indigenous belief system, practiced since the first Koreans set foot on the peninsula. "Shamanism is the primitive ethos of the Korean people. It is the basic instinct of the masses. . . . All Korean religious ideas and ceremonies are influenced by it, and at some point coalesce with it." From the fourth to the fourteenth centuries, Buddhism and Confucianism shared influence in a sometimes mutually supportive, sometimes adversarial relationship; then Confucianism reigned by itself till the end of the nineteenth century. With the demise of the Chosŏn dynasty and the fall of the *yangban* aristocracy, which had fostered Confucianism, and through Japan's occupation, for a period of about fifty years no single belief system dominated. Then, between Liberation in 1945 and the Olympics in 1988, Confucianism lost its official status; Buddhism and shamanism also lost some strength, then gradually regained it. Christianity came to enjoy greater popularity here than in any other Asian nation except for the Philippines.

Shamanism

It is 1938. Korea just before Liberation is only a tattered remnant of former times. The monarchy, which had ruled the peninsula through one dynasty or another for two thousand years, is gone now. It was abolished at the turn of the century by the Japanese, who have been assimilating the peninsula into their empire by eradicating everything Korean. Kyŏngju, only a few miles from Mohwa's dilapidated abode in "The Shaman Painting," back in the fourth century was the great capital of the state that unified the Korean peninsula. Shamans were royalty. In Mohwa the shaman's day, Kyŏngju amounts to nothing more than a provincial town, and Mohwa lives in neglected isolation.

Truly, things in 1938 are not as they once were. Korea's hermetically sealed doors have been forced open to the world; the monarchy, symbol of Koreans' self-rule, has yielded to rule by foreigners, and shamanism, already humbled by Buddhism and Confucianism, has found a new and more virulent threat in Christianity. A new world is imposing itself on shaman Mohwa and on Korea.

Looking back from the twenty-first century, if Mohwa had used her shaman powers to look forward half a century, she might not have reacted to this new enemy in the extreme manner that she did. Shamanism survived to the degree that it helped shape Korean Christianity, as it had previously worked on Buddhism and Confucianism; and, though the ritual (the *kut*) is not performed quite as frequently as it once was, shamanism maintains a strong presence in twenty-first century Korea.

Several of Korea's early chieftains and kings were shamans. Later, as the political authority and duties of the kings expanded, they handed their religious duties over to shaman priests, who nevertheless retained substantial political influence. In the fourth century Buddhist and then Confucian leaders usurped this influence from the shamans. Throughout the next few centuries, however, the shamans retained strong power among the people because with their magic rites they were more able to minister to the people's immediate needs. While Buddhists were willing to co-exist with shamanism, the Confucian ruling class saw these "witches" as a threat to their absolute control over the common people, and the shaman was relegated to "lowborn" caste, in the same bottom-rung social class as *kisaeng* (similar to the Japanese geisha) and itinerant groups of entertainers. In the Confucian-dominated Chosŏn dynasty, the official punishment for participation in shamanic practice was a hundred lashes in public. But shamanism lived on, even in highest society. Privately, the aristocracy continued to use the services of shamans, females directly and males indirectly (through their women), as long as they were not too obvious about it.

Shamanism continued to be officially shunned in post-Chosŏn times. When the Japanese occupied Korea they persecuted shamans, and tried to replace shamanism with Shintoism by moving the national shrine Kuksadang away from Namsan (geomantically, one of Seoul's foremost mountains).[20] After Liberation, President Park Chung Hee, who took power in 1961, pronounced shamanism a superstition and a deterrent to the nation's advancement. Korea was still a very poor country and much that was traditional was regarded by most Koreans as a cause and a symptom of that poverty. One of the primary points of Park's New Community Movement (also referred to as New Village Movement) in the 1970s was extermination of shamanism, and the practice of shamanism was thus outlawed,

20. Holstein, 1994, pp. 17–18. They replaced it with the central Shinto shrine and moved it to Inwang Mountain. Cumings, p. 182: "The colonizers even forced Koreans to worship at Shinto shrines, although Shinto was a strictly Japanese religion. . . . Korea in the 1940s had many Shinto shrines."

resulting in the destruction of shamanist shrines, suppression of rites, and the harassment of shamans. Shaman ritual continued to be performed in very remote villages and occasionally even in the city.

After Park Chung Hee departed the scene (1979), shamanism experienced something of a revival. Now it was no longer illegal, and shamans set up their shrines in the open and drew more patrons. Many who did not participate in it nevertheless popularized it. University students in the 1980s used the mask dance, which had originated in shamanist ritual, to stimulate young people to join the anti-dictatorship and pro-democracy movement. Shamanism and its ritual also developed as a wholesome form of entertainment, in contrast to the vacuity of pop art. It was also popularized as a national culture form. Now the most prominent shamans were designated by the government as human national treasures, and government and media referred to them with their official title of "master." Most in the middle and upper classes patronizingly regarded shamanism as quaint and harmless. They did not, however, recognize it as a belief system that any truly "modern" person would adhere to.

Since the 1988 Seoul Olympics, shamanism has continued to gain in popularity. It is accepted by nonparticipants much as Westerners accept palm readers—something they would not do, but not something to prohibit. More importantly, it is also recognized (or admitted) by many as a subconscious influence on Korean behavior, as "the fundamental religious worldview underlying the mental landscape of Koreans."

A participant in a shamanist ritual can also be a Buddhist or a Confucian or a Christian.[21] Almost every Buddhist temple

21. Baker, 2001: "Until the second half of the twentieth century, most lay Koreans did not identify themselves as Buddhists rather than Confucians, or conceive of Buddhism and shamanism as mutually exclusive reli-

complex, for example, has an auxiliary chapel for the Mountain Spirit (personified in an old man with a tiger, which is itself a combination of shamanism and Chinese Taoism). And in Seoul's shaman village, where the Chosŏn dynasty's main shamanist shrine is now located, Buddhist temples and shamanist shrines share turf and patronage. Amalgamation of ancient and newer religions is not rare in traditional societies; throughout Asia, for example, the intermingling of shamanism, Hinduism and Buddhism is obvious.

It is not easy to come up with a number for adherents of shamanism, because it is not an institution with a hierarchy or centralized organization; most patrons of shamanism do not actually "practice" shamanism, since it has no regular meetings for worship—a rite is an *ad hoc* sort of thing, performed only for a special need—nor established, documented moral code. Many of those who would participate in a shamanist ritual or who have animist beliefs do not feel that this excludes participation in organized religion, and vice versa. For what it is worth, though, the operative word in many articles on the Internet is "revival," and we come across estimates like 300 shaman shrines within an hour of Seoul and 300,000 practicing shamans in the country. Professor Sŏ Chŏng-pŏm, a sociologist, wonders why there is a revival: "One would think that with the progress in civilization and culture, shamans would die off, but actually, every year, we see the number of shamans increase by about one percent." Haines Brown thinks that the answer is found in the vicissitudes that shamanism promises to help cope with: "The practice is symptomatic of circumstances in which people either had too little power to change their fate (as in early societies) or whose personal power is insufficient in a world that

gions." Indeed, many say that shamanism is the progenitor of all religions. Today it co-exists with many religions throughout the world.

seems overwhelming or threatening (as under modern capitalism)."[22]

There are several shaman houses in almost every neighborhood—fewer per capita in the more wealthy neighborhoods (though a multistory hall for rituals was built just a few years ago in affluent P'yŏngch'angdong and over twenty of the new "fortune-telling cafés" have sprung up recently in wealthy Apkuchŏngdong). Older and less affluent neighborhoods host whole ghettos of fifteen or more shaman houses.

That Chosŏn dynasty blend of rejection and acceptance survives in modern Korea. The wealthy and middle classes, who consider themselves enlightened moderns, offer condescending tolerance, not a few of them publicly denying the shaman's powers but privately making use of her services. In neighborhoods where shamans run their business, many of the denizens—including those who use the shaman's services—dislike having one near their home, uncomfortable with the proximity of the netherworld or an element that they associate with an inferior class. At the same time, one informant told me that his sister-in-law, a middle-class Christian who considers herself a very modern woman, is going to ask a shaman for the best date to have her cesarean section; she does not believe in it, of course, "but why not?"

Internet presence provides some indication of shamanism's

22. Brown. Kim Chong-Ho, however, reports that shamanism is not accepted in some sectors. He conducted an extended field study of shamanism in a small village and found a strong sense of antagonism toward it. He claims, in fact, that "shamanism has never been welcome, but always despised, no matter what Koreans took as their ruling ideology in different periods." His opinion is suspect, though, because, while he says that shamanism was "always despised," we know that in ancient times shamans were kings, and shamanism was popular even among the aristocrats during the years that Buddhism was the politically dominant belief system.

growing popularity. Two major sites are www.shaman.co.kr and www.mudang.co.kr.

Taoism

The three Taoist immortals in "The Gulls" (1958) keep mostly to themselves, and, like Taoism in Korea, play a quiet but important role in the story. In most discussions of Korean systems of belief, Taoism is largely ignored, but it always has been a formative element in every belief system in the country, even shamanism.[23] The shaman Mohwa demonstrated the animistic features of Taoism that are an essential part of shamanism:

> It was not only to the grownups that she demurely twisted her shoulders and bowed in respect; even children awed her, and upon occasion even a dog or a pig would be the object of her embarrassing demonstrations. Cats too, and frogs, and worms, or a lump of meat, a butterfly, a potato, an apricot tree, a fire poker, a clay pot, a stone step, a straw shoe, the branch of a jujube tree, a swallow, a cloud, wind, fire, rice, a kite, a gourd ladle, an old straw cattle-feed pouch, kettles, spoons, oil lamps . . .

Taoism was, as Goulde says, "an important part of Korean culture from as early as the Three Kingdoms period and throughout the Silla, Koryŏ and Chosŏn periods" (in total, spanning from 57 BC to AD 1910) and its philosophical and religious aspects are part of ancient and contemporary beliefs and practice. The attitude of Confucianists toward Taoism is not clear. Some historians, according to Goulde, claim that

23. Covell (p. 16) uses the term "Tao-Shamanism," and adds on p. 23 that Korean shamanism "absorbed Taoism and its magic lore."

> "from [Taoism's] first appearance, it was rejected both by Confucian and Buddhist elites as subversive of normal social and ethical behavior, as is evidenced by the repeated condemnation of Taoism in standard historiographic sources. . . . When standard historiography is read critically or when alternative sources . . . are examined, accounts of Korean Taoist ritual practices and positive valuations of Taoist ideas vis-à-vis Confucianism and Buddhism are overwhelmingly present."

Whether it was publicly rejected, grudgingly tolerated or actively embraced, we do know that kings in all of the dynasties offered rites to Taoist divinities. And behind the thrones of Chosŏn dynasty kings was the multipanel screen depicting Taoist animist characters (turtle, deer, etc.) representing long life and prosperity.

In "Loess Valley," writer Kim Tong-ni used major elements of Taoism—geomancy and its agent *chi* (*ki* in Korean)—to depict Korea's mortal condition in the latest and harshest years of occupation by Japan. The legend of the dragons who fought and colored the valley with their blood, recounted at the beginning of the story, reflect the reality of the times, of Korea being violated by both external and internal forces. To this day it is believed that the Japanese used Taoist geomancy to further their policy of cultural assimilation of Korea by impaling stakes in the slopes of Pukak Mountain, at whose foot lay the Korean king's palace (the heart of the country). This was done to interrupt the flow of the vital life force *chi* from the mountain through the king to the rest of the nation. In another attempt to block this beneficent force they tore down many of the palace's ancillary buildings and, in their place, erected the governor-general's offices, thereby destroying the harmony of the carefully planned mountain-and-palace configuration.

Taoism did not disappear with the demise of the dynasty, nor with Liberation. We can witness the vitality of Taoism these days too, in the many Taoist artistic motifs (the yin-yang symbol and the hexagram in the Korean national flag being two of the most popular) in every artistic media and many commercial designs. Taoism is represented in the Mountain Deity's shrine in Buddhist temples; in the centers that offer Taoist therapy and exercise; in the continuing use of geomancy in burial of the dead and in the design of buildings; in the peculiar spontaneity of traditional style that lives in modern pottery and design (Laozi said, "Great ingenuity is something like artlessness or rusticity"); and in the thriving science and business of oriental medicine, which is based on Taoist principles of yin-yang and *chi*.[24] Streetside fortunetellers, who consult the *Book of Changes*, are increasing in number and doing good business.

Buddhism

Mohwa the shaman felt no hesitation in getting the nearby Buddhist temple to accept her son as a novice, and saw no contradiction in later telling her son that "Buddhism is the Way." And to most Koreans at the beginning of her transition, if Buddhism wasn't their main religion it was a complementary, not opposing, system of belief.[25]

24. Baker, 1995. Baker presents data showing a large increase in the numbers of clerics, self-proclaimed believers, and "buildings serving a religiously-active population [and this increase] could not have occurred without a corresponding increase in the size of that population." Andrew Eungi Kim, in an article in the year 2000, reports that "together, Protestants and Catholics thus make up close to a third of the total population in the nation."

25. Hogarth, p. 152: "Korean *mudang* and their followers often maintain that their religion is really *pulgyo* (Buddhism)."

Buddhism arrived in Korea around the fourth century and quickly became the dominant religion among the upper classes, thus nudging shamanism into the background. At the same time, Buddhists gave a home to shamanist music[26] and deities in their temples and in some rituals.[27] Buddhism was a philosophy as well as a religion, and was favored by the royalty and aristocracy until the sixth century, when Confucianism gained equal attention. During the Koryŏ dynasty (918–1392), Confucians gradually took the place of Buddhist monks in politics and government, and Buddhist monks withdrew into a less public, more contemplative life.

> Native Korean values, however, dictated that the conversion of the Koryŏ aristocracy to Confucian rationalism would be less than whole-hearted. Koryŏ Confucianists by no means rejected Buddhism. Regarding it as the doctrine for achieving spiritual tranquility and otherworldly salvation, they felt that it complemented and could coexist with Confucianism. Accordingly, many men were versed in both.

In fact, almost every one of the Koryŏ kings was a devout Buddhist. As the dynasty came to its last days, however, the Buddhist clergy was accused of having gone rotten. The Confucian complaint about Buddhism reminds us of the Reformation in

26. Eckert, 1990, p. 39: "The *hyangga* genre ['native songs'] represents a transformation of shamanist incantations into Buddhistic supplications." Heyman, p. 24: In modern times, monks in the Chogye order "have done away with all dances, accompanying musical instruments, and practically all the sacred songs in order to disassociate themselves from Shamanism."

27. Covell, p. 16: "When tinctured with the lore of Tao-Shamanism, Buddhism became a distinctly Korean entity which builds, carves and paints visions far removed from the simple origins of [Buddhism]."

Europe around the same time: it had, like the Catholic Church, amassed too much temporal wealth, and too many of its monks were morally corrupted. With the beginning of the Chosŏn dynasty (1392), Confucianism pushed Buddhism into the mountains. From this time Buddhism was practiced mainly by women." As an institution, Buddhism retained this reputation and status until the twentieth century.

At the end of the Chosŏn dynasty (1910), Buddhism was still purely a religion that "survived in isolation, among the oppressed and those disenchanted with life," and had no overt influence in public affairs. The Japanese, during their colonization of Korea, tried to replace the Korean Buddhism, which even in its forced isolation still saw itself in its former Koryŏ dynasty role as "protector of the nation," with a more contemplative and passive Japanese Buddhism. This is probably why, in censuses conducted by the Japanese in the 1920s and 1930s, only around 200,000 Koreans identified themselves as Buddhists and why statistics show more Christians than Buddhists. It was reported in 1944, a year before Liberation, that "Buddhism has died out."

Reports of its demise, however, were premature; the clergy were working underground to return the religion to its former Koryŏ role. It is true that, after Liberation in 1945, in spite of the reform movement within Buddhism took a while to make its comeback. It seems that up to 1960, fifteen years after the Japanese left, Buddhism still did not have much influence in the public arena. Sociologist Lee Man-gap stated at that time that there was no evidence that Buddhism had any strength, that it was not strong enough to have, as some accused, "a negative effect" on the country's efforts at modernization.[28] As a religion

28. Lee Man-gap, p. 231. He said the same about Confucianism: "Confucianism is no longer a serious obstacle to the industrialization of Korea."

of the people, though, it resided in the core of their being. The Anglican village priest Rutt noted in 1964, "For here is mysticism, beauty and love, with some measure of self-abandonment. Buddhism is deeply engrained in Korean popular culture, however little the laity may understand it." Just a few years ago, though, Hogarth claimed that "the reform movements with Korean Buddhism that started under Japanese colonial rule continue to this day. . . . In recent years Korean Buddhism has been enjoying a revival." Baker (2001) notes that, along with the revival of spirituality in Korea toward the end of the twentieth century, the numbers of people identifying themselves as Buddhist climbed significantly:

> In 1962 Buddhist denominations claimed almost 700,000 followers in South Korea, three times as many as were found on the entire peninsula when it was ruled by the Japanese. . . . By 1985, the percentage of the population calling itself Buddhist had reached rough parity with the percentage of the population calling itself Christian. The census in 1995, for example, found 10.3 million Buddhists in South Korea, compared to 8.7 million Protestants and slightly less than 3 million Roman Catholics. . . . [T]he number of Buddhist monks and nuns tripled from less than 10,000 in 1962 to over 30,000 in 1993. . . . [And we see] the modern Buddhist temples in urban areas—temples which run kindergartens, publish glossy magazines, and sing hymns at Sunday worship services . . .

It is apparent that Buddhism, like Korea's other belief systems, experienced a change during the period of transition—revival from a reclusive mountain religion to a participatory urban movement. This enduring philosophy and religion has had a strong influence in the formation of the Korean people's character and has become a vital force once again in Korea. From the time of its arrival in Korea it has been teaching moral principles through its doctrine of karma and rebirth in Paradise. Throughout its two centuries of political prominence, with its doctrine of all-encompassing harmony it fortified in the minds of the people the legitimacy of centralized and authoritarian monarchy. These qualities were conducive to amiable personal relations and social stability; at the same time, though, they nurtured a spirit of fatalism and passive acceptance in the face of misfortune and injustice, a quality that is evident at several points in the stories in this book.

Confucianism

Confucianism does not readily lend itself to comparison with Korea's other systems of belief, because it is difficult to regard it as a religion. While one scholar of comparative religion points out that Confucianism does have an abstract supreme being (several cosmic and conceptual forces which can collectively be termed Heaven), it deals mainly with human relations in society. But that has made it a major formative element of the Korean mentality and behavior.

The historical public role of Confucianism in the dynastic era has already been discussed in its relationship with Buddhism. Now we might have a look at Confucianism in its influence on the people. (In these pages, the Chosŏn dynasty's neo-Confucianism, a rigidly conservative school, is referred to simply as Confucianism.) It is the opinion of many that the upper (*yangban*) class was more deeply influenced by Confucianism than the lower classes, and that notion is understandable when we consider the time- and resources-consuming ritual and etiquette that the *yangban* had to follow both in the home and in society. We might also consider the vulgar, rowdy un-Confucian behavior of the peasants in "Loess Valley." Ultimately, however, commoners were also affected by Confucianism. Confucianism fortified the society's rigid system of hierarchy (class, age, gender) that commoners were subject to; if it was almost impossible for a man born as a peasant to elevate his status and if he had no hope for his children to rise either, he was influenced by Confucianism.

Nevertheless, Confucianism was not what it used to be. Even before modern times there was a noticeable weakening in the influence of Confucianism. This was caused by such events as the Kabo reform of 1894, which abolished the official status of *yangban*. And later, during the Japanese occupation, agricultural reform cost many former *yangban* their lands; while not directed at Confucianism itself, this weakened the social class that constituted the strongest support for Confucianism.[29] Christianity, which entered Korea in full force toward the end of the nineteenth century, also helped to weaken Confucianism, because the doctrine taught by missionaries—that all are equal in the eyes of God—threatened Confucian patriarchal caste society.

Liberation precipitated the weakening influence of Confucianism. In the general elections of 1948, the first in Korea's history, Koreans of both genders and all classes were given the vote. This naturally strengthened the voice of commoners and women, both of whom had been suppressed by Korea's Confucian patriarchs. When the agricultural society gave way to an industrial society, and young men and women left the farm for the city, the family was physically sundered—and with it, the

29. Lett, 1998, p. 32–33: "During the last century of the dynastic era there was intense rivalry among yangban; the defeated were deprived of a place in government, which was the only honorable way for a yangban to earn a living, and they were, in effect, exiled to the countryside. In addition, advances in agricultural techniques enriched many commoners, which ultimately resulted in the upward mobility of commoners."

centrality of ancestors and patriarchy. A survey conducted in 1959 found that around two percent of families had stopped performing rites to honor their ancestors, and another one in 1978 reported that over 16 percent had given up the practice. Over the next few decades laws were enacted to empower laborers and women, which necessarily further weakened the patriarchal hierarchy of Confucianism. In articles and books written between Liberation and the Olympics, Confucianism is pronounced all but dead.[30]

But if Confucianism were really dead, why the countless signs of its survival in our stories throughout the transition? The strong class distinction in speech register in all of the stories (though it is not directly translatable in English), the respect shown the scholar-writer in "House of Idols" and the school teacher in "The Gulls," the oppressive power of education in "River" and "First Love," and gender distinction (in speech and behavior) in several of the stories are only a few examples of Confucianism's continuing influence.

Christianity

Christianity is thriving in modern Korea. Where Christians compromise only one percent of the population in Japan and China, they comprise nearly a quarter of Korea's population.

One might place the arrival of Christianity at 1784, in the person of Yi Sŭng-hun, when he returned to Korea after having

30. Lee Man-gap, p. 231; McBrian, p. 122; Hong, p. 7. Hart, p. 56: "Confucianism, an ideology that once represented, interpreted, and proscribed life in an agrarian world, now represents more idealism than practical thinking in an industrial world. Its connections to the social and economic realities of life are increasingly tenuous."

been baptized a Catholic in China. He and his fellow Confucian *yangban* "Practical Learning" fellow travelers had already been studying some scholarly treatises written by the Jesuits—e.g., Matteo Ricci's "The True Meaning of the Lord in Heaven"—in the hopes of finding ideas to help them reform the decaying, corrupt dynasty. Such literature became representative of all "Western Learning" (*sŏhak*); Chong Yak-yong (Tasan), a high official and one of the most respected neo-Confucian scholars of the nineteenth century, spent eighteen years in exile when his interest in this became known. Meanwhile, the new religion spread, but before it could spread far its adherents were suppressed because of the insular mentality of the Chosŏn dynasty and because the ruling class felt that Christianity and contact with the West, along with talk of reform, were a threat to Confucianism, to the monarchy, and to maintenance of their own privileged status. Christianity had a tenacious hold on its advocates, though, and it survived and was finally officially permitted toward the end of the nineteenth century.

Christianity spread as Korea began to shed its "hermit nation" identity. Two treaties did much to open the country to the rest of the world—the Treaty of Kanghwa (in 1876, with Japan) and the Korean-American Treaty (in 1882). While a small number of Catholic missionaries had already arrived during the preceding decades, the treaty with America opened the door to a relatively large number of Protestant missionaries.

Around the turn of the century, however, the Japanese came to govern all Westerners in Korea when they annexed the country in 1910. These new rulers—from a country that had never accepted Christianity and who saw in any religion other than Shintoism a danger to their scheme to colonize Korea—at times made it difficult for foreign missionaries to achieve their religious and social goals. The March 13, 1944, issue of *Time* magazine reports, for instance, that the Japanese ousted the missionary who was president of Chosen Christian College; they "dictated what should be taught" in schools, controlled sermons in church, and even prevented missionaries from visiting Korean homes. By publicly obstructing the missionaries in their social goals, however, the Japanese inadvertently contributed to the growth of Christianity. While the colonizers tried to exterminate the Korean spirit and did little if anything to improve the welfare of the masses, the Christian missionaries established institutions to satisfy the need for modern (i.e., Western) medical care and to provide modern (i.e., Western) education for all classes. To make things worse for the Japanese, the Christian missionaries preached the popular and obviously un-Japanese concepts of human rights, democracy and equality, the same notions that had threatened the Confucian establishment.

The missionaries—undoubtedly including the Presbyterian missionary in "The Shaman Painting"—had to walk a fine line between supporting the Koreans and avoiding the boot of the Japanese if they were going to maintain their presence in the country, and there was strong disagreement among them as to how actively they should involve themselves in the Koreans' cause. One example of this was the conflict in the Korean Catholic Church: it seems that the foreign leadership actively proscribed participation in the resistance movement, while many of the lower clergy, foreign and native, participated indirectly. On the whole, the Christian missionaries went to great lengths to protect their parishioners, though they tried to appear to the Japanese as impartial. Many, in order to protect their flock, counseled against open resistance to the Japanese, and some, early on, even regarded the Japanese as providing sorely needed reform. In spite of the missionaries' counsel against violent resistance, however, when the Declaration of Independence was proclaimed in 1919, several of the thirty-three signers (all

Koreans) were Christians.[31] Christianity therefore gradually came to be identified as both a potential rescuer of the country from Japanese occupation and, at the same time, the representative of modernization.

After the Japanese left, new adversities in Korea furthered the growth of Christianity. From the '50s into the 1980s, Christians played a significant role in the fight against indigenous dictatorship. The nation's poverty, which lasted into the 1970s, also provided fertile ground for Christianity to grow; its mission representatives were the conduit of contributions in money, food and clothing.

> Because the Church provided the basic tools of modernization and assumed a central role in the economic, political, and social modernization of South Korea, many Koreans viewed the acceptance of the Gospel not only as a means of entry into modern society but also as an access to what [was] believed to be a more advanced civilization. In this way, Christianity held out a vision of how things might or ought to be, and in due time, conversion to Christianity came to mean enlightenment. . . . The identification of Christianity as a gateway to modernity and success, both personal and national, acquired even more impetus during the period of rapid economic development from the early 1960s to the end of the 1980s. Koreans' admiration of Western culture and its economic achievements played a decisive role in encouraging such identification.

31. Adams, Daniel (p. 16) says that half were Christian and only "two or three were Buddhist," but other sources imply that there was a rough balance of representation among Buddhism, Ch'ŏndogyo and Christianity.

Most sources estimate that Christianity, along with its Koreanized versions like the Yŏŭido Full Gospel Church, has become the religion of around 25 percent of South Koreans, in comparison with around the same number who are Buddhist.

Syncretism: Shamanist Features in Christianity

Christianity tends to be seen in contrast to shamanism, and most Christians will deny any connection between the two. They certainly were a contrasting pair in "The Shaman Painting," the main point of which was the class between the two belief systems and the different worlds that they represented. On the other hand, one reason that Christianity took hold so quickly and has prospered so in Korea may be that Koreans are masters at the pragmatic skill of syncretism.

> Recently Korean churches have been so influenced by shamanism that it is hard to distinguish shamanism from Christianity. So our biblical and Christian traditional identity as churches has been tainted. We feel that we are at a deep crisis because of the influence of shamanism, which has been at the root of Korean thinking.

Many shamanist traits appear in Korean Christianity. An example of shamanism's representation in Christianity is the name they chose for God; Hananim (or Hanŭnim, for some) is a derivative of the shamanist name for their highest deity, Hanŭnim, or the god of Heaven. Adams adds that the Christian trinity of Father, Son and Holy Spirit resembles shamanism's recognition of several deities, and goes on to list other shared features of mainstream and non-mainstream Christianity: "all night prayer meetings; the establishment of prayer retreat houses in the mountains; the belief in and practice of exorcism in cases of emotional, mental, and severe physical illness; and the expression of intense emotional states while praying. In addition, there is the commonly held belief that one receives spiritual and material blessings in direct proportion to one's financial giving." Korean Pentecostal Christianity, with its proportionately high number of adherents in comparison with other countries, invites an ecstatic participation similar to the trance of the shaman. Another feature shared by shamanism and a large number of Christians in Korea—and, for that matter, throughout the world—is "prosperity theology" (or "prosperity gospel"), the view of worship of the supreme being more as a means of gaining favors than of something due the supreme being.[32]

Professor Dwight Strawn, a Methodist missionary who has lived four decades in Korea, offers an insight on the relationship between Christianity and shamanism:

> Shamanism has provided the basic system of values and religious beliefs for the people of Korea since ancient times, and . . . "foreign" religions such as Buddhism and Christianity have often been interpreted and understood in terms of the prevailing system of beliefs based on Shamanism. . . . Much of what goes on in Buddhist temples and in Christian churches in Korea is neither "Buddhist" nor "Christian" in any "pure" sense but is an amalgam made up of beliefs and values from those religions and the shamanistic system of beliefs which are still the basic core of Korean culture. In short, Buddhism and Christianity were both "Koreanized" by the local culture.

32. Ro Bong-nin: "In Asian countries of great affluence, such as South Korea, 'Prosperity Theology' has long been taught from the pulpits. At its core is this reasoning: The more you give to God, the more he will bless. Forget him, and hard times are bound to come. In South Korea, such thinking reflects a strong shamanistic influence."

Harvey Cox, in fact, "goes further [than seeing shared features], arguing in his book, *Fire from Heaven,* that the very success of Christianity in Korea—in particular, the Pentecostal variety—lies in its incorporation of shamanistic beliefs and practices."

It appears, paradoxically, the very sects of Christianity that are most strongly syncretized have a tendency toward intolerance, and are wont to insist that Christianity is the only path to "salvation." In real-life Korea, not a few Buddhist temples and animist and Taoist symbols have been burned and vandalized by radical Christians. Kim Kŭm-hwa, a shaman who has achieved status as a human national treasure, reports that she has been interrupted several times by Christians barging in and shouting "Go away, Satans!" Another shaman relates that

> One night in 1993, when we [her *kut* team members] were performing a *kut* ritual in a mountain near Seoul, forty or so Christians interrupted us. They surrounded us closely with fire sticks in their hands. It was a really scary situation. Shouting, "Go away, Satans!" they drew a cross on our backs with red paint and even on the head of the pig we were using for the ritual. Because they outnumbered us so much, we had no choice but to bear the humiliation.

The behavior of the shaman Mohwa was not at all representative of the attitude of adherents of shamanism, Taoism and Buddhism, which are quite tolerant of Christianity.[33]

33. Hogarth, pp. 3, 4: "Christianity has generally frowned on any syncretistic movements, although historically there is strong evidence to suggest that its practices have been influenced by other religious beliefs in many localities . . . On the other hand, Buddhism . . . has been far more tolerant towards the indigenous belief systems of the areas to which it has spread."

The difficulty that fundamentalist Christian sects have in recognizing the value of Korea's other belief systems will probably not cause too much damage. Throughout Korea's history, the pragmatic inclination to embrace several belief systems—as they now embrace Western values with traditional values—has been a fundamental element in the people's nature. This inclination to welcome different belief systems promises continued movement toward a more pluralistic society and mentality.

Human Relationships

> And these old men pass on to us the Legend of the Mating Dragons. In this tale, too, a brace of yellow dragons was about to begin that ascension to heaven that they had waited for so long. But the Emperor of Heaven learned that they had defiled this occasion by mating the night before, and in his rage he seized their magic stones and stowed them away deep in his realm. The dragons went wild with grief and tore into each other with such fury that the blood they shed inundated the entire valley and left that reddish hue for eternity.

Kim Tong-ni gives us this metaphor of Korea at the beginning of "Loess Valley," which he wrote in 1939, to describe the frustration and desperation that Koreans felt in this life under the occupier. The occupier's hand was ripping apart the ties that had bound Koreans together, and turning Koreans against one another. In addition to the Koreans in the police, many Korean overseers on Japanese farms and foremen in Japanese factories and even teachers in the schools collaborated with or served the occupier, willingly or unwillingly.

For centuries before the Japanese came, Koreans had a system of relationships in which everyone knew his and her place and could depend on others to interact accordingly. Confucianism seems to have served more than any other belief system as the paradigm for the instincts of human nature in human relationships, both in the family and in the rest of society. Manifestations of the various forms of Confucianism's three primal bonds (ruler and subject, father and son, and husband and wife) appear in every relationship. As recently as 1994, sociologist Koo wrote that Confucianism still "prescribes ideal human social relations across age, generation, gender, and status, establishing clear hierarchies between elder and younger, male and female, and ruler and ruled. . . . [T]he primary social values can be considered an extension of these basic relationships."

While society retained the Confucian matrix of relationships, however, that system was substantially weakened in the transition from traditional agricultural to modern industrial society. Most of the stories in this book would not have been written if human relationships among Koreans had not been going through the change that they were during the transition period. New developments were happening at such a wild speed that there was no possibility of gradual adaptation to changing conditions. Korea's opening to the West, the Korean War, rapid urbanization and "condensed" industrialization loosened ties within the family. (These developments are discussed in detail in the section "Quality of Life.") Social relationships also became looser: 80 percent of Koreans were snatched from a collective life in the village and dumped in the individualistic anonymity of the city, where they had to replace broken bonds with new kinds of bonds that did not provide the same degree of support. The street urchins in "The Game Beaters," for instance, banded together and lived on the streets because family bonds had been severed in the great migrations from the north and abroad that took place just after Liberation.

The Family

The few families that appear in our stories span the range from dysfunctional ("The Shaman Painting") to normal ("The Visit") to ideal ("The Gulls"). One would expect the story with the ideal family to appear in the traditional era, before Liberation, and the troubled family to appear in stories of more modern times. Alas, the family is not such a simple unit. There was a basic trend, however: through the transition period, as society modernized, family ties became elastic: a strong sense of loyalty endured, even as ties eased. The definition of family, however, may now have to be narrowed to just two generations.

In traditional times, before 1945, the Korean family was a large, close-knit unit. There is some disagreement over whether the average traditional family was actually extended, with three and four generations under one roof. Conventional wisdom says that it was, but sociologist Lee Man-gap[34] says that it was mainly the aristocratic family that was extended, possibly because only aristocrats could afford to house so many people. In 1965 a quarter of all households held three or more generations; by 1980, only 17 percent had three or more. And when Seoul hosted the 1988 Olympics, at the end of the transition period, the Korean family had become a small, dispersed unit.

"Dispersed unit" is a fitting Korean oxymoron, because the individual members of one family, though they soon separate physically, still belong to a strong unit—stronger, at least, than

34. Lee Man-gap, p. 236. "In spite of widespread opinion that the extended family system was popular in Korea, empirical studies have shown that it had not been the prevailing system, though it had probably been maintained and appreciated by the wealthy yangban." Lee got his information from a 1938 Keijo Imperial University study of the Korean economy ("Observations on the population in the Yi-dynasty by Social Status").

in the West.[35] Since the beginning (in 1945) of the transition period, the form of the family has changed, and the divorce rate has increased alarmingly, but family remains the most important focus of each member's life. In 2004, sociologist Choi Seong-a reported:

> There has been a remarkable increase in nuclear families in recent years. And because of the success of the government's active family planning campaign [in the 1960s and 1970s], the size of the family has become remarkably smaller. However, the changes can be deceptive: the male-dominated value system that has supported the asymmetrical power structure of the patriarchal family remains firmly entrenched. Despite the changes in the physical organization of the family, the traditional Confucian ethics which stress patrilineage, filial piety, solidarity among brothers and the importance of domestic harmony are still pervasive in the Korean family.

While some say that family solidarity is still strong, there are those who think that this value weakened during the transition period. Kim Ha-jong, during the second half of the transition, observed that

> . . . fathers and mothers are driven from their children and condemned to an incomparably sorrowful and lonely old age. This phenomenon appears to be even more common among the parents of children who have received a modern education or have studied overseas. . . . It appears

35. Steinberg, p. 9: "The relative strength of clan and family varies among Confucian societies, but in all of them these institutions are far more important than in most Western contemporary cultures."

> to be a widespread, general phenomenon that emerged in our society as our traditional extended family system collapsed and the nuclear family system of Western individualism began its spread into Korea.

During this period, the demands of the male's traditional patriarchal role, coupled with the demands of the modern workplace, put a heavy strain on the relationship between father and children. Choe Sun-yuel illustrates this in a study of the years 1972 to 1987. He already knew that, because of traditional Confucian relationships in the family, the father was expected to distance himself from the family in order to more effectively exercise supreme authority. He discovered that this distance had been made greater by the period's rapid industrialization—the family came to spend more and more time outside the home, at work and school, leaving little time for family interaction. It was naturally the breadwinner of the family that was away from the family the most.

Meanwhile, women's increasing self-assertion was helping to loosen ties within the extended family. Throughout the transition period more and more women began working outside the home, families were moving out of single-family homes and into smaller apartments that did not comfortably accommodate three generations, and the egocentric demands of a distorted concept of individualism (introduced so abruptly, individualism was understood and practiced as a "me first" philosophy) began to grow more insistent. As recently as the 1970s, for example, many first-son or only-son college students complained that it was difficult for them to find a spouse because when the prospective spouse learned of her suitor's status in his family she knew that she would be saddled with the burden of taking care of his parents who would come to live with them. To be fair to the new Korean woman, though, ". . . as labor force participation of married women increases, the need for daily care of elderly and infirm parents cannot be solved by co-residence."

In addition to the opposing opinions on the strength of the Korean family, those who have some familiarity with the situation in modern Korea see a paradox between the assertion of strong family ties and the country's combination of soaring divorce rate (second among OECD countries in 2003) and plunging fertility rate (in 2003 it was 1.19, one of the lowest in the world). This paradox might be explained by Seoul National University Professor Chang Kyung-Sup's description of "familism" in Korea as a product of multiple aspects, one of them being instrumentality. He explains that instrumental familism, particularly strong in Korea, develops from the needs of its members. Closely related to this are social, economic and political factors: the state, throughout the nation's impoverished history, had comparatively few resources to provide support to individual citizens, and even the wealthier nation of today, perhaps mainly from habit, depends on the family to provide this support. Professor Chang observed, "There has been one coherent feature of the family policy of the state. It has always encouraged private families to fulfill all the functional burdens of feeding, protecting, educating, disciplining, consoling, supporting, and even nursing its citizens without demanding state assistances." These two factors—instrumental familism and the continuing socio-economic factors that instigated it in the first place—work together to maintain strong familism even in the face of a sharp fertility decline and a high divorce rate. The Korean family, then, might still be described as an extended family—under more than one roof.

In our earliest story ("The Shaman Painting") the problem between mother and son grew irreconcilable and she ended up killing him. But theirs was hardly a typical traditional family. The more traditional family, toward the beginning of the transitional period, was very tightly knit, though the intensity of the bond was not verbalized. This is evident in "The Visit," a story that takes place during the war between North and South. In traditional Korea, the son is the apple of the Confucian eye, and in this story an impoverished farmer feels that he must see his son, who is in some army unit on the other side of the Korean peninsula. He puts up his land as collateral for a loan to pay for the trip, which requires of this ailing and aging man five exhausting days of hiking and hitching rides. True to the distant patriarchal Confucian relationship between father and son, when the two finally meet, the extent of their conversation is the son's query as to his mother's health and the father's efforts to get the son to eat more.

The bond between father and children is just as close in "The Gulls," but is more evident. Though the setting is temporally the same as that of "The Visit," the relationship between parents and children in this story represents a gradual development toward the more open and explicit expression of the close bonds that we see today. When the daughter in "What's To Be Done?" leaves home against her father's wishes we see how those bonds, which seem to be traditionally close, have begun to relax. We sense with confidence that the separation is only temporary.

Kong Chi-yŏng (author of "What's To Be Done?") pointed out in private conversation that a college student in the 1980s, born well after the Korean war ended in 1953, could not understand why her elders were making such a fuss about communist infiltration in the unions. In the decades between Liberation and the Olympics it often seemed that the generations did not know each other. Each succeeding generation grew up in a different milieu. In 1973, just thirty years after Liberation, Kim Ha-jong offers an insightful metaphor: "We frequently hear that there are three generations living together in Korea, the

Chinese generation, the Japanese generation, and the Korean generation—depending on what they learned to read as youths."[36] A member of the "Chinese" generation would have been born around 1880; one had to know Chinese characters, not Chinese language, to understand most publications and documents. During the Japanese colonization of Korea, Japanese language was required to accomplish anything of an official nature; it was not until the 1930s that the Japanese tried to totally eliminate the use of Korean. The "Korean" generation is the post-Liberation generation, who did not have to use Japanese.

Even if the generations could communicate, the oldest generation might not be there to communicate with. O Chŏng-hŭi (author of "The Face") was asked in an interview whether she could have written the 1983 story "Wayfarer" in the 1950s or 1960s, because the interviewer felt that, in Korea's traditional society, the mother in the 1983 story would not have been placed in an institution for long-term health care. She replied, "Things like that did not happen [in those days]. And nobody even thought of putting elderly in a nursing home, because they felt responsibility for them. Now, though, the elderly often have to take care of themselves."

Within ten years of the nominal close of the transition, the situation evolved into the one that we are so familiar with today. In O Chŏng-hŭi's "The Face," published in 1999, an elderly couple live by themselves; one gets the feeling that the children do not come around anymore. And, as if that is not bad enough, the bedridden old man is even afraid that his wife might leave him. According to O, each member of the family now has his and her own life to live.

The Korean family, then, if we define it as those living under

36. Kim Ha-jong, p. 217. See Fulton, 1997 (pp. v–vii), for a description of the social function of hangul, the Korean script.

one roof, has loosened its hold on its members while retaining their intense sense of loyalty. It is a question, though, whether the elderly generation, which used to belong whether living with them or separately, can still be considered part of the family.

Male and Female

The sick, impoverished farmer in "The Visit" (1951) put up his land as collateral for a loan and made an arduous journey to visit his young son at his army unit during the war. Would he have done the same for a daughter?

When we read Korean history we are usually presented with nineteenth-century American missionary James Scarth Gale's representation of the conventional view of the relationship between male and female:

> [The Korean male] has a profound contempt for woman, speaking of her generally as *kejip* [sic] or female. . . . She is a subject altogether beneath the consideration of a member of the male sex. . . . He . . . never loses an opportunity of showing how little is the place she occupies in his extensive operations.

In addition to the importance of family, the most commonly noted feature of Confucian relationships is the leadership position of the male in the family (and, by extension, society). A woman was expected to follow the "Three Obediences" in the three phases of her life: obedience to parents, to husband, and to her son. Each phase was ruled by a male. Even in the phase of "obedience to parents"; would be expected to obey her father first, since the husband ruled the wife.

There has always been a debate, however, over how much power the male actually has in Korea. Gale concluded his remarks about male superiority and dominance thus:

> If the truth were told, however, we would know that the little woman within that enclosure is by no means the cipher he pretends her to be; but that she is really mate and skipper of the entire institution, and that no man was ever more thoroughly under petticoat government than this same Korean gentleman.

Half a century later, another missionary, the Anglican Richard Rutt, who served in a country village for several years in the 1960s, reported:

> Still we hear it said that this is a man's country, that Korean men are selfish, that their womenfolk are depressed and little better than slaves. This is for sure the biggest hoax ever pulled in all of Korea's two thousand years of uninterrupted history. . . . Formal relations and etiquette are one thing; real power is another.

The confusion may come from focusing on two different classes and two different settings. *Yangban* families were bound by the rules of Confucian behavior more tightly than commoners were; Rutt was definitely writing about commoners, and both Rutt and Gale were writing about the woman inside the home, not the woman in public.

We do know, though, that both *yangban* and commoner were bound by Confucian law, and legally (in employment, divorce, inheritance, etc.), a woman—whether *yangban* or commoner—had very low status. In ordinary domestic circumstances a woman may have enjoyed equality, but when a male wanted to assert the privileges granted him by Confucian mores and laws, the woman had to yield.

She took her first steps out of her restricted domestic domain into the realm of the male in the late nineteenth century. Christianity helped women initiate a change in their status in the person of the "bible woman," Koreans who assisted missionaries in bringing Christianity into the women's quarters (the *anbang*) of the home. Historically, the shaman, often in visits to the women's quarters, gave guidance not only on psychological and emotional issues but also for matters in home-making and child-rearing.

Throughout Korean history, female shamans addressed some of the spiritual needs of Korean women and women sought out the counsel and skills of female shamans in order to secure health and blessings for their families. Thus, female shamans were a long accepted authority in the women's anbang about how to live a good and long life. At the turn of the twentieth century Bible Women inherited, or co-occupied the women's space and benefitted from the centuries-old female authority in that *anbang*.

Along with teaching women to read, which set many women and their daughters on the path to continued education, Bible Women alongside women missionaries shared ideas of more efficient home management, hygiene and healthy baby-rearing methods. Thus, the Bible Woman, ostensibly the bearer of new religious ideas, also brought new skills, like literacy, and new social ideas to women that helped women to move beyond the confines of the anbang (women's quarters of the home) and into the public sphere.[37]

During the entire transition period, though the constitution (implemented in 1948) guaranteed women equal status with

37. Lee-Ellen Strawn, 2009. RAS Lecture *Protestant Christianity and Korean Women*. May 26, 2009. Seoul.

men, laws that contradicted the constitution were written, and even existing laws that conformed to the constitution were often interpreted in favor of men or were simply ignored when a ruling favorable to the male was not possible. Women suffered discrimination in marriage, inheritance, divorce, and employment. Lee Hye-kyung reported as recently as 1994, several years after the Seoul Olympics, the view that many women had of their status: "The tradition of patrilineal succession continues to work effectively in the relation between men and women. . . . The notion of gender hierarchy is well preserved in the division of labor in the household work. Many women themselves believe that household work and child care are their major, if not exclusive, responsibility." Such an attitude is the most likely explanation why, in "First Love," the student's elder sister worked all day in the factory and skipped meals so that her younger brother was able to get away without working at least part-time, so that he could keep studying after middle school classes and eventually go on to college.

The women's rights movement in the West took form in the second half of the nineteenth century, whereas women in Korea, who have never had a movement *per se*, did not begin their very slow journey in earnest for another century, around the commencement of the transition period. Christian missionaries had actually assisted women in the first step of their journey when they opened their schools to both genders toward the end of the nineteenth century. However, when the Japanese colonized the country they allowed most Koreans to finish only elementary education, thus eliminating the channel for women's advancement that the missionaries had provided. More progress was made after the Japanese left, when the country started to Westernize and many abandoned the traditional notion that girls did not need to be educated. By 1980, women were receiving almost equal education to men.

> By 1980, primary and secondary male-female enrollment ratios were about equal; among older children, 97.1 percent of males and 92.1 percent of females attend middle school. Women are a minority at university level, however, not because of institutional discrimination, but because parents put their limited resources into the education of their sons. . . . The average number of years of education for the group of twenty- to twenty-nine-year-olds in 1980 was 10.3 years for males and 9.4 years for females.

Education, however, has not been as influential in other areas of gender equality as one would expect. In 1989, at the end of the transition period, factory women's salaries amounted to only half that of men's. A miniscule minority of corporate and government executive positions—a total of five cabinet ministers since Liberation, for instance—were held by women. Only 2 percent of National Assembly members were women, and most of them were appointed.

The dissident subculture showed more progress. Kong Chiyŏng ("What's To Be Done?") noted that, though women did not participate in the dissident movement to any substantial degree in the 1970s, they were together with the men in the front lines in the 1980s. The fact that in Kong's story all of the trainees were women and all of the instructors were men suggests gender segregation; this might be explained by pointing out that the male trainers were dissidents who guided according to experience that they had gained in the 1970s, when women were not participating. The fact that the training group in Kong's story were of the same gender also causes us to suspect segregation based on discrimination, but the female narrator herself tells us that this was felt necessary by both parties to avoid romantic distractions and achieve undivided focus on their task. In that same story we see one more sign of the changing times: the story's narrator defied her father when she left home against his wishes and joined the dissident group. Such behavior was unthinkable at the beginning of the transition period.

If we focus on how much women managed to accomplish in the way of improved status, we realize that the transition period between Liberation and the Olympics was not much of a transition for them. Until the appearance of the student dissident in the 1980s story "What's To Be Done?" we find no "normal" or socially acceptable female protagonist in our stories (there are one lowly shaman in "The Shaman Painting," two kept women in "Loess Valley," and two prostitutes in "River" and "End of the Road"), and this absence indicates the minor role that women continued to play in society through the first half of the period. Major women writers who featured female protagonists in their stories started to appear on the scene in the 1970s, but they were still a very small minority. Apparently, the embryo of the liberated Korean woman was gestating during the transition period, nurtured by other forces such as expanded education, industrialization, Western ideas; she was not born until after the transition period.

After the transition, women's status improved substantially, when democracy became more fully installed and laws were passed that gave women exercisable legal rights in the family. Post-transition women show a new spirit of independence and self-assertion, one that inspires the reader of "The Face" to wonder at the end, "Did she actually leave him?"

General Society

During the transition, as one would expect, the hierarchical rigidity of social relationships eased. The system, however, is still hierarchical.

From long before the transition to long after it, social relationships—between older and younger generations, state and citizen, insider and outsider—have been based on Confucianism, and the bedrock of Confucian social relations is the family. In Chosŏn Korea, members of a traditional Confucian family observed a rigid hierarchy; they were loyal to the family before any other group. Kinship ideologies and organizations were at the center of social, political and economic organization. This continued through the years of the Japanese colonial period, when law and the practice of it were based upon the ideology of the "family state."[38] Traditional relationships began to weaken when, at Liberation in 1945, the Japanese were replaced by Americans as Korea's new occupiers. The Japanese had presented government as an extension of the family; the new occupiers tried to keep the family out of government.

Though the family model for relationships did indeed weaken during the transition, it certainly did not disappear. In government, for example, even in 1989, a year after the end of the transition, and forty years after the installation of a nominally democratic system, government operated as a family. Steinberg noted "the strong emphasis in Confucianism on the family as the intellectual and ideological analogy for state governance."[39]

Politics also weakened traditional bonds. With the increased intensity in fighting between left and right over what kind of government should lead the country if it ever got its sovereign-

38. Lee Hye-kyung, pp. 294–295: "[T]he Japanese law and practice in colonial years were based upon the ideology of 'the family state,' stressing the hierarchical order and unconditional loyalty to superiors."

39. Steinberg, 1989, p. 99. Koo, p. 266: "[W]hile kinship ideologies and organizations have diminished importance in capitalist, industrial society, in pre-capitalist societies such as pre-twentieth century Korea they were central to social, political, and economic organization, and to daily life and ritual practice."

ty back, residents in villages and members of families turned against each other. Relations were not good between southerners and northerners when refugees from the north, fleeing communism, poured into the south. They were looked upon, in the words of Professor Yue Mahn-gunn, as "northern beggars." In his discussion on Korean literature in the 1960s and 1970s, Hong Chŏng-sŏn says that most of the issues covered in that period's fiction were problems of traditional relationships that were weakening and new relationships that were becoming antagonistic.

> [I]n politics Korean society simultaneously experienced democracy and military dictatorship; economically it was experiencing the collapse of the traditional communal agricultural society and formation of urban society, and socially it witnessed the formation of and confrontation between proletariat and bourgeois strata. Moreover, in the dimension of mentality and ethics, the traditional Confucian system of values was being replaced by a Western system of values based on individualism. . . . Writers wrote about the issues of rigid political opposition between North and South, individual and social liberty and ideology, the collapsing village and urban poor, the confrontation between capitalist and laborer, the alienation and helplessness felt in individualistic society.

During the transition, one aspect of language—indicating the social relationship between the speaker and the one that the speaker is talking to or about—changed to reflect the country's shift to a more egalitarian society. Register is as important in modern Korea as ever: "If the choice [of register] is inappropriate in the given speech situation, some serious consequences follow for the social relationship between [speaker] and [hearer]." While register is still important, its expression has changed somewhat.

Abolishment of the elite *yangban* caste did not eliminate the aspiration to be regarded upper class, and being able to use *yangban* manner of speech, or a close equivalent, was one way to accomplish this. With the widening access to education, more people got access to cultured speech. The educated common man came to gentrify his language by appropriating a tool—*apchonpŏp*—hitherto used by the aristocracy. Professor Shin Gi-Hyun of Australian National University explains this strategy of expressing deference:

> [T]he traditional politeness rule in this culture, known as *apjonbeop*, or "rules for suppressing respect", . . . [is] a verbal repertoire amongst Yangban speakers in traditional Korea, and is essentially a means to recognize [the hearer's] seniority over [the speaker] by suppressing respect to [referents] who are "closer" to [the speaker] than to [the hearer].[40]

For example, in traditional times a young *yangban*, referring to his father in conversation with an older *yangban* outside his family, to show respect to the older would "suppress respect" for his own father and set him below the older person, by using the corresponding word from the *yangban's* repertoire: *chunbujang*. (The equivalent in ordinary speech is *abŏji*.) This repertoire, however, was extremely extensive and difficult to learn, and during the transition, with its values of democracy and equality,

40. Shin, p. 288–289. See the discussion about language register in "Stumbling Across a Language Barrier," in this volume.

people did not want to bother to learn all of these words. In modern times, therefore, in order to show fine breeding and at the same time to honor the value of equality, the educated young person, in conversation with an older person, will use the "educated" register to elevate the referent (his father) to equal status with the older person. He would use the word "*abŏnim.*" This method, then, both gentrifies the speaker in the eyes of the listener and, at the same time, honors the spirit of modernity. Given the appropriate situation, the narrator in "House of Idols" would probably have used this method, while the anarchic protagonist would probably not have bothered.

Another interesting development in language had to do with gender. In standard speech, a young woman in her teens or early twenties addresses her older brother and older male friends (and seniors of the same generation) as *oppa*. A young man addresses his older brother and older friends (and seniors) as *hyŏng*. During the 1980s, young women, like the narrator in "What's To Be Done," took up the currently gestating spirit of gender equality and probably succeeded in nurturing it by addressing older male friends (and senior school mates) as *hyŏng*.

Group and Individual

Before 1945, a Korean was less an individual than now, and more a member of the group. Korean fiction reflects this change, in its general shifting of focus of story plots from social events to psychological observation of the individual. Nevertheless, the group still has a strong hold on the individual.

As recently as 1994, sociologist Park Yong Shin claimed that there was still what Goldberg describes as a "familistic value pattern . . . an interpersonal solidarity that ties and holds together the members of a social group just like a family." One feature of traditional community and group consciousness was the *dure*, a village cooperative group. The most obvious element of this system was the villagers' practice of working together in rice planting and harvesting, encouraged by the village band. This scene is illustrated in our second story, "Loess Valley," written shortly before Liberation. (While Goldberg pronounced that the *dure* was disappearing before Liberation, Rutt witnessed it as late as 1964.)

MacDonald, describing the Korea that he found at the end of the transition period, provides a paradigm that suggests a change in the nature of group consciousness from traditional to modern times. "Korean behavior is the result of three main factors: the traditional Confucian ethic; an underlying individualism that is somewhat at odds with that ethic; and an overlay of Western ideas. In the traditional Confucian order, harmony among men was the supreme goal." Before Liberation, that "overlay of Western ideas" was not a part of the Korean mentality. But MacDonald's second factor of "an underlying individualism" tells us that even before 1945, in traditional society, a Korean was not the robot of a Confucian operator, and this may help explain the unusual individualism of the shaman's son in "The Shaman Painting," and Tŭkbo and the *femme fatale* Buni in "Loess Valley."

While there was a degree of individualism before the transition, strong expression of it was more the exception than the rule. The group was more important than the individual. In "Loess Valley," Ŏkswae loses all sense of meaning in life when, because he stood out from the group, he is exiled from his family and his home village. His friends Tŭkbo and Buni also got into trouble when they allowed their "underlying individualism" to surface.

The narrator in Kong Chi-yŏng's "What's To Be Done?"

(set in the 1980s) manifests the "overlay of Western ideas" that happened after Liberation.[41] She displayed this in leaving her family (against her father's wishes) and in disobeying the rules of the dissident organization by allowing herself to fall in love with her team's instructor. But her attachment to the group showed when, in retelling the story even several years later, she acknowledged an internal intellectual struggle with such behavior, and regret over its consequences.

Though a strong group consciousness endured through the transition period, it could not retain its traditional features. In 1988, the last year of the transition period, MacDonald observed that "In urban areas . . . there is not a strong sense of community responsibility; rather, there is the usual anonymity and isolation of industrialized city life," but he goes on to say that "Part of the role of family and community has been taken over by groupings based on common local origin, common school experience, and common workplace. People withinsuch groups have a strong sense of shared identity and mutual responsibility." In support of this, writer Kong described to me how dedicated the characters in her story were to the group, that many student dissidents even felt a certain obligation to marry someone involved in the struggle; her example is the instructor in her story, who married a woman who had become a paraplegic when she was thrown out of a window by the police. Many of these marriages ended in divorce in the nineties, after the movement died. In fact, the same story relates how later the members of the movement abandoned the cause and went their separate ways as soon as the political winds shifted.

During the transition period, as the population center shifted to the city and that "overlay of Western ideas" took root in

41. Kwon, Youngmin, p. viii: He regarded "consciousness of oneself as an individual" as a feature that appeared only after 1960.

the Korean soul, the lifelong bonds of the traditional village group apparently gave way to the more temporary bonds of the modern functional relationship.

Adversarial Relationships

The Outsider

The transition period decreased the number of outsiders in Korean society. It is now a more inclusive and tolerant society because of what happened during the transition.

Shamans have never been completely accepted in Korean society. To review our discussion in the section on "Shamanism," Mohwa the shaman, who was popular enough when her services were required, was nevertheless an outsider because she practiced magic, which was censured by the Confucian establishment. After 1945, though the constrictions of Confucianism weakened, the shaman's status in society remained low. Christianity replaced Confucianism as her institutional tormentor; to make her situation more difficult, in the eyes of many, shamanism represented the forces that had been preventing the social and economic development that everyone wanted. In a collection of essays by Richard Rutt, the Anglican missionary who served as village priest back in the 1960s, we find that "[the sorceress] is socially ostracized, together with her family. Her house is set apart, and people do not mix in its society." Anthropologist Kendall reported as late as 1987 that "The *mansin* [the shaman] shares in the ambiguous status of other glamorous but morally dubious female marginals, the actress, the female entertainer, and the prostitute." However, as mentioned previously, although shamanism was outlawed for a brief period in the 1970s, in the following decade, because of the growing new pride in traditional culture, the shaman moved from outside society to its fringes.

Before the war forced reconsideration of traditions, moving to a village other than one's birthplace opened one to treatment as an outsider. The author of "The Shaman Painting" expressed the traditional disdain for outsiders when he described the outsider Mohwa's low status by lowering the status of the village that she lived in. By naming her village the equivalent of "Many-names Village," he told us that the village wasn't "purebred"—its residents weren't mostly of one clan—which had an effect similar to Westerners labeling a village "Gypsy Run." Ŏkswae and Tŭkbo ("Loess Valley," 1939) were outsiders, and exiled, because they were different—Ŏkswae was uncommonly strong and Tŭkbo violated social norms. And when they settled in a new village they were ostracized—as people from another village they lacked the credentials required for membership in the new group:

> The concept of *kohyang* and the notion of individual legitimacy are closely related. . . . The incentive to stay at home, to remain in one's kohyang, for the rest of one's life must have been very strong in the traditional society. Only very difficult circumstances would lead one to seek a new life away from the place where one's roots were. . . . [As the aphorism goes,] "To leave one's kohyang is to become despised. . . ." The outsider, then, is the man who has renounced his "roots" and, thereby, his legitimacy.

The friendship between Ŏkswae and Tŭkbo may have been a subconscious attempt at replacement of family ties sundered by exile. As mentioned earlier, the street kids in "The Game Beaters" (1948) were outsiders, accused of thievery even in the absence of evidence that they were thieves. One imagines that they were refugees from the north—they had left their hometown and had no money to reestablish themselves in their adopted home. "Radio and newspapers called those returning from Japan and Manchuria 'returned brethren,' but people called them 'Japanese beggars' and 'Manchurian beggars.'"

A few years after this story took place, though, with industrialization's increased urban migration, antipathy toward those outside their hometown would eventually weaken—soon 80 percent of the population would be "outside" in the city—and with industrialization and the new class mobility, the surviving street kids in the story would be able to divest themselves of their indigent status. Still, they would feel like outsiders until they established ties with a group. The traveling companions in "River" (1960) were typical of millions uprooted from their hometown by industrialization in finding solace in the close ties of the surrogate family that they formed in their boardinghouse.[42]

The wine house girl in "River," an occasional prostitute, is an outsider whose status was not improved during the transition. She knows that she will never be able to marry respectably, and sighs with longing admiration at the college student, who she feels could make her an insider. The transition from traditional to modern society has changed nothing for her. In the Chosŏn dynasty even her higher-class ancestor, the *kisaeng*, though she was much sought after by the *yangban* gentry and more highly cultured than many of them, was officially relegated to the very lowest caste. This is the theme of Korea's favorite classic "Song of Chun Hyang," which tells of the *kisaeng*'s daughter and the son of the *yangban* who could not legally marry. (In the popular modern version of the tale, they live "happily ever af-

42. Many single expatriates (myself included) had such invaluable experiences in the boardinghouse, where family-like ties were formed and later maintained for many years.

ter"; in most older versions, Chunhyang meets a realistically tragic end.[43]) After 1945, Koreans held on to their Confucian sense of morality as far as such people were concerned, and spreading Christianity, with its own set of morals, also condemned prostitution.

The prostitute in "End of the Road" (1966) is even more an outsider than the wine house girl in "River." She is an outsider twice over, a prostitute for foreigners, the camptown whore of American soldiers. Katherine Moon, in her book on this kind of prostitute, explains this specially virulent brand of ostracism: "[T]heir pariah status is due to the unique demographic and cultural constitution of the camp towns in which they live and the particular prejudices of Korean people regarding race, class, and Western influence." The two young toughs in "End of the Road" provide a powerful example of the contempt in which these women were held. The political importance of this prostitute, however, was in reverse proportion to her social status. Moon claims that the Korean and American governments "sponsored and regulated" the prostitution system "as a means to advance the 'friendly relations' of both countries and to keep U.S. soldiers . . . happy."[44]

43. See Cleary's "Song of Chun Hyang" in Holstein, 2005. More on Chun Hyang's tragic end on p. 222.

44. Moon, p. 1. Also read Choe, Sang-Hun: "Now, several former prostitutes in South Korea have accused their country's former leaders of . . . encouraging them to have sex with the U.S. soldiers who protected South Korea from North Korea. . . . Transcripts of parliamentary hearings also suggest that at least some South Korean leaders viewed prostitution as something of a necessity. In one exchange in 1960, two lawmakers urged the government to train a supply of prostitutes to meet what one called the "natural needs" of allied soldiers and prevent them from spending their dollars in Japan instead of South Korea. The deputy home minister at the time, Lee Sung Woo, replied that the government had made some improvements in the 'supply of prostitutes' . . . for U.S. troops."

"End of the Road" introduces another outsider in Korea, the Westerner. Until 1876 Korea avoided contact with the West and was suspicious of all foreigners; the term "hermit kingdom" (which has recently come under fire by some as being politically incorrect) evolved from the Chosŏn dynasty's closed-door policy, which it applied to every nation except China and Japan. Since Japan pried the doors open in 1876, however, relations with Western peoples have been relatively amicable. As previously mentioned, Westerners (mostly in the form of missionaries) were the source of mass education and modern health care and aid. Mohwa's son Woogi ("The Shaman Painting") is an unfortunate example of the influence of the missionaries' contributions. Westerners were regarded by the general public as supporters of the people in their struggle against government oppression during both the Japanese occupation and Korean autocratic regimes. And Westerners were also admired for their relative affluence. It was quite conspicuous against the background of general poverty, in fact, until the 1980s, when Korea became economically independent.[45] Except for the last years of the transition period, Westerners occupied a special position in Korean society; though Koreans always considered them outsiders, they often forgave the Westerners' indiscretions and afforded them preferential treatment.[46] At the same time, as a

45. Clark, p. 16: Clark's description reminds us of Goldberg's description (earlier) of the traditional Korean attitude toward those who are from outside the village. At the beginning, while the poor in the countryside generally accepted the missionaries, "[O]fficials and other upper-class Koreans, however, continued to see Westerners in general and missionaries in particular as troublemakers. . . . What kind of people would abandon their own parents to live in a foreign land? Perhaps they were exiles or fugitives from justice, or somehow rejects from their own societies."

46. Two examples: they were legally exempted from three decades of the nightly curfew, and traffic police ignored driving transgressions (like driving under the influence of alcohol).

group the Westerners were also resented; Koreans resented the stronger nations (Britain, Germany, France, the United States) that had not helped protect Korea against Japan.[47]

"The Game Beaters" (1948) provides a few glimpses of the privileged status of people from the West and of the hankering that many Koreans felt for the things that the Westerners brought with them. Author Hwang Sun-wŏn was no jingoist, but he was concerned about the toadyism that naturally existed in the poor, morally defeated society of that time. The "beaters" in the story are the group of passersby—with their foreign trappings like the fedora hat, designer sunglasses, and fighter-pilot jacket, which were very dear in those days—who tried to flush the street urchin from his hiding place in the drainage pipe. These beaters represent those in society who were either actively or passively collaborating with the new colonial master; they are beating the urban bush to flush game for the Western hunter (represented by the owner of the big house). The urchins, their prey, represent the common people, who in those days often found themselves with the perpetually downtrodden. In the end, though, the urchins' persecutors become conscious of a certain self-identification with the kid in the sewer pipe, demonstrating the author's hope that Koreans would eventually develop a proper sense of self-esteem.

Along with the admiration that Koreans had for things Western, they suffered from a serious inferiority complex. This was one aspect of their excessive admiration for things Western. One good example of this complex is the young man in "End of the Road" (1966), who sarcastically asked the GI prostitute, "So you stoop to doing Koreans too?" At times, when ordinary

47. They were too deeply involved in their own imperialistic business. France was preoccupied in Indochina, Germany in China, the United States was trying to quell the independence movement in the Philippines, and England allied with Japan to protect its own colonies.

Koreans compared themselves with the Westerners and their Korean protégés, they felt like outsiders in their own country.

The American military was welcomed when they first appeared in Korea as conquerors of the Japanese. Then relations deteriorated when the Americans announced that they would rule Korea for the time being, and resentment grew when the Americans recruited Japanese and former Japanese collaborators to help run the occupation bureaucracy. (The late Horace Underwood, who was in Korea at the time, reported that "The American tended to think in terms of occupying enemy territory, not the Liberation of a friendly nation.") And when, in 1946, they announced trusteeship with the Russians over Korea—which meant the division of their country into North and South—America's only friends were those whom the Americans were providing jobs and political backing.[48] It was only when American aid started arriving, and then American troops helped beat back the North Koreans in the war, that relations improved.

Even after the war, though, some, like Ch'oe In-hun ("House of Idols" and "End of the Road"), presented the bullying side of the Americans (in "House of the Idols") and the vulgarizing influence that the overwhelming American presence had on the society ("End of the Road").[49] Ch'oe had served in the Korean army in the 1960s and witnessed the sad situation in the "Texas" red-light districts—with their bars named "Honey Cats" and

48. Park Se-kil, p. 50: "The American military occupation government turned the history of the Korean people right back into the dark tunnel [formerly] known as the Japanese colonial period." So, to many at that time and to many historians these days, the proverbial light at the end of the tunnel was the headlight on the American troop train.

49. Ch'oe In-hun, interview, July 2, 2005. It was apparent in this interview that his attitude toward individual Americans depends entirely on the individual.

"Pink Heart"—that clustered around U.S. army bases, and the huge Marlboro billboards that blighted the highways; a critical review of this story commented that, for the people there, "the American military serves as their main referent: their identities are defined almost solely through their interaction with the soldiers. The Korean countryside is defiled by monstrous American trucks and weapons of destruction." Ch'oe had also witnessed the indiscriminate American bombing of civilians in Wŏnsan during the Korean War, described in the eerie image of the silent aerial juggernaut in "House of Idols."

Still, conservative Koreans, who constituted a majority of the population, admired America, if not the American military. Affairs between the two continued in a relatively amicable state until 1980, when the American army was suspected of having supported coup d'etat leader General Chun Du-hwan's brutal suppression of the Kwangju uprising.[50] American aid had stopped in the 1970s and, because of the booming economy, was not needed anymore. The Korean War, which the younger generation hadn't experienced, was long in the past and the continued presence of 35,000 American troops was regarded by the younger generation as unnecessary and an aggravation to the South's troubled relations with the North; they also saw American gov-

50. The charge was that Chun used units that were under ROK–U.S. Combined Forces Command (CFC), which would mean that he had to get the approval of the U.S. commander, and such approval would in turn point to U.S. support. U.S. Embassy: "Neither troops of the SWC [Special Warfare Command] nor elements of the Twentieth Division, employed by the Martial Law Command in Kwangju, were under CFC OPCON [operational control], either at the time they were deployed to the city or while operating there. None of the Korean forces deployed at Kwangju were, during that time, under the control of any American authorities. The United States had neither prior knowledge of the deployment of SWC forces to Kwangju nor responsibility for their actions there."

ernment and capitalists as exploiting Korean labor. The student dissidents in "What's To Be Done?" harbored a strong antagonism against the American government and military and corporations.[51]

For the average American soldier the feeling was mutual. Stationed in Korea against their will and serving for a tour of just one year, they knew little or nothing about Korea beyond their experience of the Koreans who worked on their compound. (Reference to the "slicky boys," who were workers who cleaned the barracks and performed other menial services on the base, is made in "The Game Beaters.") In the early days, before the country improved economically, GIs spoke among themselves of "the land that God forgot," "a desolate Oriental country of sullen peasants," and, relevant to the girl in Ch'oe In-hun's "End of the Road": "It is the only thing—the availability of women—that makes Korea bearable."[52] Throughout the period of transition many retained the hardship tour image of Korea—the M.A.S.H. image of Korean quaintness, corruption and ineptitude—that was implanted when the American army first arrived in 1945.

The relationship between most Koreans and Americans who were not associated with the U.S. military was, for the most part, one of mutual warmth and respect. During the transition period, the largest contingents of these Americans were missionaries and the Peace Corps (which served in Korea

51. The setting for "What's To Be Done?" is the 1980s. Kong, the story's author, told the interviewer that students were basically not anti-American in the 1970s.

52. Wade, James. Respectively, pp. 13, 229, 230. Wade witnessed a 1954 encounter between American GIs and Korean villagers and reported it in a moving story that Ch'oe In-hun would appreciate; it can be accessed at www.koreamosaic.net/wade.pdf.

from 1966 to 1981); many former Peace Corps volunteers even now maintain their relationship forged forty years earlier with their "second home," in academia, business and the diplomatic corps.

Another outsider in Korea is the homosexual, who moved during the transition from total denial to the outskirts of acceptance. The author of "First Love" never clarified whether the lovelorn middle school student was homosexual or bisexual or just dabbling, but the story is one of the first to present the issue of alternative sexual orientation. (Tellingly, it was written in 1995, but its setting is the 1970s.) The absence of a more specific characterization of the relationship between the middle-school narrator and his ambivalent schoolmate reflects the attitude of young educated Koreans of the 1970s toward homosexuality: denial. When such behavior was not totally ignored, it was explained away as "just playing around," or a reclining form of somnambulism.

Although instances of homosexuality do appear in both classical and contemporary documents, until recently most Koreans denied its existence in their culture. Toward the end of the transition period, when the first AIDS cases were confirmed, Koreans finally recognized the existence of Korean homosexuals. One would expect that acceptance might follow recognition, but, until now, that does not seem to be the case. Two decades after the end of the transition, although sympathy is occasionally expressed by heterosexuals on a personal level, homosexuality is ridiculed and censured publicly; while homosexuality itself is not illegal, "[I]n July 2001, the Ministry of Information and Communications adopted an Internet content-rating system classifying gay and lesbian websites as 'harmful media' that must be blocked on all public computer facilities accessible to youth (e.g., schools, public libraries, and Internet cafés)."

Left against Right, North against South

In dynastic Korea, materially there was not much of a gap between the classes. Only the very highest in the aristocracy were wealthy. The fall of the dynasty and the aristocracy combined with industrialization and class mobility to ignite a struggle between haves and have-nots. For the Koreans, under the oppressive foot of Japanese rule, it was natural that the Russian revolution would engender hope for justice and equality, and Korean socialist and communist parties were formed as early as 1925. As happened in other colonies (like Vietnam under the French), the two causes of nationalism and socialism worked hand in hand, but, more and more, one cause's interest came into conflict with the other's. The only thing that held the country together was the heavy-handed autocratic rule of the colonial government.

When this restraint was removed with the departure of the Japanese, the left and right took the gloves off. Right and left frequently met in armed clashes in the streets of the cities and villages during these years. Three men who were in their teens at that time recalled in interviews that many of those participating in the fighting, ignorant of the difference between the two ideologies, were recruited by one side or the other as they were needed for the particular occasion. The majority of the people did not concern themselves about ideology itself during this period of extreme poverty; they were concerned more with keeping themselves and their families from starvation.

Eventually, the leftist North and the rightist South would meet in war, causing the people untold suffering, again for the sake of ideology. The writer of the 1955 story "A Moment's Grace," the setting of which is the Korean War, makes the point that ideology is not only irrelevant, it is destructive, ultimately trivializing and demeaning the individual.

A few years after the war, the battle between left and right erupted again among South Koreans, this time between autocratic regimes and the dissident student movement. This has been covered in more detail in the section "State and the People."

All in all, the transition period between Liberation and the Olympics brought several changes in human relationships. It eradicated hereditary caste relationships, changed the form but not the importance of the family and group, weakened the bond between generations, began the process of equalizing relationships, and intensified some adversarial relationships but eased others.

Standard of Living, Quality of Life

Between Liberation and the 1988 Olympics, Korea transformed itself from a land of despair to a nation of hope.

Before Liberation

In the setting and characters of "The Shaman Painting" (1936) and "Loess Valley" (1939), Kim Tong-ni metaphorically described the frustration and despair that people felt under Japanese rule. The common people exhausted themselves, on the land and in factories, producing food and goods that fueled the expansion of the Japanese empire and lined the pockets of a few collaborating Koreans. Half of the rice crop was exported, causing per capita consumption of rice to decrease 45 percent. Those three elderly gentlemen who were interviewed at Chongmyo spoke of the severe hunger their countryside village had experienced. One recalled that six or seven out of ten were unable to eat properly, and gave witness to the oft-heard account of villagers being forced to eat the bark of trees to survive. Scholar and painter of Buddhist art Brian Barry helps us sense the degree of despondency that Koreans were feeling at the time: in his survey of 135 paintings of the Mountain God with his tiger companion in the forty-volume *Korean Buddhist Paintings,* he found that all of those with a serious or angry tiger were painted after 1910, when the Japanese took full control of Korea.

It was not only the villagers that suffered under the occupiers. Commercial policy under the governor-general favored Japanese entrepreneurs, leaving few Koreans with such an inclination to have much hope of establishing anything much bigger than a small shop. If a Korean succeeded in growing his business into a substantial enterprise, he was often "squeezed out" when an interested Japanese asked the government to help him acquire the fruit of the Korean's labors.[53] This and other practices of the occupiers impoverished the entire society.

> During the war years, the Japanese drew heavily on Korean resources. . . . Factories were diverted to military production; forested hillsides were stripped for timber and fuel; industrial plants depreciated; metals, including family heirlooms of brass, were ruthlessly collected and melted down to make ammunition . . . galloping inflation . . . the Koreans were left without managers, markets, or (in South Korea) raw materials for a rundown industrial plant that was not designed to serve Korean needs.

53. Underwood, p. 127. He adds: "A few Koreans were able to rise in business, though they were mostly squeezed out if those businesses became too large, and only a very few rose to government offices above clerk level. . . . When the Japanese were expelled, the country was left with only a small handful of trained personnel in any field."

Liberation

On August 15, 1945, Japan surrendered and Koreans celebrated the dawn of a new era that would not only restore sovereignty but would also provide a higher standing of living. "On August 15, 1945, 'Establishment of a sovereign nation,' 'land reform,' 'liquidation of Japanese property' and other catchphrases abounded as the great tidal wave of change swept the country." Most of the population shed their fatalistic mentality and took on a constructive spirit, and felt a strong sense of potential.

Just as soon as they started celebrating, they were faced with reality. As mentioned above, the Japanese occupation and World War II had left the country desperately short of food and resources, there weren't enough people with experience in running government and industry because only about one percent of the population had been allowed to study beyond secondary school and receive training in the relevant subjects. In addition, millions of Koreans who had been conscripted for the war effort and almost as many escaping communism in the North were flowing into the South, exacerbating the food shortage. What food was available could be bought only at extremely inflated prices. At the risk of redundancy we recall Yue Mahn-gunn's account of the hordes of North Korean refugees represented in "The Game Beaters," who settled around Seoul in shanties and tents and had to scrounge for food, begging on the street, burrowing in garbage dumps, and burgling every house they could.[54] "On the broad flats [of the river Han] where U.S. Army trucks dump the city of Seoul's garbage, Ye stopped to watch a swarming tangle of noisy, ragged small fry clawing over the piled-up refuse. The urchins were looking for any scrap of coal or tin or

54. Yue Mahn-gunn, interview, February 21, 2005. Clark, p. 352: "[T]hievery . . . was endemic in late 1940s Korea. Burglars, pickpockets, and petty thieves were everywhere."

paper that could possibly be sold. . . . They were a poor and filthy rabble."

The occupation of the peninsula by the United States and the Soviets exacerbated the economic misery for the South.

> Most of the natural resources, heavy industry (including fertilizer production), and electric power generation were concentrated in the north. . . . [T]he U.S. occupiers . . . removed wartime economic control. Hoarding, speculation, food shortages, and galloping inflation resulted. . . . An influx of Korean repatriates from Japan and elsewhere and a flood of refugees from the Communist regime in the north—perhaps four million or more in both categories by 1951—increased the population by 20 percent. Food production was hindered by fertilizer shortage. South Korean daily caloric intake fell to less than 1,500 per person in 1946–47."

But there was some hope. The Japanese had installed a capitalist system,[55] and had laid a foundation for extraordinary post-Liberation economic growth.

War

That foundation was rendered almost worthless in June of 1950, when the North attacked the South. In 1953 a truce was signed, leaving the peninsula a charnel house. For all that destruction, nothing at all had been gained by either side: the boundary be-

55. See the argument presented by Eckert, 1991, pp. 2–3. Some scholars, however, argue that the seeds of capitalism had already been sown in Korea by the beginning of the twentieth century, before the Japanese gained political influence.

tween the two remained generally where it had been before the start of the war.

The amount of destruction was incredible: much of the peninsula's newly installed infrastructure had been wiped out along with more than half of its industrial capacity and a third of its housing. Cumings' description reminds us of other accounts of life just before the war, and underscores the war's spectacular futility:

> South Korea in the 1950s was a terribly depressing place, where extreme privation and degradation touched everyone. Cadres of orphans ran through the streets, forming little protective and predatory bands of ten or fifteen; beggars with every affliction or war injury importuned anyone with a wallet, often traveling in bunches of maimed or starved adults holding children or babies; half-ton trucks full of pathetic women careened onto military bases for the weekend, so they could sell whatever services they had.

This war is the setting for two of our stories, "A Moment's Grace" and "The Visit." The former is O Sang-wŏn's defiant response to the destruction—here, in the form of degradation of the human spirit—that ideology and institutions inflict on individuals. Similarly, Kim Tong-ni's "The Visit" is a condemnation of these same human institutions that ravage humans like Sŏkgyu, who put his small farm at risk to pay for a trip across the peninsula to visit his son in the army for what, for all he knew, might be the last time he would see him. Both of these stories represent the desperation and grief of millions of Koreans like him who were losing family to the war. The South alone, in fact, suffered over 1.3 million "military and civilian casualties—Koreans who had been killed, executed, wounded, kidnapped, or gone missing."

The "great equalizer" that was war put the last nail in the coffin of the formerly dominant *yangban*. Economically, the new domestic masters were those who had milked the war; they were the charter members of a new middle class, who prospered by lending money, by putting to their own use money that came in the form of aid or the war budget, or by providing the goods and services peculiar to a society at war. What had once been a largely non-materialistic society—in which even royalty and aristocracy, in comparison with their counterparts in other countries, lived in austere simplicity—became a materialistic one that valued not only the quick buck but also the ostentatious flaunting of it.

> During the Chosŏn dynasty, less tangible qualities, such as a good family background, education, occupation, performance of ritual, and adherence to certain family behavioral norms, were more important than material considerations in determining status, although one was often linked to the other. . . . In the Korea of today, where status is no longer legally defined or inherited and especially in the urban centers where not everyone knows everyone, conspicuous consumption has become an important means of asserting status regardless of educational level.

The supplies and people that flooded in to conduct the war, and the huge amounts of cash in aid, spawned a strong subculture of "people who serviced the foreign presence: drivers, guards, runners, valets, maids, houseboys, black-market operators, money changers, prostitutes, and beggars."

Choe In-hun's "House of Idols" (1960) describes how the war distorted people's perceptions, and in its schizophrenic protagonist provides an example of the neurosis of the soul that developed from this war. The dislocation that the war caused is illustrated in Lee Pŏm-sŏn's "The Gulls" (1958): all of the main characters on the island are refugees from the war. The atmosphere throughout this story whispers to the reader that the war is over but its memories and sorrows linger.

Another of Lee's works, "The Stray Bullet" (*Obalt'an*), describes the crippled mentality left in the wake of the war. One passage describes the family in that story:

> [T]he mother who lost the basis for a comfortable life and emotional stability when she left her hometown, the war-crippled unemployed wandering younger brother, the younger sister turned GI prostitute in order to reduce life's hardships, the lethargic wife who has lost her youthful vivacious beauty through hardship and despair, and enervated and timid Chŏl-ho, who walks 30 or 40 *li* to and from work every day waiting for his "salary that's less than the streetcar fare" so he can take his mother with her toothache to the dentist. The family is melancholy and mute.

As was the whole country. Ch'oe In-hun's view of society at that time is similar to Lee Pŏm-sŏn's. At the beginning of "House of Idols" he treats the reader to an image of a Seoul in shambles in the war's aftermath. The protagonist's family, refugees from the North, had not been destroyed financially, as many others had been, but the son in that family was severely scarred psychologically.

Another result of the war was the expanded influence of the military. The Americans, who had first come at Liberation, then left, and then returned to fight the war, now had no thought of leaving again. Forty thousand of them stayed, increasing the speed of Westernization and de-Koreanization of the culture, as described previously in the section "The Outsider." The Korean army, which amounted to a few hundred soldiers at Liberation, was now, seven years later, a force of 600,000, the largest and most efficient institution in the country. In less than one decade, with Park Chung Hee's coup in 1961, it would tyrannize the country, and would not relinquish its hold until just before the 1988 Seoul Olympics.

But in that pile of ashes that the war left, there were embers of renewal. In Yi Pŏm-sŏn's "The Gulls," the army captain assigned security of the island noticed a crowd gathered around a body that the war had taken and the ocean had returned, and stopped to investigate. When he turned to get back into his jeep, he found his father, which the war had separated from him.

> The two had lived alone together until the outbreak of war, when the boy was called into the auxiliary forces. When the soldier finally returned his home was a pile of ashes and no one could tell him his father's whereabouts. He kept on searching, everywhere, never giving up. But in his heart he knew he was searching for nothing less than a miracle.

The story, then, tells us the tragedy of that war, and of the unexpected miracle that followed it.

Industrialization and Growth

The phenomenon that is often referred to as "phoenix-like growth" and "the miracle on the Han" is well known in a superficial way. What is not so well known are the problems that at times and in varying degrees seemed during the transition to render that growth meaningless to many in the country.

A denizen of the stagnant first two decades of the transition could not have imagined the amazing growth that would invigorate its remaining decades. In 1946 it was observed that "the fundamental population problem of Korea remains what it has been throughout the centuries: the achievement of even minimum acceptable levels of living for a people too numerous to subsist adequately by primitive agrarian techniques on the land available to them." In 1966, *Korea Times* columnist James Wade worried that little progress had been made over two decades: "The warning of twenty years ago remains valid." Wade's comment was based on an annual per capita income of only $105 in 1965. That income, however, was quite a jump when we consider the fact that per capita income had jumped about 30 percent, from $76 in 1962. In 1962 the country had just entered a GNP growth rate of 9.7 percent that would provide an annual per capita income of nearly $3,000 in 1985, and the 41 percent figure for absolute poverty in 1965 would decrease to 9.8 percent in 1980. From the early-1960s to 1988 it was full steam ahead, except for a setback at the beginning of the 1980s.

A few reasons for this rapid growth were a plentiful supply of cheap, hungry labor, the hierarchical, family-oriented mentality of Confucianism, and a generous infusion of foreign aid and inflow of foreign capital. The military government, however, with its oppressive hold on the economy, stifled creativity and natural adjustment to the market, thereby causing imbalances in the social economy and very troublesome labor-management relations. (This is covered in more detail in "State and the People.")

Nonetheless, even the victims of the booming economy were infected with a spirit of hope. By the time the 1988 Olympics heralded the end of the transition period, two-thirds of those who had been tenant farmers or laborers at Liberation, living in absolute poverty, had lifted themselves out of their extreme circumstances. In concrete terms, in 1959 there was one television per 10,000 households, and in 1985 there were more televisions than households; in 1960 there were 2,208 people per private car, and in 1988 there were 49. In 1976, 50 percent of Seoulites had running water, compared with 97.5 percent in 1985. This did not mean, of course, that Koreans were wealthy—the great majority would have to wait till the next millennium for their family car and vacation abroad. But during this transition period Koreans built up the momentum to power themselves into a much more comfortable life in the modern period.

Education

One of the most important fruits of economic growth is access to education. Koreans' fervid desire for education fueled phenomenal growth in access to it. During the Chosŏn dynasty (1392–1910), almost the only legitimate way to join the aristocracy and enjoy the good life was by passing the higher civil service exam; the post-Liberation explosion of education fervor among commoners must have been fueled by centuries of witnessing the elevating power of education: education equals *yangban* status. In the days of the dynasty the peasants had, in effect, no access at all to the education needed for upward mobility.

During the reform movement that began toward the end of the nineteenth century, approximately three thousand schools were founded for providing to all levels of society instruction in the new Western learning, subjects like history, geography, arithmetic, algebra and civics. When the Japanese took control of the country at the beginning of the twentieth century, they allowed the schools to continue operating only with government approval, using only authorized textbooks, and many of the schools were forced to close because the government deemed them "hotbeds of the nationalist movement." The Japanese built schools and provided education in vocational subjects that developed manual skills employed under Japanese bureaucrats and technicians. Officially, all children were permitted to attend primary and secondary school, a small fraction of the population were allowed to continue training in subjects like agriculture and in skills for lower positions in bureaucracy and industry, and an even smaller number were allowed to attend the one university in Korea or go abroad for tertiary education.

When the Japanese left, for the first time in Korea's history the doors of academia were thrown open to all. Between 1945 (Liberation) and 1947 the number of secondary schools doubled, by 1946 the number of universities jumped from one to four (Seoul National, Korea, Ewha, and Yonsei Universities), and university attendance increased from around 500 in 1945 to 20,000 in 1948.

The numbers kept growing in similar exponential terms over the following years, till the War put the brakes on it for a few years. As soon as the truce was implemented, in 1953, the country focused its energy again on education, and, by 1964, 95 percent of kids of primary school age were attending school (as opposed to 40 percent in 1945), college attendance had risen 180 percent over the 1945 figure, and literacy, which was around 25 percent in 1945, reached 98 percent in 1989.[56] Several Korea scholars think, with Rutt, that "It would also probably be fair to attribute to the lingering influence of Confucius the fantastic eagerness which everybody has for education."

While the transition years saw a phenomenal increase at all levels of education, not everyone went to college. Expense was a factor, but apparently not an insurmountable one; most parents made tremendous sacrifices to help their children (and the family through their children) take this last step to getting into

56. Nahm, p. 96. Compare with 99.5 percent in 1990.

the middle class, and many a penniless household somehow managed to scrape enough together to send at least one child to college. Our student in "River" (1968) was able to enter college and stay there even if he was always "tightening the belt another notch to quiet that grumbling stomach, lugging that heavy old hand-me-down ox-hide school bag under the arm because the handle's about ready to snap again, how oh how to come up with next term's tuition." And even our hero in "First Love" (with its setting in the 1970s), whose sister supported the two of them with what she earned from her sweat-shop job, would somehow find a way to afford it.

Starting in the mid 1960s, the main reason that not everyone went to college, the one stumbling block that could trip up even rich students, was the college entrance exam. The competition to enter prestigious universities (essential for real success in this group-oriented society) depended on the popularity of the department, ranging as high as 18:1 for some. Students from rural schools—like Hun's kids in "The Gulls," the student in "River," and the narrator in "First Love"—stood little chance of beating the competition for entrance to universities in Seoul (which was essential for getting a good job after graduation, since all roads lead to Seoul); they had to attend secondary school in one of the major cities to get a proper college-prep education. The college entrance exam was a nightmare that haunted even students in Seoul, as the narrator in "First Love" (whose family sent him to Seoul) will attest. Beginning in the 1970s, when the college entrance exam was introduced, high school students whose families could afford it attended classes at a "cram school"[57] after regular classes, where they gorged on all the mi-

57. At one of the stricter cram schools, as Maass describes in 1989, "[T]eachers and administrators carry truncheons that they regularly use to whack the behinds of students who commit such offenses as being late for class, falling asleep or scoring badly on quizzes. There is no clowning

nutiae that might appear on the college entrance qualifying exam. If they couldn't afford cram school classes, they spent their semester nights and vacation days and nights in a cram center, where they crammed by themselves.[58] The college student in "What's To Be Done?" probably did not have much difficulty getting into university. She was apparently from a middle class family, who could afford to send her to a college entrance exam prep institute or arrange private tutoring.

Income Distribution

From before 1945 up till a few years after the war, in the late 1950s, Koreans were equally poor, for the most part. Colonization had abolished the gentry class and, up to Liberation, the Japanese owned 90 percent of industrial assets; land reform after Liberation parceled the land with relative fairness, and the war had wrought impartial and general destruction. It was not until the 1960s that economic classes began to form to a noticeable degree, when the government, with billions of dollars in foreign aid, launched its drive to stimulate the economy. A

around when the teacher turns his back—television cameras are mounted in each classroom to allow supervisors in a control room to keep tabs on the students, and on the teachers. Students sleep 24 to a barracks-style room, and wear identical sweat suits and crew cuts. Many of them also wear a headband that says in blood-red ink, 'Must Win.' This is the school's slogan, repeated like an academic mantra to bring success to those who shout it loudest."

58. Entrance to high school, until the 1990s, was also competitive, but it wasn't as intensely so; as the narrator in "First Love" tells us, "In the junior high room practically all they learned was things like connecting electric lines to metal chopsticks in an old powdered milk can to boil ramyon, and masturbating."

growing income gap was the natural result of a growing economy that did not focus on equitable distribution.

In its rush to get the economy going, Park Chung Hee's government ignored the manual laborers, who expected to benefit from a prosperous economy with everyone else. Everything was focused on development of industry. Our 1970s story "First Love," while it does not directly address these inequities associated with the immature economy's growth, evokes a sense of the grim situation that its victims faced. Whether or not the author intended so, in the following image the reader sees the capitalist-industrialist casting scraps of bread to the laborers that he is exploiting.

> That day too a truck loaded with bakery stuff passed by. The kids playing soccer on the street dropped their game and tailed the truck close. These trucks sometimes dropped stuff as they bounced and rattled on down the road. Today, though, unlike other days, I didn't join the kids. But a whole case—not just one or two pieces—jumped out of the truck and landed right in front of my nose. "There's some!" Within a second dozens of kids gathered around me. A cloud of dust rose as they scrambled over each other and punched and bit each other to carry off their booty.

Corporate Korea (including the government) claimed that resources had to be accumulated in order to build up capital, while smaller voices demanded that resources be distributed. Some assert that distribution was reasonably equitable. Choo, for one, analyzed economic figures from the 1960s to the late 1970s and concluded that the country's distribution of income was more evenly balanced than in most other countries, roughly equal to that of Japan and Taiwan. And Lindauer observes that, although there was unequal distribution of wealth in the 1970s and 1980s, most Korean workers benefited substantially from the economy's growth. While statistics convinced some that income distribution was relatively fair in Korea, perceptions differed according to one's economic status. The ordinary citizen and the laborer saw the conspicuous consumption of the middle and capitalist classes[59]—"These newly rich are engaged in an extravagant, flamboyant and competitive display of wealth" —and thought that the Park regime needed to give more attention to distribution. Even the newly emerging middle class was dissatisfied when it looked upward. In 1967, Lee Man-gap reported:

> Their economic conditions are much better than those of the lower class, but sometimes they may be even more dissatisfied with their standing than the latter. When they evaluate their own social status, they usually refer to the people who are in somewhat better conditions than themselves.

With the Fourth Five-Year Plan (1977–1981) the authorities began to think more about social development. Evidently, they did not go far enough in this direction; the most virulent dissident activity occurred during the 1980s. The Sixth Five-Year Plan (1987–1991), at the end of the transition period, set the goal of striking "a balance between continued economic expansion and meeting the demands of different segments of soci-

59. Lett, 1998, p. 97: "In the Korea of today, where status is no longer legally defined or inherited and especially in the urban centers where not everyone knows everyone, conspicuous consumption has become an important means of asserting status."

ety." It was in these years, coincidentally, that the activity of the dissident movement began to diminish.

Social and Economic Classes

Most of the main characters in our stories are from the working and lower classes. None of our main or major characters are of the upper class, and only in "House of Idols," "What's To Be Done?" and possibly "The Face" do representatives of the middle class appear.

At the time of our first two stories, just before Liberation, the largest class was the peasants. Mohwa ("The Shaman Painting," 1936) was, as a shaman, in a class even below the peasantry. Ŏkswae, in "Loess Valley," farmed his own land, so he belonged to the peasantry. At the time, there was also a growing petite bourgeoisie class, which included traders and craftsmen and large landowners, and a new group, small capitalists, which the Japanese allowed to exist as long as they contributed to the empire. Officially, the *yangban* aristocracy had been abolished before the turn of the century, but there was no shortage of those former *yangban* gentry in denial:

> In the capital there are many people who have no business—that is to say, they are gentlemen of leisure. They are gentlemen, and gentlemen are not supposed to meddle with such sordid matters as manufacture and merchandise—no, not even office work, unless it be an office connected with the government.

Between 1945 and the early 1960s, social class distinction, like income distribution, was not so apparent. Two-thirds of the population were farmers, and all the other classes made up the other third, which consisted of "the old middle class or petite bourgeoisie (about 13 percent), the new middle class (7 percent), industrial workers (9 percent), and the urban lower class (6 percent)."[60] From the mid 1960s through the 1980s, social stratification became more complex, so much so that there is a lot of disagreement among analysts over how to characterize it. Analyst Lim Hy-Sop integrated their views:

> The population share of the middle class increased from 20 percent in 1960 to 39 percent in 1980, and it is still growing. Moreover, the proportion of the population that subjectively identifies itself with the middle class also increased, exceeding 60 percent. . . . Korean society can be said to have become a middle-class society and is becoming more so as the proportion of the middle-class population continues to increase. . . . In the early 1960s, the working-class population did not exceed 10 percent of the total population. As industrialization progressed, the population of this class gradually expanded and reached 22 percent by 1980. . . . The independent farmers' class, comprising nearly half of the total population in early 1960, has shrunk to only one-fifth.

Lim's analysis is based on a very broad definition of middle class, but it does provide an informative description of the changing pattern.

As Korea moved into the 1980s, industrialization contributed to the growth of the labor class. In 1960 it comprised roughly 10

60. Lim Hy-Sop, p. 13. "Moreover, the traditional landowner class disintegrated as a result of the land reform of 1949, but a new capitalist class had not yet emerged. Thus, Korean society in the early 1960s was fairly homogeneous, characterized by considerable equality in class status and income."

percent of all workers, then rose to almost 30 percent (40 percent of which were urban workers) in 1980. In numbers, this class was "the most significant social class in . . . South Korea."

Urbanization

As in other developing countries, Korea experienced an unsettling transformation from rural to urban society. This transformation can be termed a revolution if we consider its speed and intensity. Toward the end of the monarchy, at the beginning of the twentieth century, under 200,000 lived in Seoul, with no more than 5 percent living in all of the nation's cities. The move to the city began in a small way with Japan's annexation, in tandem with industrialization. One reason that Japan colonized Korea was its need for cheaply manufactured products, and it set up its mills and factories near the cities; at the same time, many peasants were losing their land because of the colonial government's agricultural policies and were not able to find jobs in the countryside.

At the time the Japanese left, around 15 percent of Koreans lived in cities, with Seoul's population around 5 percent of the nation's total. The urban population—especially Seoul's—jumped dramatically upon Liberation, when millions returned from migration abroad and fled from communism in the north. This urban population rose at a higher rate in the 1960s, when the nation began to focus most of its attention on industrialization. In 1974, Seoul's population of six million was 16 percent of the nation's population, and by the 1988 Olympics, 25 percent lived in Seoul (with almost 70 percent of the nation's population living in cities).[61] This was a complete reversal of the situation at the start of the 40-year transition period.

61. Lee, Hee-yeon, p. 105. In 1995 almost half of the nation's popula-

This reversal, of course, fundamentally changed the people's lives. One of the biggest changes for ordinary citizens was the sundering of family ties. It was not whole families that moved to the city, and those that did move—like the characters in most of our stories—found themselves without the support of family and hometown. The effect that this had on the individual is described in more detail in the section "Human Relationships."

A one-word adjustment to the popular adage describes the traditional household: The family that produces together stays together. When the family lived on the farm, they worked together to produce most of what they needed. In the city they were unable to produce those same goods and did not need to, since industrialization supplied them with these goods.[62] Not only was this a factor in splitting up the family, it also changed the individual's relationship with work. This altered relationship, and the abruptness with which it changed, caused greater distress for the individual and society than it did in societies where the transition from rural life to urban life happened much more gradually, not in two decades but over a century or more. The street urchins in "The Game Beaters" are a good example of what happened to the uprooted in the late 1940s, and the small village in "River" gives us a sense of the dying countryside of the 1960s and the desperation of the young to escape from it.

For the "refugees from the countryside" who could not afford to pay the soaring prices of housing, migration to Seoul

tion lived in Seoul's metropolitan area, which included Incheon and Kyŏnggi Province.

62. Hart, p. 47: "Larger families became anachronistic as they were no longer necessary to survival, and the new smaller dwellings of the city made them physically inconvenient."

also meant miserable living conditions. The concentrated populations and high prices in the cities required living in apartments, which were much smaller than the old homestead in the countryside. When a whole family moved to Seoul together, five or six (often parents and children and a couple of country cousins) in a one-room rental was not unusual. In the 1960s and 1970s, most workers in the factories could find housing only in the squatters' villages on the hills of Seoul, or in the outskirts of the city, where "the darkness and the dust and the noise and the stench and the coal gas" filled the lives of denizens like those in "First Love." Here's a general description of the situation in the late 1960s and early 1970s:

> [N]ew migrants are pouring into the city . . . , most of whom eventually end up in these shantytown neighborhoods, or squatter slums. . . . The city provides very few services of any kind to the slums . . . there may be one water spigot for 40 or 50 families, and very often it is a private concession so that people have to pay a few cents for each can of water. . . . Electricity reaches a very small percentage of the shacks.

The urban poor did not live only in ghettos close to the center of the city. Also available to them were rented rooms in dismal industrial neighborhoods on the outskirts of Seoul, like the settlement that provides the background in "First Love":

> [Our teachers] came on the bus from another world and taught us kids and then picked up their lunch boxes and went back to that other world. After these people from the other world took off, all that was left was the darkness and the dust and the noise and the stench and the coal fumes and fat older sisters.

The land in the urban squatters' villages was mostly government land, which meant that these people built their shanties and continued to live in them only at the grace of civil servants, who quite often served rich land developers. When the developer cast his eye on one of these urban villages, the government sometimes provided the crumb of another parcel of land to the village residents—a couple of hours outside Seoul; when they did not leave of their own accord, the developer's thugs descended upon them to help them move.

Urban migration also changed the quality of life in the countryside. It was mainly the young that moved to the cities, leaving behind in the countryside an older population, who now found it more difficult to do the farming and fishing. The nation's focus on industry meant less attention to rural areas, with the result that electricity and paved roads and the other features of modern life did not reach the countryside till long after they were common in the cities. "The South still had a long way to go in providing electricity to its villages in the 1970s when as many as 79 percent of them were still not electrified," which explains the village inn's gloomy darkness and its oil lamp in "River." As noted above, education in the rural areas also suffered; one could not expect to get a good job here—and much less in the city—if he graduated from a college in the provinces. The student in "River" tells us more about the rocky road to getting an education in the capital.

After the government made several half-hearted and ineffective attempts to reduce the disparity between city and countryside and to instill a spirit of self-reliance there, in 1971 it got serious and introduced the New Community Movement. In more specific terms, the goals were improvement in transportation, irrigation, housing, electrification, sanitation and many other areas, and attraction of manufacturing facilities that could use materials and surplus labor available in the local area to entice more young people to stay on the farm. Another goal was to encourage creative and dynamic leadership at the village level. It was a self-help program, in which the government would supply the financing (loans and grants) and guidance, and the village would supply the human resources. After a lot of trial and error, by the 1988 Olympics, the program and its various offspring seemed to have achieved some success in those original goals. To evaluate in material terms:

> The rural transportation infrastructure, carefully constructed in the 1970s, turned Korea from a series of individual, isolated valley economies into one national market. There were only 812 kilometers of paved roads in the nation in 1958; in 1985 there were 20,072 kilometers. [Whereas 79 percent of the countryside lacked electricity at the beginning of the Movement,] electricity reached every village. Although farm family lives are still hard, improvement has been remarkable.

Though the Movement achieved some success in its general aim of improving living standards and quality of life in Korea's rural areas, the exodus from the countryside did not let up. In 1986, only 35 percent of Koreans lived in the countryside. It was still a hard life: "Rural houses . . . were generally equipped with traditional dirt-floor kitchens, and few had flush toilets or separate spaces for bathing. Many rural households used firewood for cooking and heating," and only 23 percent had a telephone line. But it certainly beat "the good old days."[63]

63. About the "good old days," Underwood, who spent his whole life in Korea, wrote, "There are those who regret the loss of old Korea's morning calm, who yearn for the slow-moving countryside, beyond the sound of motors, and who mourn the loss of the good old days that really were

Attitude

Throughout the summer night, tears lovelier than pearls
settle on each waiting leaf like the pain which forms in
my soul.
I climb the morning knoll, dew and sun-bathed knoll;
such beauty gathered through the night to show in the
light of the day.
Growing smile lights my heart as glowing Sun lights my
way.
To its height it climbs, master now, searing bitterness
away.
Now back down to that blooding frontier of the soul,
leave agony behind to rot and nurture grassy knoll.[64]

It wasn't as rosy as a journey from "pain" to "dew and sun-bathed knoll"; what Koreans did during the transition was to "leave agony behind to rot and nurture grassy knoll." The transition did not make everything all right, but it was a start.

Kevin O'Rourke, a scholar and prolific translator of Korean literature, believed in 1973 that "the national attitude of the typical Korean intellectual has been pessimistic, defeatist and negative, a trait which [is] . . . true in the short story today." Through much of the transition, it was not only the intellectual that this pessimistic literature represented. Except for a couple brief periods of false hope, until well into the 1980s the general public had pretty much the same attitude, including a hefty dose of fatalism.

not so good. Such mourners for the past are mostly those who did not have to live in it" (Underwood, p. 294).

64. A government-censured song, "Morning Dew" ("*Achim Isŭl*"), popular in the 1970s and 1980s; melody and lyrics by Kim Min-gi, translation by Holstein.

This feeling is strongest in the first stories in this book. In "The Shaman Painting" (1936), the nation's mood is described as "this weary, rundown haunted house," the son of the shaman Mohwa simply withered away after his mother attacked him, and Mohwa herself committed suicide. The whole of "Loess Valley" (1939) was a metaphor for the people's passive, fatalistic but resentful mentality. Previous to Liberation, the general mood was one of despondency; from Liberation to the Olympics it was a mix of melancholy and hope, with the former state of mind gradually weakening as the latter strengthened. By the time Seoul celebrated its Olympics, most Koreans had pretty much shed the negative attitudes that had burdened those of just one or two generations before. This shows more in the details of the stories' settings than in the stories' overall mood. (O'Rourke correctly observed, after all, that universally the short story as a genre is pessimistic.) In "First Love," for instance, we know that the narrator will eventually get out of the slum, in "What's To Be Done?" the dictatorship is destroyed in the end, and in "The Face" the problem is not one of poverty or social disenfranchisement but of individual psychological struggle.

Han is Korea's operational word for the negative state of mind felt before and during much of the transition. It is one way or a combination of several ways of feeling bad about other people or a situation or one's fate in general.[65] Most Koreans think it is unique to their culture, and proprietarily insist that a non-Korean could never begin to comprehend it. It is regarded by many as the defining Korean emotion—most regard it as an essential element in the collective Korean consciousness[66]—and,

65. Deautsche describes *han* as "profound broken-heartedness, bitterness, grief, and the abyss of anguish, anger and resentment."

66. Standish presents a detailed and informative discussion on *han*, and on "the *han/chŏng* dyadic relationship which binds [all Koreans] together."

in fact, it would be understandable if a non-Korean mistook the "han" character in country's name Hanguk as the *han* discussed here. Psychiatrists and essayists and culture critics have written long treatises on it, and for decades it was the governing sentiment in film, literature and song. Fundamental to any description of *han*, more than the feelings themselves, is the *way* the feelings are expressed. This aspect of it may, in fact, be peculiarly Korean—the long, poignantly stoic bearing of accumulated negative feelings, and then their explosive release at the trigger of a word or touch, in a shaman rite, a Christian revival meeting, or a serious drinking session (like those in "Loess Valley").

Since the Olympics, though, *han* has been witnessed less and less. A book critic wrote in his 1997 review of "River" that "The depressing mood that governs 'River' is the angst-ridden state of mind of that period. It is rarely mentioned these days, and many young people think that expression of the feeling is a sign of weakness. Nowadays we think that *han* state of mind is incomparably silly."[67] The most likely reason of this feeling's disfavor may be that young people these days were born after the dynamics that many believe to have caused *han*: invasions (in the dynastic era and the Korean War), the patriarchal system and oppression by aristocracy in the dynastic era, the Japanese occupation 1910–1945, military governments and exploitative industrial capitalists from Liberation to the late 1980s, poverty from the dynastic era into the 1980s, and the strong gender discrimination that existed until recently.

67. Nam, Jin-u. He was somewhat ahead of his time. It was not unusual to find *han* expressed by name in many poems, songs, stories and movies until the end of the 1980s. One of Korea's all-time great movies (and winner of several international awards), the 1993 film *Sŏ-pyŏn-je*, featured *han* as its main theme.

On the other hand, *han* may be something like Confucianism, down but not out. Even in our second millennium,

> Yun Suk Ho, director of four TV serials that have been smashes in Japan, talks of han, a Korean word for a deeply felt sense of oppression: "Korean dramas express sadness particularly well. The writer of [current hit] *Autumn in the Heart* would cry when writing his script. The actors, during rehearsals, started crying too." Shin Hyun Taik, a film producer who runs a government-funded foundation promoting cultural exports, emphasizes another aspect of han: a grudge mentality, with resentments directed at everyone from U.S. troops to Japanese politicians. "A grudge is part of our national sentiment," he says. "We have a talent for expressing this."

Expressing sentiment and carrying a grudge are not necessarily the same as nursing *han*. As I suggested before, an essential feature of *han* is its explosive expression, which has become less evident over the years.

Conclusion

In 2005, on the sixtieth anniversary of Liberation, a poll was taken to determine the nature of Korean patriotism. "The survey shows that the nation is a source of pride for the younger generation while the older generation associate it with toil and suffering."

An instructive perspective on the transition from Liberation to Olympics is the society that it led to. Korea's hosting of the 1988 Seoul Summer Olympics was a celebration of its admission to the league of modern nations. Since Liberation in 1945, this autocratically ruled country with a largely illiterate populace and one of the world's feeblest economies had developed into a country with a 98 percent literacy rate, a budding democracy, and one of the world's most robust economies.[68] The country was not fully democratic yet, nor rich. As historian Cumings described, on the downtown streets of 1988 Seoul, we did not see the suave middle-class employees from offices in glass skyscrapers, the professional shoppers, the stylishly dressed students that we see in 2009. In 1988 we saw

> cab drivers honking in the gridlocked traffic, shoeshine boys, tearoom waitresses bustling by with a take-out order, grandmothers selling apples, young office workers in black pants and white shirt, bus girls in blue uniforms leaning out of the back door of a bus to announce the destination, old men heaving along under A-frames or pulling two-wheeled carts, women with sleeping babies strapped to their backs trying to maneuver enormous sidewalk vending wagons festooned with hats and wigs, delivery boys balancing ten auto tires behind the seat of their motorbike, scooting in and out of traffic.

Korea was still a difficult place to make a good life, and many workers and farmers, a substantial part of the population, resented their exclusion from the good life that they had worked so hard for, only to see others so blatantly enjoying it at their expense. Nevertheless, most of them were feeling the energy and hope essential to keep the momentum going for achieving the true democracy and mature society that was just around the corner. Most were feeling what economist Arthur Lewis wrote: "The advantage of economic growth is not that wealth increases happiness, but that it increases the range of human choice."

68. This book is being published in 2009, in the middle of the global economic crisis, when no country can describe its economy as "robust."

The choice, even of those that were dissatisfied, was to continue along the same path that they had traveled through the transition period—with a few adjustments for quality of life.

In second-millennium Korea, six decades after Liberation, we still see the cab drivers, of course, and grandmothers selling apples, and the delivery boys on motorcycles. But we see hardly any shoeshine boys now, nor tearoom waitresses—nor tearooms, for that matter, though a few can be found if you look hard enough; the intrepid bus girls (one of whom makes a scene-stealing appearance in "River") have all disappeared, as have most of the A-frames. Women carry their babies in strollers instead of strapped to their back; but now, most women of that age are at work, and their children at the daycare center, or we are almost as likely to see fathers with their one or, at most, two children. The tear gas from student and labor demonstrations has long since cleared from the streets.

In 2008, South Korea had a fully functioning democracy and held its fifth round of free presidential elections at the end of the year. Its gross domestic product in that year ranked thirteenth in the world, while per capita income, which had jumped more than ninety times since Liberation, ranked thirtieth.

Even the most modern, mature nations have their problems, and Korea is no exception. The nation is still divided into North and South. The nation's suicide rate in 2005, because of "the fast pace of social change," is higher than it was during less wealthy years of the transition and is highest among OECD nations. The Korean family seems to be in trouble: the divorce rate rose from 1.7 in 1996 to 2.6 in 2006—third highest in the world. Korea's elderly, in this most rapidly aging nation on earth, are being deserted by their families and effectively ignored by the government.[69] The Seoul metropolitan area is straining un-

69. Choi, Sung-Jae: "Families, which have generally been the safety net

der a population of half of the country's entire population (it held one quarter of it in 1988), and the rural areas are still suffering from depopulation—now down to only 22 percent of the nation's total population—and that decreasing rural population is aging even faster than the national rate.[70] Workers are making demands that lower the competitiveness of Korean goods and discourage investment.[71] Despite an anti-prostitution law promulgated in 2004, the trade in 2007 amounted to $13 billion, "roughly 1.6 percent of the nation's gross domestic product."

Extreme poverty exists side by side with extreme wealth in this land that in 2004 joined the world's exclusive trillion-dollar club. On the outskirts of Dongduchŏn, a satellite city about

for older persons, are now challenged, threatened, assaulted and eroded in terms of both structure and function. Social and familial values of filial piety, familism and communalism are apparently withering away, and individualism and an orientation toward the nuclear family are developing and expanding in their place." Lee, Hyo-sik (in 2005). He adds: "The suicide rate for South Korea's elderly has increased more than five-fold over the past 20 years as more senior citizens opted to terminate their lives due to economic hardship and loneliness. . . . The sharp rise reflects the transformation of the Confucian Korean society into a Western-style nuclear family structure where the elderly are less supported by their [children] than under the big family system." Soh, 2004: "The country's rising suicide rate is a stark contrast to some 20 years ago in 1982, when the suicide rate was relatively low at 6.8 per 100,000 people." A *Dong-a Ilbo* editorial (2006) tells of many who can't afford the monthly payments into the national pension plan.

70. Choi Sung-Jae, 2002: "[T]he proportion of older persons in the population aged 65 and over has also greatly increased, from 2.9 percent in 1960 to 7.2 percent in 2000," and is expected to reach 23 percent in 2030.

71. *TIME*, 2003: "Foreign investment in South Korea has plunged by more than a third since 1999, partly due to strike fatigue. 'Korea is losing its competitive edge,' warns Sunny Yi, a management consultant at Bain & Co. 'Unions are making things worse.'"

thirty kilometers north of Seoul, is a community whose economy depends largely on the nearby U.S. military base, Camp Casey. Now that the base is planning to close down, the people living there, who depended on the camp for a living that never amounted to more than scraping by, are in dire straits. Many of the children in high school are so poor that they cannot afford lunch, and, just like the middle school students in the 1970s' "First Love," gorge with tap water to fill empty stomachs.

Liberation in 1945 was not the first step toward Korea's modern way of life. The social caste system had begun to wither before that, in the eighteenth century, with the decline of the *yangban* aristocracy; political reform was being contemplated as early as the middle of the eighteenth century and was attempted in the second half of the nineteenth century; industrialization and urbanization had already begun in earnest during the Japanese occupation. Just as Liberation was not the first step, the 1988 Seoul Olympics was no culmination. It was not until a few years after the Seoul Olympics that people felt they had a government that truly represented the people, that a woman did not have to regret being born a woman, that laborers earned a decent living, that industry was exporting technically advanced, high-value products.

But that period from Liberation to Olympics was a special period. The essentials for transition to modern life—traditional and new, domestic and foreign—fused during these forty-three years; new developments took root, and were not reversed or nullified, as they had been in previous times. Without this transition and its people and events, Korea would be a much different story from what it is today.

Endnotes

270: "common business interests with the Japanese" —Pihl, 1973, pp. xvi–xvii. Lee, Ki-baik, p. 315

270: "about 38,000 indigenous personnel" —Eckert, 1990, p. 257

271: "held together by the power of the colonial state." —Eckert, 1990, p. 329

271: "and promise brightened their future." —Chŏng, Ho-ŭng, p. 7. My translation

272: "collaborators from positions of political power and influence," —Eckert, 1990, p. 332

272: Russian and American influence" —O'Rourke, p. 4

273: earmarks of a conquered country" —*Time*, July 14, 1947

273: struck it rich during colonial days —Cumings, p. 203

274: remained intact and were in force. . . . —Lee, Hye-kyung, 1994, p. 299

276: outside the formal political structure —Eckert, 1990, p. 347

277: unit labor costs down and economic growth up." —Lee, Joung-Woo, p. 81

277: before they thought of themselves. —Kim, Dong-chun

277: social justice and political democracy. —Kim, Kyong-Dong, p. 202

278: and installed their repressive regimes. —Koo, Hagen, 1994, p. 137

278: against the threat of communism. —Vogel, p. 96

279: the growth of any base for political opposition." —Lim, Hy-Sop, p. 20

279: was controlled by the government; —Vogel, p. 97

279: labor laws favored management. —Vogel, pp. 97–98

279: from around 4,000 to 2,635. —Ch'oe, Bae-gŭn, p. 281

279: These "watchdogs of political morality" —Steinberg, p. 79

279: incarnation of the sovereign people" —Oh, p. 149

281: their number and influence have been negligible." —Oh, p. 145

282: "March for the Martyrs." —*Nim-ŭl uihan haengjin'guk*. (Composer unknown.)

283: two evils, usually seen as interconnected. —Eckert, 1990, p. 379
283: the author of "What's To Be Done?" —Interview with Kong Chi-yŏng, January 6, 2005
283: ("PD"; *minjung minju undong*). —Walhain, p. 194
287: from around 2,700 to over 4,000. —Ch'oe, Bae-gŭn, p. 281
287: the previous twenty-five years combined. —Vogel, p. 105
288: valid and natural social order." —Park, Yong Shin, p. 113
288: at some point coalesce with it." —Palmer, p. 4
290: a hundred lashes in public. —Kim, Chong-Ho
291: and the harassment of shamans. —Goldberg, p. 101
291: underlying the mental landscape of Koreans." —Kim, Andrew Eungi
291: shamanist shrines share turf and patronage. —Holstein, 1994, pp 16–21
292: shamans increase by about one percent." —Kim, Min-hee
293: in wealthy Apkuchŏngdong). —Kim, Tong-hyung
294: the Silla, Koryŏ and Chosŏn periods" —Goulde
296: like artlessness or rusticity" —Yoon, Chang Sup
296: and doing good business. —Lee, Jin-woo
297: Accordingly, many men were versed in both. —Eckert, 1990, p. 80
298: and those disenchanted with life," —Hogarth, p. 152
298: passive Japanese Buddhism. —Hogarth, p. 152
298: statistics show more Christians than Buddhists. —Baker, 2001
298: "Buddhism has died out." —*Time*, Mar. 13, 1944
299: however little the laity may understand it." —Rutt, 1964, p. 65
299: Buddhism has been enjoying a revival." —Hogarth, p. 153
300: centralized and authoritarian monarchy. —Eckert, 1990, p. 51
300: regard it as a religion. —Ch'oe, Mun-hyŏng, pp. 117–123, and personal communication
302: over 16 percent had given up the practice. —Hart, p. 54
303: *yangban* "Practical Learning" —"Silhak" in Korean. It is also known as the "New Learning" school
303: "The True Meaning of the Lord in Heaven" —Kim, Young-Gwan
304: participated indirectly. —Kim, Chin-so
305: role in encouraging such identification. —Kim, Andrew Eungi
306: at the root of Korean thinking. —Cha, Young Gil
307: one's financial giving." —Adams, Daniel, pp. 11–12

307: "Koreanized" by the local culture. —Personal e-mail communication with Dwight Strawn, Sept. 29, 2005
308: shamanistic beliefs and practices." —Suh, Sangwon
308: "Go away, Satans!" —Kim, Chong-Ho
308: to bear the humiliation. —Baker, 2001
310: these basic relationships." —Koo, 1994, p. 265
310: rapid urbanization and "condensed" —Lee, Joo-hee
311: only 17 percent had three or more. —Lee, Hye-kyung, 1994, p. 302
312: pervasive in the Korean family. —Choe, Sang-Hun, p. 259
313: individualism began its spread into Korea. —Kim, Ha-jong, pp. 217–218
313: away from the family the most. —Choi, Sun-yuel, p. 262
314: cannot be solved by co-residence. —Bell
314: description of "familism" —Chang, Kyung-Sup, p. 597
316: the 1983 story "Wayfarer" —"Sullyeja ŭi norae," 1983. See Fulton, 1997, for the English translation. The original story first appeared in *Munhak Sasang* (Seoul) in 1983
316: her own life to live. —Interview with O, Chŏng-hŭi, July 2005
317: his extensive operations. —Gale, p. 189
317: and to her son. —Lee, Hye-kyung, 1994, p. 300
318: this same Korean gentleman. —Gale, p. 189
318: real power is another. —Rutt, 1964, p. 166
320: if not exclusive, responsibility." —Lee, Hye-kyung, 1994, p. 302
321: 9.4 years for females. —Steinberg, p. 77
321: most of them were appointed. —Steinberg, p. 77.
321: the front lines in the 1980s —Interview, January 6, 2005
322: a very small minority. —See Fulton 2003 for an informative discussion of women's literature
324: Professor Yue Mahn-gunn, —In an interview held May 22, 2005
324: in individualistic society. —Hong, Chŏng-sŏn, p. 7
324: relationship between [speaker] and [hearer]. —Shin, p. 288
326: just like a family. —Park, Yong Shin, pp. 118–119
327: as late as 1964. —Goldberg, p. 101. Rutt, 1964, pp. 67, 73–74, 88–89
327: the supreme goal." —MacDonald, p. 80
329: people do not mix in its society." —Rutt, 1964, p. 190
329: and the prostitute." —Kendall, p. 63

330: "roots" and, thereby, his legitimacy. —Goldberg, p. 99
331: 'Manchurian beggars.' —Kwon, Chŏng-saeng
332: and Western influence." —Moon, p. 6
335: the Liberation of a friendly nation." —Underwood, pp. 297-301
336: weapons of destruction." —Kim, Susie Jie Young
336: juggernaut in "House of Idols." —Interview with Ch'oe In-hun, July 2, 2005
338: contemporary documents, —Rutt, 1961, pp. 57–60, 103–104
338: and Internet cafes)." —Choi, Hyung-Ki
339: rule of the colonial government. —Eckert, 1990, p. 329
340: consumption of rice to decrease 45 percent. —Fairbank, p. 881
341: when the Japanese took full control of Korea. —Barry, p. 44
341: not designed to serve Korean needs. —MacDonald, p. 183
342: change swept the country." —Chŏng, Ho-ŭng, p. 7
342: training in the relevant subjects. —Underwood, p. 127
343: a poor and filthy rabble. . ." —*Time*, Feb. 16, 1948
343: 1,500 per person in 1946-47." —MacDonald, pp. 183–184
343: post-Liberation economic growth. —Kuk, Bom Shin, p. 161–162
344: whatever services they had. —Cumings, p. 303
344: kidnapped, or gone missing." —Eckert, 1990, p. 345
345: regardless of educational level. —Lett, 1998, p. 97
345: prostitutes, and beggars." —Cumings, p. 302
346: its memories and sorrows linger. —Kim, Chŏng-shin, p. 358
346: "The Stray Bullet" —Translated by Kim, Chong-un
346: melancholy and mute. —Kim, Chŏng-shin, p. 356
348: the land available to them." —Taeuber, p. 306
348: "The warning of twenty years ago remains valid." —Wade, James, p. 40
348: 30 percent, from $76 in 1962. —Wade, L. L., p. 51
348: decrease to 9.8 percent in 1980—Park, Yong Shin, p. 108
348: troublesome labor-management relations. —Ch'oe, Bae-gŭn, p. 256–257
348 / 349: their extreme circumstances. —Lim, Hy-sop, p. 24
349: in 1988 there were forty-nine. —Hart, pp. 71, 74
349: compared with 97.5 percent in 1985. —Chira
349: "hotbeds of the nationalist movement." —Lee, Ki-baik, p. 332
350: the number of secondary schools doubled —Underwood, p. 129

350: which everybody has for education." —Rutt, 1964, pp. 117–118
351: ranging as high as 18:1 for some. —Oh, Byung-hun, p. 132
352: 90 percent of industrial assets —Choo, p. 303
354: that of Japan and Taiwan. —Choo, pp. 301–302
354: benefited substantially from the economy's growth. —Lindauer, p. 6
354: competitive display of wealth" —Brandt, "Mass Migration and Urbanization in Contemporary Korea," *Asia* (Winter 1970–1971), as quoted in Kim, Kyong-Dong, p. 201
354: better conditions than themselves. —Lee, Man-Gap, p. 238. It appears that this paradoxical correspondence of dissatisfaction and increasing wealth was not peculiar to Korea. Kamp reports that "[b]y nearly every measurable indicator . . . in 2003, lie for the average American had gotten better than it used to be . . . [yet] political scientists and mental-health experts detected a marked uptick since the midcentury in the number of Americans who considered themselves unhappy."
354 / 355: different segments of society." —Kim, Jong-Gie, p. 124
355: connected with the government. —Moose
356: has shrunk to only one-fifth. —Lim, Hy-Sop, p. 20–21
357: social class in . . . South Korea." —Koo, Hagen, 1987, p. 178
357: 16 percent of the nation's population —Oh, Byung-hun, p. 131
358: "refugees from the countryside" —Pihl, 1993, p. xvi
359: small percentage of the shacks. —Brandt, "Mass Migration and Urbanization in Contemporary Korea," *Asia* (Winter 1970–1971), as quoted in Kim, Kyong-Dong, p. 201
360: 79 percent of them were still not electrified," —Keim, p. 23
360: labor available in the local area —Kim, Jong-Gie, p. 145
361: improvement has been remarkable. —Steinberg, p. 151
361: only 23 percent had a telephone line. —Kim, Jong-Gie, p. 134
362: true in the short story today." —O'Rourke, pp. 2–3
365: "We have a talent for expressing this." —Spaeth, p. 17
365: toil and suffering." —*Chosŏn Ilbo*
366: scooting in and out of traffic. —Cumings, p. 333
366: the range of human choice." —Lewis, p. 420
367: "the fast pace of social change" —Lee, Hyo-sik, 2006
367: from 1.7 in 1996 to 2.6 in 2006 —KNSO
368: the nation's gross domestic product." —Kim, So-hyun
369: tap water to fill empty stomachs. —Kim, Jong-han

References

Adams, Daniel J. 2004. "Church Growth in Korea: Perspectives on the Past and Prospects for the Future." *Transactions* 79: 1–32. Seoul: The Royal Asiatic Society, Korea Branch.

Adams, Robert M. 1972. *Proteus: His Lies, His Truth; Discussions of Literary Translation*. New York: Norton.

Baker, Donald. 1995. "Taoism in Contemporary Korea." *Abstracts of the 1995 AAS Annual Meeting: Taoism: The Forgotten Strand in Korea's Religious Heritage*. Downloaded July 29, 2005, from http://www.aasianst.org/absts/1995abst/korea/kses73.htm.

Baker, Donald. 2001. "Looking for God in the Streets of Seoul: The Resurgence of Religion in 20th Century Korea." *Harvard Asia Quarterly* V, No. 4 (Autumn 2001). Downloaded in May 2004 from http://www.fas.harvard.edu/~asiactr/haq/200104/0104a002.htm.

Barry, Brian. 2008. "Potpourri." *Korea Heritage*, Vol. 1 (Summer 2008). Seoul: Korea Cultural Heritage Administration.

Bell, Patricia A. 2004. "The Impact of Rapid Urbanization on South Korean Family Composition and the Elderly Population in South Korea." *Population Review*, 43(1). Downloaded in November 2005 from http://muse.jhu.edu/journals/population_review/toc /prv43.1.html.

Brandt, Vincent. 1970. "Mass Migration and Urbanization in Contemporary Korea." *Asia* (Winter 1970–1971).

Brown, Haines. 1997. "Korean Shamanism." Downloaded in August 2005 from http://www.hartford-hwp.com/archives/55a/092.html.

Cha, Young Gil. "The Influence of Korean Shamanism on Korean Churches." Downloaded August 6, 2003, from http://my.netian.com/~jsschrst/shamanism.html.

Chang, Kyung-Sup. 2003. "The State and Families in South Korea's Compressed Fertility Transition: A Time for Policy Reversal?" Supplement to *Journal of Population and Social Security* 1 (June 2003). National Institute of Population and Social Security Research, Japan. Downloaded in

November 2005 from http://www.ipss.go.jp/webj-d/WebJournal.files/population/ps03_6.html.

Chira, Susan. 1987. "Boom Time in South Korea: An Era of Dizzying Change." *New York Times*, April 7, 1987.

Ch'oe, Bae-gŭn, et al. 1999. *Hanguk Kyŏngje-ŭi Ihae: Hanguk Kyŏngje Sŏngjang-ŭi Hoigo-wa Jŏnmang (Understanding the Korean Economy: Retrospective and Outlook on the Growth of the Korean Economy)*, 249–285. Seoul: Pŏpmunsa.

Ch'oe, Mun-hyŏng. 2002. *Dongyang-e-do Shin-ŭn Issnŭn-ga? (The East's Concept of God)*. Seoul: Baeksan Sŏdang.

Choe, Sang-Hun. 2009. "After Korean War, brothels and an alliance." *International Herald Tribune*, January 8, 2009. Downloaded in February 2009 from http://www.iht.com/articles/2009/01/08/asia/korea/php.

Choi, Hyung-Ki, Yi Huso. 2004. "South Korea." In *International Encyclopedia of Sexuality*, ed. Francoeur and Raymond Noonan. CCIES at the Kinsey Institute. Downloaded in February 2009 from http://www.kinseyinstitute.org/ccies/kr.php#homoerot.

Choi, Sun-yuel. 1994. "Sex Role Socialization in the Korean Family." In *Gender Division of Labor in Korea*, ed. Hyoung Cho and Chang Pil-wha, 256–271. Seoul: Korean Women's Insitute Series, Ewha Womans University Press.

Choi, Sung-Jae. 2002. "National Policies on Ageing in Korea." In *Ageing and Long-Term Care: National Policies in the Asia-Pacific*, ed. David R. Phillips and Alfred C. M. Chan. Singapore: Institute of Southeast Asia Studies. Downloaded July 25, 2005, from http://web.idrc.ca/es/ev-28475-201-1-DO_TOPIC.html.

Chosŏn Ilbo. 2005. "Poll Finds Pragmatic Patriotism Among the Young." *Chosun Ilbo*, August 15.

Choo, Hakchung. 1980. "Economic Growth and Income Distribution." In *Human Resources and Social Development in Korea*, ed. Park Chong Kee, 277–335. Seoul: Korea Development Institute.

Chŏng, Ho-ŭng. 1995. "Gil-ŭi Yŏllim-gwa Gkŭnghgim" ("Opening and Closing of the Way"). In *Haebang 50 nyŏn han'guk-ŭi sosŏl (Fifty Years After Liberation: Korean fiction)*, 2 (1960–1980): 7–14, ed. Hong Jŭng-sŏn et al. Seoul: Han'gyŏre shinmunsa.

Cicero. *Libellus de optimo genere oratorum* IV:14. In Baynard Q. Morgan, "A critical bibliography of works on translation" (1959). In *On Translation*, ed. Reuben A. Brower. Cambridge, MA: Harvard University Press.

Clark, Donald. 2003. *Living Dangerously in Korea: The Western Experience, 1900–1950*. Norwalk, CT: Eastbridge Books.

Cleary, William. 2005. "Chun Hyang Song." In *A Yang for Every Yin: Dramatizations of Korean Classics*, by John Holstein, 177–218. Seoul: Seoul Selection.

Covell, Jon Carter. 1981. *Korea's Cultural Roots*, 3rd edition. Salt Lake City: Moth House Publications.

Cumings, Bruce. 1997. *Korea's Place in the Sun*. New York: W. W. Norton.

Deautsche, Lauren W. 2005. "DMZ Diary: Surviving the Future Past Tense." *Kyoto Journal* 60. Downloaded July 4, 2005, from http://www.kyotojournal.org/Korea/deutsch.html.

Dong-a Ilbo. 2006. "National pension plan has 'blind spots.'" *Dong-A Ilbo*. February 14, 2006. Downloaded June 2007 from http://english.donga.com/srv/service.php3?biid =2006021408548&path_dir=20060214.

Eckert, Carter J., Lee, Ki-baik, et al. 1990. *Korea Old and New: A History*. Seoul: Ilchokak.

Eckert, Carter. 1991. *Offspring of Empire: The Koch'ang Kims and the Colonial Origins of Korean Capitalism 1876–1945*. Seattle: University of Washington Press.

Fairbank, John K., Edwin O. Reischauer, and Albert M. Craig. 1973. *East Asia Tradition and Transformation*. Boston: Houghton Mifflin.

Fulton, Bruce, and Ju-Chan. 1997. *Wayfarer*. Seattle: Women in Translation.

Fulton, Bruce. 2003. "Women's Literature." In *The Columbia Companion to Modern East Asian Literature*, ed. Joshua Mostow, 638–643. New York: Columbia University Press.

Gale, James S. 1898. *Korean Sketches*. Reprint 1975. Seoul: The Royal Asiatic Society, Korea Branch.

Goldberg, Charles N. 1979. "Spirits in Place: The Concept of Kohyang and the Korean Social Order." In *Studies on Korea in Transition*, ed. David McCann, John Midleton, Edward Schultz. Honolulu: Center for Korean Studies.

Goulde, John. 1995. "Taoist Alchemists in Mid-Choson Korea." *Abstracts of the 1995 AAS Annual Meeting: Taoism: The Forgotten Strand in Korea's Religious Heritage*. Downloaded July 29, 2005, from http://www.aasianst.org/absts/1995abst/korea/kses73.htm.

Hart, Dennis. 2001. *From Tradition to Consumption: Construction of a Capitalist Culture in South Korea*. Seoul: Jimoondang.

Heyman, Allen. 2006. "Buddhist ritual music and dance." *Transactions* 81: 23–31. Seoul: The Royal Asiatic Society, Korea Branch.

Hirohito. 1945. "Hirohito's Surrender Broadcast, 15 August, 1945." Downloaded on December 25, 2005, from http://www.kyokipress.com/wings/surrender.html.

Hogarth, Hyun-key Kim. 2002. *Syncretism of Buddhism and Shamanism in Korea.* Seoul: Jimoondang.

Holstein, John. 1994. "Seoul's Shaman Village." *Asiana* 6 (2): 16–21.

———. 1999. "The McCune-Reischauer Korean Romanization system." *Transactions* 74 (1999): 1–21. Seoul: The Royal Asiatic Society, Korea Branch.

———. 2005. *A Yang for Every Yin.* Seoul: Seoul Selection.

Hong, Chŏng-sŏn, Chŏng Ho-ŭng, Kim Jae-yong, eds. 1995. "Sahoijŏk, yŏksajŏk salmŭro-ŭi hoigui" ("Revolution of Social and Historical Life"). *Haebang 50 nyŏn han'guk-ŭi sosŏl (Fifty Years After Liberation: Korean fiction),* Vol 2 (1960–1980): 7–11. Seoul: Han'gyŏre shinmunsa.

Horace. The Art of Poetry. *Horace: Satires. Epistles. The Art of Poetry.* Trans. H. Rushton Fairclough. 1969. Loeb Classical Library. Cambridge, MA: Harvard University Press.

Ishikawa, K. I. "Difficulties in Translating Japanese into English and Vice Versa." *Pacific Spectator* 9: 95–99.

Johnson, Samuel. 1890. *Lives of the Poets.* I:437. London: J. M. Dent. 1925. *The Penn State Archive of Samuel Johnson's Lives of the Poets,* ed. Kathleen Nulton Kemmerer. Downloaded September 24, 2003, from http://www.hn.psu.edu/Faculty/KKemmerer/poets /dryden/life1.htm.

Kamp, David. 2009. "Rethinking the American Dream." *Vanity Fair,* April 2009. Downloaded in April 2009 from http://www.vanityfair.com/culture/features/2009/04/american-dream200904.

Kang, Hildi. 2001. *Under the Black Umbrella.* Ithaca, NY: Cornell University Press.

Kang, Ku-yŏl. 2005. "Chŏn Duhwan Sŏch'odong Ttang Naenyŏn 1-2 Wŏl Tchŭm Kyŏngmae" (Chun Du-hwan's Sŏch'odong Land to Be Auctioned Next Year January or February). *Sekye Ilbo,* Nov. 9, 2005.

Karlsson, Anders. 2005. "Kyung Moon Hwang. Beyond birth: Social Status in the Emergence of Modern Korea." *Sungkyun Journal of East Asian Studies* 5 (2): 237–240.

Keim, Willard D. 1979. *The Korean Peasant at the Crossroads: A Study of Attitudes.* Bellingham, WA: Western Washington University.

Kendall, Laurel. 1987. *Shamans, Housewives, and Other Restless Spirits.* Honolulu: University of Hawaii Press.

Kim, Andrew Eungi. 2000. "Christianity, Shamanism, and Modernization in South Korea." *Cross Currents,* Spring-Summer, 2000. Downloaded July 25, 2005, from http://www.findarticles.com/p/articles/mi_m2096/is_2000_Spring-Summer/ai_63300897.

Kim, Chin-so. 1996. "Iljeha Hanguk Ch'ŏnju Kyohwoe-ŭi Sŏn'gyo Banchim-gwa Minjok Ŭishik" (Nationalism and Mission Policy of the Korean Catholic Church during the Japanese Occupation). *Kyohwoesa Yŏn'gu (Research in Church History),* Vol. 11. Seoul: Hanguk Kyohwoesa Yŏn'guso (Korean Church History Research Institute).

Kim, Chŏng-shin. 1995. "Sobakhan Saram-dŭl-ŭi Sobakhalsuŏpnŭn Sang-chŏ" ("The Not So Simple Wounds of Simple People"). In *I Pŏm-sŏn Taep'yo Chung-tanpyŏn Sŏnchip (Collected Novelettes and Short Stories of Lee Pŏm-sŏn),* ed. Kim Chik-sŭng, 355–362. Seoul: Dosŏchulp'an Chaek Sesang.

Kim, Chong-Ho. 2001. "Cultural Politics or Cultural Contradiction? Prejudice against Shamanism in Korean Society." Presentation to KSAA Conference. 2001. Downloaded in July 2005 from http://www.arts.monash.edu.au/korean/ksaa/conference/papers /03chonghokim.PDF.

Kim, Chong-un. 1978. "Images of Man in Postwar Korean Fiction." *Korean Studies* 2: 1–27.

Kim, Dong-chun. 2001. "Nodongja-wa Nodong Chŏngch'aek" (Labor Policy and the Laborer). Downloaded July 8, 2005, from http://www.kdatabase.com/SchRstBook.aspx?schKeyword=1125

Kim, Ha-jong. 1973. "The Dark Later Years." In *Listening to Korea,* ed. Marshall R. Pihl, 217–219. New York: Praeger.

Kim, Jong-Gie, and Jae-Young Son. 1997. "Rural-Urban Disparity and Government Policies for Rural Development." In *The Strains of Economic Growth: Labor Unrest and Social Dissatisfaction in Korea,* ed. David Lindauer, Kim Jong-Gie, et al, 123–153. Cambridge, MA: Harvard University Press.

Kim, Jong-han. 2004. "Saving Dongducheon." *Korea Herald,* September 2, 2004.

Kim, Kyong-Dong. 1979. *Man and Society in Korea's Economic Growth: Sociological Studies*. Seoul: Seoul National University Press.

Kim, Min-hee. 2003. "45 years with Korea's Shamans." *Korea Herald,* July 26, 2003.

Kim, Richard. 1998. *Lost Names: Scenes from a Korean Boyhood*. Berkeley: University of California Press.

Kim, So-hyun. 2007. "Sex trade accounts for 1.6% of GDP." *Korea Herald,* September 19, 2008. Reprinted in the Korea Women's Development Institute web site: http://ww2.kwdi.re.kr.

Kim, Susie Jie Young. 1999. "Remembering Trauma: History and Counter-Memories in Korean Fiction." *Manoa* 11 No. 2 (1999): 42–46, University of Hawai'i Press. Downloaded July 4, 2005 from http://muse.jhu.edu/demo/manoa/v011/
11.2kim01.html

Kim, Tong-hyung. 2006. "Fortune-Telling Emerges as Thriving Business." *Korea Times,* Feb. 1, 2006.

Kim, Young-Gwan. 2002. "The Confucian-Christian Context in Korean Christianity." *B. C. Asian Review* 13 (Spring 2002): 70–91. Downloaded in December 2005 from www2.arts.ubc.ca/bcar/no13/articles/young kim/article.pdf in.

KNSO (Korea National Statistics Office). 2007. "Divorce statistics in 2006." Downloaded in June 2007 from http://www.nso.go.kr/eng2006/e01___0000/e01b__0000 /e01bi_0000/e01bi_0000.htm.

Kong, Chi-yŏng. 1995. "In'gan-e-daehan Yeŭi (Human Decency)." *Ingan-e-daehan Yeŭi* (Human Decency), 270–307. Seoul: Dong-a chulpansa.

Kong, Chi-yŏng. 2002. "Uri-nŭn Nugu-i-myŏ Ŏdisŏ Wassŏ Ŏdiro Kanŭn'ga?" ("Who Are We, Where Did We Come from, Where Are We Going?"). In 2002 *Olhae-ŭi Munje Sosŏl* (This Year's Issue Stories: 2002), eds. Han'guk Hyŏndae Sosŏl, 50–85. Seoul: Purŭn Sasangsa.

Koo, Hagen. 1987. "The Interplay of State, Social Class, and World System in East Asian Development: The Cases of South Korea and Taiwan." In *The Political Economy of the New Asian Industrialism,* ed. Frederic Deyo, 165–181. Ithaca, NY: Cornell University Press.

Koo, Hagen. 1994. "Middle-Class Politics in the New East Asian Capitalism: The Korean Middle Classes." In *Culture, Politics, and Economic Growth: Experiences in East Asia,* ed. Richard Harvey Brown, 127–151. Williamsburg, VA: Dept. of Anthropology, College of William and Mary.

Koszul, A. H., ed. 1910. "Shelley's prose in the Bodleian MSS." *The Cambridge History of English and American Literature in 18 Volumes (1907–21),* Vol. 12: The Romantic Revival. Cambridge, England: University Press.

Kuk, Bom Shin. 1979. "Technology and Transformation in Korean Education." In *Studies on Korea in Transition,* ed. David McCann et al., 160–173. Honolulu: Center for Korean Studies, University of Hawaii.

Kwon, Chŏng-saeng and Lee Ch'ŏl-su. 2000. *Mong-sil Eonni.* Seoul: Changbi.

Kwon, Youngmin. 1993. "Foreword." *Land of Exile: Contemporary Korean Fiction,* ed. Marshall Pihl and Bruce Fulton, vii–ix. Armonk, NY: M.E. Sharpe.

Lanier, Sidney. 1892. *The English Novel and the Principle of Its Development.* New York: C. Scribner's Sons. Revised edn. 1911.

Lee, Dong Jae. 1975. "Some problems in learning Korean second-person pronouns." In *The Korean Language: Its Structure and Social Projection,* ed. Homin Sohn. Occasional Papers of the Center for Korean Studies, #6, The Center for Korean Studies, University of Hawaii.

Lee, Hee-yeon. 2000. *Korea: The Land and People.* Ed. Organizing Committee of the 29th International Geographical Congress, 98–122. Seoul: Kyohaksa.

Lee Hye-kyung. 1994. "Gender Division of Labor and the Authoritarian Developmental State: Korean Experience." In *Gender Division of Labor in Korea,* ed. Cho Hyoung and Chang Pil-wha, 292–321. Seoul: Korean Women's Insitute Series, Ewha Womans University Press.

Lee, Hye-Kyung, and Park Yeong-Ran. 2003. "Families in Transition and the Family Welfare Policies in Korea." Canada-Korea Social Policy Research Co-operation Symposium, Seoul, Korea, November 22, 2003, pp. 73–103. Downloaded in February 2006 from http://www.kihasa.re.kr/board/seminar/file/HyeKyung_lee-Yeong_Ran_Park.pdf.

Lee, Hyo-sik. 2005. "Elderly Suicide Rises 5-fold in 20 Years." *Korea Times,* July 20, 2005.

———. 2006. "Korea's Suicide Rate Highest in OECD in 2005." *Korea Times,* September 18, 2006.

Lee, Jin-woo. 2004. "Fortunetellers Enjoy Year-end Boom." *Korea Times,* December 20, 2004.

Lee, Joo-hee. 1997. "Class Structure and Class Consciousness in South Korea." *Journal of Contemporary Asia* 19, No. 3: 135–155.

Lee, Joung-Woo, and David Lindauer. "The Quality of Working life." In *The Strains of Economic Growth: Labor Unrest and Social Dissatisfaction in Korea,* eds. David Lindauer, Kim Jong-Gie, et al., 77–92. Cambridge, MA: Harvard University Press.

Lee, Ki-baik. 1984. *A New History of Korea.* Transl. Edward W. Wagner with Edward J. Shultz. Seoul: Ilchokak.

Lee, Kwang-shik. 1999. *Han'guk Hyundae Munhak 100 Nyŏn, Tanp'yŏn Sosŏl Best 20 (Korean Contemporary Literature 100 Years: 20 Best Short Stories).* Seoul: Doseo/Garam.

Lee, Man-gap. 1967. "The Structural Change of the Korean Society and Her Modernization." In *Korea: A Nation in Transition,* ed. Kim Se-Jin and Kang Chi-Won, 224–242. Seoul: Research Center for Peace and Unification, 1978.

Lett, Denise P. 1998. *In Pursuit of Status: The Making of South Korea's "New" Urban Middle Class.* Cambridge, MA: Harvard University Press.

————. 2001. "South Korea's 'New' Middle Class." *The Korea Society Quarterly,* Fall 2001: 13–16.

Lewis, Arthur. 1955. *The Theory of Economic Growth.* London: Allen & Unwin.

Lim, Hy-Sop. 1997. "The Evolution of Social Classes and Changing Social Attitudes." In *The Strains of Economic Growth: Labor Unrest and Social Dissatisfaction in Korea,* ed. David Lindauer, Kim Jong-Gie, et al., 13–34. Cambridge, MA: Harvard University Press.

Lindauer, David. 1997. "Introduction." In *The Strains of Economic Growth: Labor Unrest and Social Dissatisfaction in Korea,* ed. David Lindauer, Kim Jong-Gie, et al., 1–12. Cambridge, MA: Harvard University Press.

Lukoff, Fred. 1978. "Ceremonial and Expressive Uses of the Styles of Address of Korean." In *Papers in Korean Linguistics,* ed. Chin-W. Kim. Columbia, SC: Hornbeam Press, Inc.

MacDonald, Donald Stone. 1988. *The Koreans: Contemporary Politics and Society.* London: Westview Press.

Mack, Maynard. "A note on translation," *The Norton Anthology of World Masterpieces. 5th Continental Edition.* New York: Norton, 1987.

Martin, Samuel E. 1954. *Korean Morphophonemics.* William Dwight Whitney Linguistic series. Baltimore: Linguistic Society of America.

Maass, Peter, and Young H. Lee, 1989. "'Must-win' South Koreans Cram for College in Schools of Hard Knocks." *The Washington Post.* June 28,

1989. Downloaded November 28, 2005, from http://www.petermaass.com.

McBrian, Charles D. 1979. "Kinship, Communal, and Class Models of Social Structure in Rising Sun Village." In *Studies on Korea in Transition,* ed. David McCann, John Middleton, and Edward Shultz. Honolulu: Center for Korean Studies, University of Hawaii.

Moon, Katherine H. S. 1997. *Sex Among Allies: Military Prostitution in U.S.–Korea Relations.* New York: Columbia University Press.

Moose, J. Robert. 1911. *Village Life in Korea.* Nashville: Publishing House of the M. E. Church, South.

Morgan, Baynard Quincy. 1959. "A critical bibliography of works on translation." In *On Translation,* ed. Reuben A. Brower. Cambridge, MA: Harvard University Press. This is a review of *Shelley's Prose in the Bodleian Manuscripts,* ed. A. H. Koszul, 1910. London: H. Frowde.

Nabokov, Vladimir. "Problems of Translation: Onegin in English." *Partisan Review* 22:496–512.

Nam, Jin-u. 1997. "Sŏ Jŏng-in Sosŏl 'Kang'" (Sŏ Jŏng-in's Story "River"). *Chosun Ilbo.* September 9, 1997.

Nahm, Andrew C. 1997. "History." In *An Introduction to Korean Culture,* ed. John H. Koo et al., 39–98. Elizabeth, NJ: Hollym.

Nelson, Laura. 2000. *Measured Excess: Status, Gender, and Consumer Nationalism in South Korea.* New York: Columbia University Press.

Newmark, Peter. 1988. *Approaches to Translation.* New York: Prentice Hall.

Oh, Byung-hun. 1975. "Students and Politics." In *Korean Politics in Transition,* ed. Edward Reynolds Wright, 111–152. Seattle: University of Washington Press.

O'Rourke, Kevin. 1981. *Ten Korean Short Stories.* Seoul: Yonsei University Press.

Palmer, Spencer J. 1967. "The New Religions of Korea." *Transactions* 43: 1–27, ed. Spencer J. Palmer. Seoul: Korea Branch Royal Asiatic Society.

Park, Se-kil. 1988. *Rewriting the History of Modern Korea (Dasi Ssŭnŭn Hankuk Hyŏndaesa).* Seoul: Dolpekae.

Park, Yong Shin. 1994. "The Socio-Cultural Dynamic of a Newly Industrializing Country: The Experience of Korea." In *Culture, Politics, and Economic Growth: Experiences in East Asia,* ed. Richard Harvey Brown, 109–125. Williamsburg, VA: Dept. of Anthropology, College of William and Mary.

Perrine, Laurence. 1977. *Sound and Sense.* New York: Harcourt, Brace, Jovanovich.

Pihl, Marshall R. 1973. *Listening to Korea,* xiii–xxiii. New York: Praeger.

Pihl, Marshall R., and Bruce and Juchan Fulton. 1993. *Land of Exile: Contemporary Korean Fiction.* New York: M. E. Sharpe.

Pope, Alexander. 1715. "Preface to the translation of Homer's Illiad." In Morgan, Baynard Quincy. 1959, "A critical bibliography of works on translation." In *On Translation,* ed. Reuben A. Brower. Cambridge, MA: Harvard University Press.

Ro, Bong Rin. 1998. "Bankrupting the Prosperity Gospel." *Christianity Today* 42, No. 13. Downloaded in August 2005 from http://www.christianity today.com/ct/8td /8td058.html.

Rutt, Richard. 1961. "The Flower Boys of Shilla (Hwarang)." *Transactions* 38: 1–66. Seoul: Royal Asiatic Society, Korea Branch.

———. 1964. *Korean Works and Days: Notes from the Diary of a Country Priest.* Seoul: Royal Asiatic Society, Korea Branch.

Sato, Paul T. 1978. "Adjectives and copula in Korean." *Papers in Korean Linguistics* (ed. Chin-W. Kim). Columbia: SC: Hornbeam Press, Inc.

Shelley, Percy Bysshe. 1822. "In Defence of Poetry," discussed in "A Critical Bibliography of Works on Translation" by Baynard Q. Morgan. In *On Translation,* ed. Reuben A. Brower, 1959. Cambridge, MA: Harvard University. This is a review of *Shelley's Prose in the Bodleian Manuscripts,*" ed. A.H. Koszul, 1910. London: H. Frowde.

Shin, Gi-Hyun. 2001. "Apjonpŏp and an Emerging New Politeness Strategy in Contemporary Korean." Proceedings of the KSAA Conference 2001, 287–295. Downloaded in December 2005 from http://www.arts.monash.edu.au/korean/ksaa/conference/papers/25gihyunshin.PDF.

Showerman, G. 1916. "The way of the translator." *The Unpopular Review,* 5: 84–100.

Soh, Ji-young. 2004. "Suicide rate grows fastest in OECD." *Korea Times,* June 4, 2004. Downloaded on November 21, 2005 from http://times.hankooki.com/lpage/200406/kt2004060414532510220.htm.

Son, Kyŏng-muk. 1994. "Sunjinsŏng-esŏ chagi doem-ŭro" (From Innocence to Self). In *Kong Chi-yŏng Sosŏl Chip: In'gan-e-daehanYyeŭi* (*Short Stories of Kong Chi-yŏng: Human Decency*), 315–328. Seoul: Ch'angjakgwa Pip'-yŏngsa.

Sŏng, Sŏk-che. 2004. "Nae sosŏl sok-ŭi sarang (15): Sŏng Sŏk-jae ŭi Chŏ's

Sarang" ("Love in My Stories [15]: Sŏng Sŏk-je's 'First Love'"). *Kyŏnghyang Shinmun*. July 11, 2004.

Spaeth, Anthony, and Donald MacIntyre. "Breaking Through." *Time*, 15–18, November 14, 2005.

Standish, Isolde. 1992. "United in Han: Korean Cinema and the 'New Wave.'" *Korea Journal* 32 (4) (Winter 1992): 109–118.

Steinberg, David I. 1989. *The Republic of Korea: Economic Transformation and Social Change*. London: Westview Press.

Suh, Sangwon, and Laxmi Nakarmi. 1997. "Fervor in South Korea: Mixing Shamanism with Christianity?" *AsiaWeek*, December 12, 1997.

Taeuber, Irene B. 1946. "The Population Potential of Postwar Korea." *The Far Eastern Quarterly*, Vol. 5 (3) (May 1946): 289–307. Ann Arbor, MI: Association for Asian Studies.

Tamplin, Ronald. 1976. "Creation, imitation, and translation." *College English*; Vol. 37, No. 8, April 1976.

Time Magazine. 1945. "City of the Bell." October 8, 1945.

——. 1944. "Voices in Bondage." March 13, 1944.

——. 1946. "Rx for Corns." October 14, 1946.

——. 1947. "Trial Balance." July 14, 1947.

——. 1948. "Presbyterian in a Packing Case." February 16, 1948.

——. 2003. "Striking to Death?" September 1, 2003.

——. 2005. "South Korea: The Miracle Workers." August 15, 2005.

Thomson, J. A. K. 1927. "Some thoughts on translation." *The Greek Tradition: Essays in the reconstruction of Ancient thought*. London: George Allen & Unwin Ltd.

Tuchman, Barbara W. 1978. *A Distant Mirror: The Calamitous Fourteenth Century*. New York: Ballantine Books.

Underwood, Horace, and Michael Devine. 2001. *Korea in War, Revolution and Peace: The Recollections of Horace G. Underwood*. Seoul: Yonsei University Press.

U. S. Embassy, Seoul. 1989. "United States Government Statement on the Events in Kwangju, Republic of Korea, in May 1980." Press Office, United States Information Service, United States Embassy, Seoul, Korea. June 19, 1989.

Vogel, Ezra F., and David L. Lindauer. 1997. *The Strains of Economic Growth: Labor Unrest and Social Dissatisfaction in Korea*. Eds. David Lindauer, Kim Jong-Gie, et al., 93–121. Cambridge, MA: Harvard University Press.

Wade, James. 1967. *One Man's Korea.* Seoul: Hollym.

Wade, L. L. and B. S. Kim. 1978. *Economic Development of South Korea: The political economy of success.* New York: Praeger Publishers.

Walhain, Luc. 2001. "Democracy on the Back-Burner: An Evaluation of South Korea's Student Movements in the 1980s." Proceedings of the KSSA (Korea Studies Association of Australia) Conferrence 2001, 190–197. Downloaded in November 2005 from http://www.arts.monash.edu.au/korean/ksaa/conference/papers/14lucwalhain.PDF#search='democracy%20on%20the%20backburner%20walhain'.

WSCF (World Student Christian Federation) Asia/Pacific, Christian Conference of Asia. 1989. EFFT. "Appendix 'B': The Korean Campus Situation Since 1980." *Ecumenical Fact Finding Team Visit to Korea 1980.* Downloaded in November 2005 from http://www.ibiblio.org/ahkitj/wscfap/arms1974/cca-wscf/Report%201985/appendix%20b.htm.

Yoon, Chang Sup. "Brief History of Korean Architecture: Palace Architecture of Ch'cagdok-kung [Ch'angdŏkgung]." Downloaded in August 2009 from http://nongae.gsnu.ac.kr/~mirkoh/palace1.html.

Recommended Reading

Brother Anthony of Taize. "A Well-Kept Secret: Korean Literature in Translation." Downloaded April 10, 2005, from http://www.sogang.ac.kr/~anthony/klt/Secret.htm.

Finch, Andrew J. 2000. "A Persecuted Church: Roman Catholicism in Early Nineteenth-Century Korea." *The Journal of Ecclesiastical History*, 51: 556–580. Cambridge University Press.

Fulton, Bruce. 1989. *Words of Farewell.* Seattle: Seal Press.

Fulton, Bruce. 1998. "O Chŏng-hu'i." *Korean Literature Today* 3 (4): 90–92.

Fulton, Bruce, and Kwon Youngmin, eds. 2005. *Modern Korean Fiction: An Anthology*. New York: Columbia University Press.

Gargen, Edward A. 2003. "Young Korean Writers Turn a Page." *Newsday*. Downloaded in July 2004 from http://www.jsonline.com/enter/books/mar03/127325.asp.

Hadle, Gabriele. "Korean Protest Culture." *Kyoto Journal* #60. Downloaded July 9, 2005, from http://www.kyotojournal.org/kjselections/korean protest.html.

Harvey, Youngsook K. 1979. *Six Korean Women: The Socialization of Shamans*. St. Paul, MN: West Publishing.

Keith, Howard. 1990. *Bands, Songs, and Shamanistic Rituals*. Seoul: Seoul Computer Press.

Jacobs, Norman. 1985. *The Korean Road to Modernization and Development*. Chicago: University of Illinois Press.

Kang, Chi-Won. 1978. "Korea in Developmental Nexus: Political Integration and Alienation." In *Korea: A Nation in Transition*, ed. Kim Se-jin and Kang Chi-Won, 243–258. Seoul: Research Center for Peace and Unification.

Kim, Doo-Sub. 1994. "The Demographic Transition in the Korean Peninsula, 1910–1990: South and North Korea Compared." *Korea Journal of Population and Development* 23 (2): 131–155.

Kim, Richard. 1998. *Lost Names: Scenes from a Korean Boyhood*. University of California Press.

Kister, Daniel A. 1997. *Korean Shamanist Ritual*. Budapest: Akademiai Kiado.

Lee, Jeong-kyu. 2002. "Christianity and Korean Education in the Late Choson period." *Christian Higher Education*, 1: 85–99.

Lyman, Princeton. 1975. "Economic Development in South Korea: A Retrospective View of the 1960's." In *Korean Politics in Transition*, ed. Edward Reynolds Wright, 243–254. Seattle: University of Washington Press.

McCann, David. 1997. "Modern Poetry and Literature." In *An Introduction to Korean Culture*, ed. John H. Koo et al. Elizabeth, NJ: Hollym International Corp.

McCann, David, John Middleton, and Edward Shultz, eds. 1979. *Studies on Korea in Transition*. Honolulu: Center for Korean Studies, University of Hawaii.

McCune-Reischauer Romanization System. The American Library Association-Library of Congress table "Korean": http://www.loc.gov/catdir/cpso /romanization/korean.pdf.

O, Chŏng-hŭi. 1979. "Evening Game." In *Words of Farewell: Stories by Korean Women Writers*, trans. Bruce and Ju-chan Fulton, 181–231. Seattle: Seal Press. 1989.

O, Chŏng-hŭi. 1983. "Sullyeja ŭi norae" ("Wayfarer"). In *Wayfarer*, transl. Bruce and Ju-chan Fulton, 184–205. Seattle: Women in Translation.

Park, Hyunmo. 2004. "King Jeongjo's Political Role in the Conflicts Between Catholicisma and Confucianism in 18-century Korea." *The Review of Korean Studies* 7 (4): 205–228. Seoul: The Academy of Korean Studies. Downloaded October 23, 2005, from http://review.aks.ac.kr/AttachedFiles/09-Park%20Hyunmo.pdf.

Rausch, Franklin. 2004. "Korean Catholicism: Finding a Place Between Heaven and Earth." Paper presented at the graduate student conference "Asia Pacific: Local Knowledge versus Western theory." Hosted by the Insitute of Asian Research and the Centr for Japanese Research at The University of British Columbia. Downloaded October 23, 2005, from http://www.iar.ubc.ca/centres/cjr/publications/grad2004/Franklin Rausch.pd

Skeldon, Ronald. "Ageing of Rural Populations in South-East and East Asia, Part 2." Downloaded August 14, 2005, from http://www.fao.org/SD/wpdirect/Wpan0029.htm.

Steinberg, David I. 1995. "The Republic of Korea: Pluralizing Politics." In

Politics in Developing Countries: Comparing Experiences with Democracy, eds. Larry Diamond et al., 369–415. Boulder: Lynne Rienner Publishers.

Suh, Sang Mok. 1980. "The Patterns of Poverty." In *Human Resources and Social Development in Korea,* ed. Park Chong Kee, 336–371. Seoul: Korea Development Institute.

Wade, L. L., and B. S. Kim. 1977. *Economic Development of South Korea: The Political Economy of Success.* New York: Praeger.

Wiley, Richard. 1991. *Festival for Three Thousand Maidens.* New York: Penguin.

Willoughby, Heather A. 2002. "Retake: A Decade of Learning from the Movie Sŏpy'yŏnje." In *The Sound of Han: P'ansori, Timbre, and a South Korean Discourse of Sorrow and Lament.* Dissertation for Columbia University. Downloaded August 14, 2005, from http://www.worldmusic.or.kr/intro/kswmactivity/journal/article/article8/willouby_article8.htm.

Yi, Yang-ha. 1973. "On Growing Old." In *Listening to Korea,* ed. Marshall R. Pihl, 210–216. New York: Praeger.

Yu, Chai-sun, and W. I. Guisso, eds. 1988. *Shamanism: The Spirit World of Korea.* Berkeley: Asian Humanities Press.

Yun, Hŭng-gil. 1977. "The Man Who Was Left As Nine Pairs of Shoes." In *Land of Exile: Contemporary Korean fiction,* trans. Marshall Pihl, Bruce and Ju-Chan Fulton. 1993, 165–199. Armonk, NY: M.E. Sharpe.

CORNELL EAST ASIA SERIES

4 Fredrick Teiwes, *Provincial Leadership in China: The Cultural Revolution and Its Aftermath*
8 Cornelius C. Kubler, *Vocabulary and Notes to Ba Jin's Jia: An Aid for Reading the Novel*
16 Monica Bethe & Karen Brazell, *Nō as Performance: An Analysis of the Kuse Scene of Yamamba.* Available for purchase: DVD by Monica Bethe & Karen Brazell, "Yamanba: The Old Woman of the Mountains"
18 Royall Tyler, tr., *Granny Mountains: A Second Cycle of Nō Plays*
23 Knight Biggerstaff, *Nanking Letters, 1949*
28 Diane E. Perushek, ed., *The Griffis Collection of Japanese Books: An Annotated Bibliography*
37 J. Victor Koschmann, Ōiwa Keibō & Yamashita Shinji, eds., *International Perspectives on Yanagita Kunio and Japanese Folklore Studies*
38 James O'Brien, tr., *Murō Saisei: Three Works*
40 Kubo Sakae, *Land of Volcanic Ash: A Play in Two Parts,* revised edition, tr. David G. Goodman
44 Susan Orpett Long, *Family Change and the Life Course in Japan*
48 Helen Craig McCullough, *Bungo Manual: Selected Reference Materials for Students of Classical Japanese*
49 Susan Blakeley Klein, *Ankoku Butō: The Premodern and Postmodern Influences on the Dance of Utter Darkness*
50 Karen Brazell, ed., *Twelve Plays of the Noh and Kyōgen Theaters*
51 David G. Goodman, ed., *Five Plays by Kishida Kunio*
52 Shirō Hara, *Ode to Stone,* tr. James Morita
53 Peter J. Katzenstein & Yutaka Tsujinaka, *Defending the Japanese State: Structures, Norms and the Political Responses to Terrorism and Violent Social Protest in the 1970s and 1980s*
54 Su Xiaokang & Wang Luxiang, *Deathsong of the River: A Reader's Guide to the Chinese TV Series* Heshang, trs. Richard Bodman & Pin P. Wan
55 Jingyuan Zhang, *Psychoanalysis in China: Literary Transformations, 1919–1949*
56 Jane Kate Leonard & John R. Watt, eds., *To Achieve Security and Wealth: The Qing Imperial State and the Economy, 1644–1911*
57 Andrew F. Jones, *Like a Knife: Ideology and Genre in Contemporary Chinese Popular Music*
58 Peter J. Katzenstein & Nobuo Okawara, *Japan's National Security: Structures, Norms and Policy Responses in a Changing World*
59 Carsten Holz, *The Role of Central Banking in China's Economic Reforms*

60 Chifumi Shimazaki, *Warrior Ghost Plays from the Japanese Noh Theater: Parallel Translations with Running Commentary*
61 Emily Groszos Ooms, *Women and Millenarian Protest in Meiji Japan: Deguchi Nao and Ōmotokyō*
62 Carolyn Anne Morley, *Transformation, Miracles, and Mischief: The Mountain Priest Plays of Kyōgen*
63 David R. McCann & Hyunjae Yee Sallee, tr., *Selected Poems of Kim Namjo*, afterword by Kim Yunsik
64 Hua Qingzhao, *From Yalta to Panmunjom: Truman's Diplomacy and the Four Powers, 1945-1953*
65 Margaret Benton Fukasawa, *Kitahara Hakushū: His Life and Poetry*
66 Kam Louie, ed., *Strange Tales from Strange Lands: Stories by Zheng Wanlong*, with introduction
67 Wang Wen-hsing, *Backed Against the Sea*, tr. Edward Gunn
69 Brian Myers, *Han Sŏrya and North Korean Literature: The Failure of Socialist Realism in the DPRK*
70 Thomas P. Lyons & Victor Nee, eds., *The Economic Transformation of South China: Reform and Development in the Post-Mao Era*
71 David G. Goodman, tr., *After Apocalypse: Four Japanese Plays of Hiroshima and Nagasaki*, with introduction
72 Thomas Lyons, *Poverty and Growth in a South China County: Anxi, Fujian, 1949–1992*
74 Martyn Atkins, *Informal Empire in Crisis: British Diplomacy and the Chinese Customs Succession, 1927-1929*
76 Chifumi Shimazaki, *Restless Spirits from Japanese Noh Plays of the Fourth Group: Parallel Translations with Running Commentary*
77 Brother Anthony of Taizé & Young-Moo Kim, trs., *Back to Heaven: Selected Poems of Ch'ŏn Sang Pyŏng*
78 Kevin O'Rourke, tr., *Singing Like a Cricket, Hooting Like an Owl: Selected Poems by Yi Kyu-bo*
79 Irit Averbuch, *The Gods Come Dancing: A Study of the Japanese Ritual Dance of Yamabushi Kagura*
80 Mark Peterson, *Korean Adoption and Inheritance: Case Studies in the Creation of a Classic Confucian Society*
81 Yenna Wu, tr., *The Lioness Roars: Shrew Stories from Late Imperial China*
82 Thomas Lyons, *The Economic Geography of Fujian: A Sourcebook*, Vol. 1
83 Pak Wan-so, *The Naked Tree*, tr. Yu Young-nan
84 C.T. Hsia, *The Classic Chinese Novel: A Critical Introduction*
85 Cho Chong-Rae, *Playing With Fire*, tr. Chun Kyung-Ja
86 Hayashi Fumiko, *I Saw a Pale Horse and Selections from Diary of a Vagabond*, tr. Janice Brown
87 Motoori Norinaga, *Kojiki-den, Book 1*, tr. Ann Wehmeyer
88 Chang Soo Ko, tr., *Sending the Ship Out to the Stars: Poems of Park Je-chun*
89 Thomas Lyons, *The Economic Geography of Fujian: A Sourcebook*, Vol. 2

90 Brother Anthony of Taizé, tr., Midang: *Early Lyrics of So Chong-Ju*
92 Janice Matsumura, *More Than a Momentary Nightmare: The Yokohama Incident and Wartime Japan*
93 Kim Jong-Gil tr., *The Snow Falling on Chagall's Village: Selected Poems of Kim Ch'un-Su*
94 Wolhee Choe & Peter Fusco, trs., *Day-Shine: Poetry by Hyon-jong Chong*
95 Chifumi Shimazaki, *Troubled Souls from Japanese Noh Plays of the Fourth Group*
96 Hagiwara Sakutarō, *Principles of Poetry (Shi no Genri),* tr. Chester Wang
97 Mae J. Smethurst, *Dramatic Representations of Filial Piety: Five Noh in Translation*
99 William Wilson, *Hōgen Monogatari: Tale of the Disorder in Hōgen*
100 Yasushi Yamanouchi, J. Victor Koschmann and Ryūichi Narita, eds., *Total War and 'Modernization'*
101 Yi Ch'ŏng-jun, *The Prophet and Other Stories,* tr. Julie Pickering
102 S.A. Thornton, *Charisma and Community Formation in Medieval Japan: The Case of the Yugyō-ha (1300-1700)*
103 Sherman Cochran, ed., *Inventing Nanjing Road: Commercial Culture in Shanghai, 1900-1945*
104 Harold M. Tanner, *Strike Hard! Anti-Crime Campaigns and Chinese Criminal Justice, 1979-1985*
105 Brother Anthony of Taizé & Young-Moo Kim, trs., *Farmers' Dance: Poems by Shin Kyŏng-nim*
106 Susan Orpett Long, ed., *Lives in Motion: Composing Circles of Self and Community in Japan*
107 Peter J. Katzenstein, Natasha Hamilton-Hart, Kozo Kato, & Ming Yue, *Asian Regionalism*
108 Kenneth Alan Grossberg, *Japan's Renaissance: The Politics of the Muromachi Bakufu*
109 John W. Hall & Toyoda Takeshi, eds., *Japan in the Muromachi Age*
110 Kim Su-Young, Shin Kyong-Nim, Lee Si-Young; *Variations: Three Korean Poets;* trs. Brother Anthony of Taizé & Young-Moo Kim
111 Samuel Leiter, *Frozen Moments: Writings on* Kabuki, *1966–2001*
112 Pilwun Shih Wang & Sarah Wang, *Early One Spring: A Learning Guide to Accompany the Film Video* February
113 Thomas Conlan, *In Little Need of Divine Intervention: Scrolls of the Mongol Invasions of Japan*
114 Jane Kate Leonard & Robert Antony, eds., *Dragons, Tigers, and Dogs: Qing Crisis Management and the Boundaries of State Power in Late Imperial China*
115 Shu-ning Sciban & Fred Edwards, eds., *Dragonflies: Fiction by Chinese Women in the Twentieth Century*
116 David G. Goodman, ed., *The Return of the Gods: Japanese Drama and Culture in the 1960s*

117 Yang Hi Choe-Wall, *Vision of a Phoenix: The Poems of Hŏ Nansŏrhŏn*
118 Mae J. Smethurst and Christina Laffin, eds., *The Noh* Ominameshi*: A Flower Viewed from Many Directions*
119 Joseph A. Murphy, *Metaphorical Circuit: Negotiations Between Literature and Science in Twentieth-Century Japan*
120 Richard F. Calichman, *Takeuchi Yoshimi: Displacing the West*
121 Fan Pen Li Chen, *Visions for the Masses: Chinese Shadow Plays from Shaanxi and Shanxi*
122 S. Yumiko Hulvey, *Sacred Rites in Moonlight: Ben no Naishi Nikki*
123 Tetsuo Najita and J. Victor Koschmann, *Conflict in Modern Japanese History: The Neglected Tradition*
124 Naoki Sakai, Brett de Bary, & Iyotani Toshio, eds., *Deconstructing Nationality*
125 Judith N. Rabinovitch and Timothy R. Bradstock, *Dance of the Butterflies: Chinese Poetry from the Japanese Court Tradition*
126 Yang Gui-ja, *Contradictions,* trs. Stephen Epstein and Kim Mi-Young
127 Ann Sung-hi Lee, *Yi Kwang-su and Modern Korean Literature:* Mujŏng
128 Pang Kie-chung & Michael D. Shin, eds., *Landlords, Peasants, & Intellectuals in Modern Korea*
129 Joan R. Piggott, ed., *Capital and Countryside in Japan, 300–1180: Japanese Historians Interpreted in English*
130 Kyoko Selden and Jolisa Gracewood, eds., *Annotated Japanese Literary Gems: Stories by Tawada Yōko, Nakagami Kenji, and Hayashi Kyōko* (Vol. 1)
131 Michael G. Murdock, *Disarming the Allies of Imperialism: The State, Agitation, and Manipulation during China's Nationalist Revolution, 1922–1929*
132 Noel J. Pinnington, *Traces in the Way: Michi and the Writings of Komparu Zenchiku*
133 Charlotte von Verschuer, *Across the Perilous Sea: Japanese Trade with China and Korea from the Seventh to the Sixteenth Centuries,* Kristen Lee Hunter, tr.
134 John Timothy Wixted, *A Handbook to Classical Japanese*
135 Kyoko Selden and Jolisa Gracewoord, with Lili Selden, eds., *Annotated Japanese Literary Gems: Stories by Natsume Sōseki, Tomioka Taeko, and Inoue Yasushi* (Vol. 2)
136 Yi Tae-Jin, *The Dynamics of Confucianism and Modernization in Korean History*
137 Jennifer Rudolph, *Negotiated Power in Late Imperial China: The Zongli Yamen and the Politics of Reform*
138 Thomas D. Loooser, *Visioning Eternity: Aesthetics, Politics, and History in the Early Modern Noh Theater*
139 Gustav Heldt, *The Pursuit of Harmony: Poetry and Power in Late Heian Japan*

140 Joan R. Piggott and Yoshida Sanae, *Teishinkōki: The Year 939 in the Journal of Regent Fujiwara no Tadahira*
141 Robert Bagley, *Max Loehr and the Study of Chinese Bronzes: Style and Classification in the History of Art*
142 Edwin A. Cranston, *The Secret Island and the Enticing Flame: Worlds of Memory, Discovery, and Loss in Japanese Poetry*
143 Hugh de Ferranti, *The Last Biwa Singer: A Blind Musician in History, Imagination and Performance*
144 Roger des Forges, Minglu Gao, Liu Chiao-mei, Haun Saussy, with Thomas Burkman, eds., *Chinese Walls in Time and Space: A Multidisciplinary Perspective*
145 Hye-jin Juhn Sidney & George Sidney, trs., *I Heard Life Calling Me: Poems of Yi Sŏng-bok*
146 Sherman Cochran & Paul G. Pickowicz, eds., *China on the Margins*
147 Wang Lingzhen & Mary Ann O' Donnell, trs., *Years of Sadness: Autobiographical Writings of Wang Anyi*
148 John Holstein, tr., *A Moment's Grace: Stories from Korea in Transition*
149 Sunyoung Park in collaboration with Jefferson J.A. Gatrall, trs., *On the Eve of the Uprising and Other Stories from Colonial Korea*
150 Brother Anthony of Taizé & Lee Hyung-jin, trs., *Walking on a Washing Line: Poems of Kim Seung-Hee*
151 Matthew Fraleigh, trs., with introduction, *New Chronicles of Yanagibashi and Diary of a Journey to the West: Narushima Ryūhoku Reports from Home and Abroad*
152 Pei Huang, *Reorienting the Manchus: A Study of Sinicization, 1583–1795*
153 Karen Gernant & Chen Zeping, *White Poppies and Other Stories by Zhang Kangkang*
154 Mattias Burell & Marina Svensson, eds., *Making Law Work: Chinese Laws in Context*
155 Tomoko Aoyama & Barbara Hartley, trs., *Indian Summer by Kanai Mieko*
156 Lynne Kutsukake, tr., *Single Sickness and Other Stories by Masuda Mizuko*
157 Takako U. Lento, tr. with introduction, *Tanikawa Shuntarō: The Art of Being Alone, Poems 1952–2009*
158 Shu-ning Sciban & Fred Edwards, eds., *Endless War: Fiction & Essays by Wang Wen-hsing*
159 Elizabeth Oyler & Michael Watson, eds., *Like Clouds and Mists: Studies and Translations of Nō Plays of the Genpei War*

160 Michiko N. Wilson & Michael K. Wilson, trs., *Of Birds Crying by Minako Ōba*
161 Chifumi Shimazaki & Stephen Comee *Supernatural Beings from Japanese Noh Plays of the Fifth Group: Parallel Translations with Running Commentary*
162 Petrus Liu, *Stateless Subjects: Chinese Martial Arts Literature and Postcolonial History*
163 Lim Beng Choo, *Another Stage: Kanze Nobumitsu and the Late Muromachi Noh Theater*
164 Scott Cook, *The Bamboo Texts of Guodian: A Study and Complete Translation, Volume 1*
165 Scott Cook, *The Bamboo Texts of Guodian: A Study and Complete Translation, Volume 2*
166 Stephen D. Miller, translations with Patrick Donnelly, *The Wind from Vulture Peak: The Buddhification of Japanese Waka in the Heian Period*
167 Theodore Hughes, Jae-yong Kim, Jin-kyung Lee & Sang-kyung Lee, eds., *Rat Fire: Korean Stories from the Japanese Empire*
168 Ken C. Kawashima, Fabian Schäfer, Robert Stolz, eds., *Tosaka Jun: A Critical Reader*
169 John R. Bentley, *Tamakatsuma—A Window into the Scholarship of Motoori Norinaga*
170 Dandan Zhu, *1956: Mao's China and the Hungarian Crisis*

CORNELL
East Asia Series

eap.einaudi.cornell.edu/publications